ALL ABOUT
MUTUAL FUNDS

ALL ABOUT MUTUAL FUNDS

SECOND EDITION

BRUCE JACOBS

McGraw-Hill

New York   Chicago   San Francisco   Lisbon   London   Madrid
Mexico City   Milan   New Delhi   San Juan   Seoul
Singapore   Sydney   Toronto

Library of Congress Cataloging-in-Publication Data

Jacobs, Bruce, 1916–
    All about mutual funds : from the inside out / Bruce Jacobs.— 2nd ed.
      p. cm.
    Includes bibliographical references and index.
    ISBN 0-07-137678-X
    1. Mutual funds—United States.   2. Investments—United States.   I. Title.

  HG4930 .J33 2001
  332.63'27—dc21

                                   2001044002

McGraw-Hill

*A Division of The **McGraw·Hill** Companies*

1 2 3 4 5 6 7 8 9 0 DOC/DOC 0 9 8 7 6 5 4 3 2 1

ISBN 0-07-137678-X

The sponsoring editor for this book was Ela Aktay, the editing supervisors were Scott Amerman and Scott Kurtz, and the production supervisor was Clare Stanley. It was typeset by The Composing Room of Michigan, Inc.

Printed and bound by R. R. Donnelley & Sons Company.

McGraw-Hill books are available at special quantity discounts to use as premiums and sales promotions, or for use in corporate training programs. For more information, please write to the Director of Special Sales, Professional Publishing, McGraw-Hill, Two Penn Plaza, New York, NY 10121-2298. Or contact your local bookstore.

This book is printed on recycled, acid-free paper containing a minimum of 50% recycled, de-inked fiber.

This book is dedicated to
my mother,
Hilda Jacobs,
who introduced me to the world of
investing,
and to my wife,
Zelda Jacobs,
whose support and encouragement
led to the creation of this book.

Bruce Jacobs, M.Ed.

CONTENTS

Chapter 5

Advantages of Mutual Fund Investing   47

Chapter 6

Risks in Mutual Fund Investing   57

Chapter 7

Investment Companies   67

Chapter 8

The Prospectus   76

Chapter 15

Costs of Ownership   156

Chapter 16

Tax Issues   166

Chapter 17

Developing a Model Portfolio   183

Chapter 18

Is Mutual Fund Investing for Me?   192

Chapter 19

Mutual Fund Investing via the Internet   203

Epilogue   208

Appendix A

Non-Technical Magazines and Newspapers   217

PREFACE

The purpose of this book is to provide, in a complete yet concise format, the information the uninitiated investor requires to enter the world of mutual fund investing with confidence. In essence, it is a step-by-step guide that will enable the would-be investor to proceed in an intelligent and informed manner toward becoming a knowledgeable, profitable owner of mutual funds. It provides an abundance of basic data and helpful background material for the novice investor. It answers some technical questions, and all of the basic ones, such as: Where do I start? What does the mutual fund jargon mean? What information should I have? How, exactly, do I go about investing in, and making decisions about, mutual fund purchases? How much must be invested? Are there risks involved? Why invest in mutual funds at all?

This second edition of *All About Mutual Funds* is completely updated, expanded, and revised. A new and informational innovation has been introduced in the form of chapter postscripts. The postscripts serve as enhancements to the chapter content, providing additional insights and interesting commentary.

In addition, a totally new chapter has been added, "Mutual Fund Investing via the Internet." It provides examples of helpful mutual fund websites available without cost to owners of personal computers.

While the second edition of the book retains all the basic concepts pertaining to mutual fund investing covered in the first edition, a more advanced approach to mutual fund investing utilizing new techniques currently available is offered. Readers of the first edition will find many new and exciting ideas. But the author's primary focus, which is helping investors achieve success in the pursuit of profits through mutual fund investing, has been maintained throughout the new edition.

INTRODUCTION

In light of the widespread publicity provided by the mutual fund industry, I was amazed to discover how many people who should be taking advantage of mutual fund investing were not. The reason, I suspected, was because they lacked sufficient knowledge about mutual funds. How do you rate? Check yourself using the questionnaire below.

Mutual Fund Questionnaire

Use the following key to indicate your level of understanding regarding mutual fund investing.

1 = very knowledgeable

2 = somewhat knowledgeable

3 = not at all knowledgeable

How familiar are you with:

1. Mutual funds in general? _____
2. The difference between open-end and closed-end mutual funds? _____
3. Tax-free funds and what makes them tax-free? _____
4. The difference between load and no-load mutual funds? _____
5. Mutual fund prospectuses? _____
6. The advantages of investing in mutual funds? _____
7. The risks involved in investing in mutual funds? _____
8. The process of opening a mutual fund account? _____

9. The costs involved in mutual fund ownership? _____
10. Tracking a mutual fund's performance? _____
11. Dollar-cost averaging? _____
12. Diversification in mutual fund investing? _____
13. The use of mutual funds for retirement accounts? _____
14. Sources of information about mutual funds? _____
15. The many varied types of mutual funds? _____

(By the time you finish reading this book, you will be able to answer every question with a "1.")

For example, people who have relied on the income from bank CDs in order to meet some of their basic financial needs are now bemoaning the recent, sharp decline in interest rates. Yet, they seem to have no idea how to *equal* or *better* the amount of interest income their CDs *used* to provide. When asked why they did not consider investing in mutual funds now that their high-paying CDs were maturing, I almost always got the same response: "I don't know enough about mutual funds, and wouldn't know how or where to begin."

I undertook to find out just how prevalent this lack of understanding about mutual funds might be. To this end, I sent a brief questionnaire (reproduced on the previous page) to 120 individuals to determine if it really is *lack of information* that keeps so many people from taking advantage of the better-paying mutual funds. Based on the results, the answer was a resounding yes. Mutual funds are still a mystery to many investors, vis-à-vis CDs.

The individuals surveyed included 60 people who owned some mutual funds as well as bank CDs, and 60 people who have never owned mutual funds but do own bank CDs. In each of the two groups of 60 subjects, 20 were professionals, 20 were homemakers, and 20 were self-employed. (Both men and women participated.)

Based on the returns, the following data were obtained.

Mutual Fund Owners

Level of Understanding:	Number of Responses at Each Level:
Professionals:	
Very knowledgeable	3
Somewhat knowledgeable	10
Not at all knowledgeable	7

Homemakers:

Very knowledgeable	1
Somewhat knowledgeable	5
Not at all knowledgeable	14

Self-employed:

Very knowledgeable	2
Somewhat knowledgeable	7
Not at all knowledgeable	11

Of the above group, which included those who own some mutual funds, the following percentages were derived in each of the three categories measured:

Level of Understanding:	Percentages:
Very knowledgeable	10%
Somewhat knowledgeable	37%
Not at all knowledgeable	53%

Non-Owners of Mutual Funds:

Level of Understanding:	Number of Responses at Each Level:
Professionals:	
Very knowledgeable	2
Somewhat knowledgeable	9
Not at all knowledgeable	9
Homemakers:	
Very knowledgeable	0
Somewhat knowledgeable	2
Not at all knowledgeable	18
Self-employed:	
Very knowledgeable	1
Somewhat knowledgeable	3
Not at all knowledgeable	16

Of the above group, none of whom had ever owned mutual funds, the following percentages were derived in each of the three categories measured:

Level of Understanding:	Percentages:
Very knowledgeable	5%
Somewhat knowledgeable	23%
Not at all knowledgeable	72%

The startling, although not unexpected, findings revealed the following:

Among mutual fund owners, only 10% were fully knowledgeable, while 53% had no real knowledge of mutual fund investing.

Among non-mutual fund owners, only 5% had any real knowledge of mutual funds, while a whopping 72% knew virtually nothing about mutual fund investing.

These results are clear evidence that lack of knowledge is the most likely reason so many people are hesitant about investing in mutual funds. This, despite the fact they are fully aware that interest rates on their bank CDs are no longer adequate to meet their needs for supplemental income.

This small sampling represents only the tip of the iceberg. There must be countless more who find themselves in the same precarious situation. It is for them that *All About Mutual Funds—From the Inside Out* was written.

POSTSCRIPT I–1

FIGURES DON'T LIE

"The average American is more attuned to television than to investing." That's the outcome of a survey conducted by the National Association of Security Dealers (NASD).

Of those polled, 78% knew a sitcom character's name, but only 12% knew anything about load and no-load mutual funds. Sports enthusiasts aren't reading the stock and mutual fund pages during the game; 63% of respondents knew the difference between a quarterback and a halfback, yet only 14% could explain the differences between a growth stock fund and an income stock fund.

"We learned very quickly," says Michael Jones, an NASD vice president, that there is a real need for quality investor education.

Since we have mentioned sports, remember this advice: "If you don't swing the bat, you can't get a hit. You may miss occasionally, but this much is *certain*, if you *don't* swing the bat you'll *never* get a hit."

A long time ago, as a high school football player, I also learned this lesson: *You can't catch your own forward pass.* Likewise in financial matters, not everyone has a sufficient background in investing to do it on his or her own. Therefore, a book such as this is definitely helpful. However, financial consultants are sometimes also needed, because even though you do try swinging the bat, a batting coach will often improve your batting average.

POSTSCRIPT I–2

AMERICANS NEED FINANCIAL LESSONS

In a survey of people who have been investing for an average of 11 years, mostly for retirement, it was found that about half have mutual funds or individual stocks. Two-fifths own bonds. Yet, their nest egg after all that time is about $33,000. Not bad, but far from rich. These are ordinary folks doing their best to plan for the future. *Trouble is, most don't know what they're doing.*

Another report on Americans' lack of financial knowledge came out recently from the nonprofit Investor Protection Trust of Arlington, Virginia. That survey found that only 18% of American investors are "financially literate" and able to answer seven out of eight *very basic questions about investing.*

"To devote huge amounts of energy to tell people how to find the best camcorder or VCR and ignore how to choose a mutual fund or create an investment plan doesn't make much sense today. These are some of the most important decisions people will make," said Barbara Roper, director of information for the Consumer Protection Federation of America. But they are making these vital decisions without the facts!

The survey found that most American investors don't know that all mutual funds, load and no-load, charge management fees, or that the value of bonds goes down when interest rates go up. Even among people who own bonds, 58% did not know this basic fact. *That's scary!*

The key question is: How can investors educate themselves? The first step is to recognize that there is a serious need in this area. The second step is to face the fact that the government may not be able to provide for one's financial needs in the future. For people in their 40s and 50s, looking at Social Security with a jaundiced eye is to face the future realistically. The next step is to become financially literate by reading financial news, watching financial TV programs, and visiting public libraries where many books on the subject of investing may be found, such as the book you are presently reading.

Mark Griffin, a trustee of the Investor Protection Trust, remarked, "We basically graduate students with barely the skill to balance a checkbook. Yet we teach them about the Punic Wars. When was the last time in most of life's pursuits that you were called upon to use your knowledge of who won the Punic Wars? I believe knowing how to handle your money will serve you *throughout your entire life.* At least our youth should know what dollar-cost averaging means, and why an 18-year-old should not use an income fund in an IRA, or to begin with, what an IRA is anyway."

ALL ABOUT
MUTUAL FUNDS

CHAPTER 1

What Are Mutual Funds?

DEFINITION

A mutual fund is a collection of stocks, bonds, or other securities purchased by a pool of individual investors and managed by a professional investment company.

When you make an investment in a mutual fund, your money is pooled along with all the other investors' money. The aggregate sum is then used by the fund to build or expand the investment portfolio that comprises the particular fund.

Each mutual fund share you own represents your proportional share of all the stocks and bonds that make up the fund's investment portfolio. Most mutual fund portfolios consist of 50 to 100 different stocks, bonds, U.S. Treasuries, etc. Thus, when you invest in a mutual fund, you buy "shares" at a price that represents the total value of all the securities in the fund's portfolio divided by the total number of shares outstanding. This is known as the *net asset value* (NAV) of a single share of the fund.

As an example, suppose XYZ Mutual Fund has in its portfolio shares of 50 different stocks, and on a given day the value of all its securities totals $5 million. Assuming there are 500,000 shares outstanding, the NAV of a single share of the fund on that day would be $10 ($5,000,000 divided by 500,000). If you owned 40 shares of XYZ Fund, your total investment would be worth $400 on that particular day.

The NAV may vary from day to day as the value of the securities held by the fund changes. Thus, on a given day the NAV may be higher or lower than the price you paid for each of the shares of the fund at the time you bought them. In essence then, a mutual fund investor is an owner, not a lender (as is the holder of a bank certificate of deposit). Therefore, as an owner, the mutual fund investor shares in the profits and losses as well as the income and expenses of the fund.

The NAV will figure prominently throughout this text.

HISTORY

Mutual funds, as we know them today, began in this country in the early 1920s. By 1929 there were 19 mutual funds with assets of about $140 million. During the Depression years of the 1930s, the growth of mutual funds was slow; by 1940 the combined assets of the 68 funds then in existence totaled less than $500 million.

During the 1950s, 1960s, and 1970s, the mutual fund industry experienced tremendous growth. By the end of 1972 there were over 400 mutual funds with assets of over $60 billion, and more than 10 million shareholder accounts. In 1986 the number of mutual funds had grown to almost 1,900, and investors had poured in excess of $708 billion into them (see Table 1–1).

TABLE 1–1

Total Assets All Funds

Mutual Fund Assets	
How mutual fund assets have grown since 1980	
Year	Total assets all funds
1980	180 billion
1983	250 billion
1986	750 billion
1989	1 trillion
1992	1.6 trillion
1994	2.5 trillion
1999	3.5 trillion

TABLE 1–2

Amounts Invested by Institutions

Year	Amount invested
1970	$6.2 billion
1980	$17.7 billion
1983	$26.0 billion
1984	$146.0 billion
1990	over $225.0 billion
1999	over $378 billion

Roye, SEC director, said, "American investors have more than $6 trillion invested in mutual funds; up more than 580% in the past 10 years.*

*Includes Tables 1–1 & 1–2 plus another $2 trillion invested in money market mutual funds.

THE CURRENT INDUSTRY

To paraphrase Al Jolson, "You ain't heard nothin' yet!" Mutual fund investing swept the nation during the 1990s and money poured in at the rate of *$1 billion per day*, according to the Investment Company Institute (ICI). By the end of the decade, there were *10,350 different* mutual funds containing *$3.7 trillion in assets*, excluding money market funds, which held additional billions in assets.

Table 1–2, compiled by ICI, shows the amounts of money institutional investors (i.e., labor unions, large corporations, professional associations, colleges and universities) have invested in mutual funds. Their pension funds, employee retirement accounts, 401(k) plans, and cash reserves are entrusted to mutual funds—a clear indication of the confidence and trust these large organizations have in the safety and worth of mutual funds.

Mutual funds provide convenience, diversification, professional management, and over the long-term have helped millions upon millions of investors to build substantial wealth. And the new millennium will continue to provide wealth-building opportunities for knowledgeable investors.

HOW TO SELECT A MUTUAL FUND

Selecting a good fund in which to invest is a simple matter. With the large number of investment companies and the tremendous variety of funds available, you should have no trouble finding a fund or two with which to establish your portfolio.

First, you should decide whether you want a load or no-load fund (see Chapter 4). If you choose a load fund, any stock broker will be happy to help you, but you will pay a commission. If you go the no-load route, *as I strongly recommend,* check your daily newspaper (see Chapter 13) or other sources of mutual fund listings (as noted in Appendix A). Next, decide on your general objectives. Are you seeking income, growth, or both? Do you want a taxable or tax-free fund? It is also helpful to define your specific objectives. These may include building an estate, increasing current income, creating a fund for education, or saving for a large purchase or for retirement. These are the preliminaries to purchasing any fund. The particulars will be carefully delineated in succeeding chapters.

As you evaluate your choices, keep in mind your risk tolerance and decide whether you would like to speculate or to sleep comfortably at night. Chapter 6 provides some help with this problem. Chapter 9 explains how to open an account once you have made a choice.

MUTUAL FUNDS ARE:

A convenient and sensible way for the novice to enter the investment field.

Safe, well-managed, well-regulated, diversified investment vehicles.

So varied and accessible that there are funds available to meet every investor's goals.

MUTUAL FUNDS ARE NOT:

Get-rich-quick investments.

Entirely risk-free, but the companies that sell them are strictly regulated and controlled.

Investments designed to be held for the short term.

Investments whose shares ordinarily make *large* moves either up or down.

STUDY GUIDE FOR CHAPTER 1

1. What is a mutual fund?
2. What is done with the money you invest in a mutual fund?
3. What is meant by "owning a proportional share" of the fund's portfolio?
4. Explain what is meant by the NAV.
5. What would be the NAV of a mutual fund with $55 million invested and 1 million outstanding shares?
6. What is the difference between being a lender, as in purchasing a bank CD, and being an owner, as in purchasing shares of a mutual fund?

POSTSCRIPT 1–1

THE NAV ANALYZED

MEANING

1. NAV stands for *net asset value* (dollar value) of one share of a mutual fund.
2. How much it costs to purchase one share of a fund (when it has no up-front load).
3. What you receive per share when redeeming shares (exclusive of back-end loads where imposed).
4. The dollar value of *one* share of a mutual fund.

HOW TO DETERMINE A FUND'S NAV

Add the value of all the securities in a fund's portfolio and divide by the number of outstanding shares. For example, realistically, the average mutual fund would have many more securities in its portfolio:

1. *Portfolio of XYZ Mutual Fund* (on a given day)

General Motors stock	value of shares	$49 million
Ford Motor stock	value of shares	$35 million
Texaco Oil stock	value of shares	$41 million
Sony stock	value of shares	$18 million
IBM stock	value of shares	$27 million
Cash Reserve	total amount of cash	$10 million
	TOTAL PORTFOLIO VALUE	$180 million

2. Number of outstanding shares: 20 million
3. Calculating the NAV: $180 million divided by 20 million shares = $9 NAV
4. An investment of $2,500 will purchase 277.777 shares at a NAV of $9 (the number of shares is always calculated to three decimal places).

EFFECT OF ASSET FLUCTUATIONS

On the date for which the above NAV was determined, GM stock traded at $49 per share. XYZ Mutual Fund owned 1 million shares ($49 times 1 million shares equals $49 million). If GM stock were to gain $2 per share, and therefore trade at $51 per share, the $2 gain times 1 million GM shares adds $2 million to the value of the fund's total portfolio. Then the fund's portfolio would be worth $182 million. The $182 million divided by the 20 million outstanding shares equals an NAV of $9.10 per share—a rise of $.10 per share.

If, on the other hand, GM shares lost $2, the total value of the XYZ's portfolio would decrease to $178 million: divided by the 20 million outstanding shares, this equals a NAV of $8.90—a loss of $.10 per share.

There are five other variables that affect a fund's NAV. They will be analyzed in the next chapter.

MUTUAL FUNDS NOW TOP BANK SAVINGS

In 1998, for the first time in history, total assets of mutual funds exceeded the total assets of all the nation's banks. The public has shifted from saving to investing. In prior years the nation's savers kept their money in federally insured bank accounts. Today, however, the nation's savvy investors are betting their future on Wall Street. And with good reason.

The shift reflected the stock market boom that raised the value of stocks and mutual funds more than 25% over three years. Given the gains made by the stock market and equity mutual funds, smaller investors by the millions were lured to Wall Street by the hopes of riches. Investors were willing to take on added risk for potentially higher gains. Consider that in April 1988 banks held $2.9 trillion of savers money, while in the same year mutual funds could only claim $809 million of investor's money. Today, however, while bank assets have grown to $4.9 trillion, mutual fund assets total an amazing $7 trillion. The gap shows every indication of continuing to grow.

Total mutual fund assets grew by 35% in the past two years, from about $3.7 trillion to today's total of $7 trillion. The preponderance of growth has been in equity-type mutual funds.

The Social Security Administration may one day permit some privatization of its system by allowing individuals to designate a percentage of their Social Security withholding to be invested in mutual funds of their own choice. If this were the case, the government stands to gain because it will be paying smaller benefits to Social Security recipients. This should help the system remain solvent for a much longer period of time than is currently anticipated. Additionally, Social Security recipients stand to gain because they will have had the opportunity to invest in higher income producing investments, such as mutual funds, thereby increasing their total retirement returns.

Under a system of partial privatization, mutual funds will experience growth unprecedented in prior years. Employee 401(k) plans already operate under a somewhat similar system. These plans have enabled participants to greatly improve their retirement benefits by using mutual funds as the investment medium for their 401(k) contributions.

POSTSCRIPT 1–3

GROWTH OF THE MUTUAL FUND INDUSTRY

As late as 1995 the total assets invested in mutual funds totaled slightly over $1 trillion. Today, mutual fund assets total better than $7 trillion. The Investment Company Institute projects that mutual fund assets will probably reach $8.5 trillion by the year 2001.

Today there are more mutual funds available to the public than there are stocks listed on the New York Stock Exchange, and the number of funds increases *every day*. The leading stock index, the Dow Jones Industrial Index, could reach 12,000 by the end of 2001. This bodes well for mutual fund shareholders!

HOW MUCH IS $1 TRILLION?

If you were to count a trillion one dollar bills, one per second, 24 hours a day, it would take 23 years before you were finished.

With $1 trillion you could buy a $100,000 house for every family in Missouri, Kansas, Nebraska, Oklahoma, and Iowa.

Then you could put a $10,000 car in the garage of each one of those houses. There would be enough left over to build ten $1 million libraries and ten $1 million hospitals for 250 cities in those five states. There would still be enough left over to build ten $1 million schools for 500 communities.

If you put $1 trillion in the bank, the interest alone would be enough to pay 10,000 nurses and teachers, plus give a $5,000 bonus for every family in those five states.

The above analysis is based on just $1 trillion. It is worth repeating that there are over $7 trillion invested in mutual funds.

CHAPTER 2

Mutual Fund Classifications

There are two kinds of mutual funds: open-end investment funds, and closed-end funds. How they are alike and how they differ will be analyzed in this chapter.

OPEN-END FUNDS

These are by far the more prevalent and better known type of mutual fund offered by investment companies. Open-end simply means that the fund has shares available for sale at all times and will sell as many shares as investors wish to buy. Conversely, the fund also stands ready to redeem as many outstanding shares as investors want to sell. The investment company sells and/or redeems shares at the net asset value as of the close of the stock market on the date it receives the request to do so.

As a result of the fund's constantly ongoing transactions, the share's NAV may vary from day to day. Changes in the fund's NAV is caused by (a) the purchasing of new securities for the portfolio, and (b) the selling of securities currently in the fund's portfolio.

Changes in the *value* of the individual securities that make up the fund's portfolio also cause the NAV to fluctuate. Every mutual fund maintains a cash reserve, usually around 5% of the total assets of the fund. The cash reserves are usually reserved to cover shareholder's redemption requests. However, should the amount required to meet the cost of redemptions exceed the money available in the cash reserves, the fund manager may have to liquidate some of the securities in the fund's portfolio in order to obtain the cash necessary to cover all the redemption requests. The total value of the securities remaining in the portfolio diminishes, thus affecting the NAV.

CLOSED-END FUNDS

Generally referred to as *publicly traded investment funds*, closed-end funds differ from open-end funds in three important respects and are similar in two major respects. They differ in (1) the method of purchase, (2) the number of outstanding shares, and (3) the relationship of share value to market value. They are similar in that both provide professional management and portfolio diversification.

The shares of closed-end funds are traded (bought and sold) strictly on the floor of the particular stock exchange where they are listed. Since they are bought and sold like any other stock, the service of a stockbroker is required, for which a commission is charged. As noted, the number of shares of open-end funds varies; the number of shares of closed-end funds remains fixed. Lastly, the trading prices of closed-end funds are determined solely by what investors feel they are worth and are influenced by investors' expectations regarding the potential value of the shares vis-à-vis their NAV. Thus, they may trade either at a discount or at a premium. Shares will sell at a discount when investors feel they are worth less than their NAV.

For example, if the NAV for a particular closed-end fund is $17.72 and the selling price of its shares is listed at $16.00, the fund is selling at a 10% discount. The discount indicates how investors think the fund will perform in the future—in this instance, they are bearish on the fund. Conversely, when the NAV of a closed-end fund's shares is $17.58 and its listed selling price is $19.75 per share, it is selling at a 12.34% premium. In this instance, investors are bullish on the fund. They feel the shares will appreciate in value and they are willing to pay a premium to purchase them. In most cases, however, shares of closed-end funds usually sell at a discount.

Closed-end funds are not listed in the mutual fund tables printed in most daily newspapers; instead, they are listed alphabetically in the stock tables of daily newspapers according to the stock exchange where they are traded. Excellent sources for closed-end fund listings are the *Wall Street Journal* and *Barron's*.

A word of advice: A beginning investor would be prudent to wait before venturing into the closed-end fund market. For now, concentrate strictly on open-end mutual funds—there are many hundreds of excellent ones from which to choose. Later chapters will help you decide which choices are best, based on your risk-level temperament and your investment objectives.

SIX REASONS FOR FLUCTUATIONS IN NET ASSET VALUE

1. Performance of the stock and bond markets (either up or down).
2. Dividend distributions (from income that the fund receives).
3. Capital gains distributions (from realized capital gains).
4. Unrealized capital gains: increase in the value of securities held in the fund's portfolio—not distributed to shareholders.
5. Realized losses resulting from the sale of securities in the fund's portfolio at a price lower than when purchased.
6. Unrealized losses caused by the decrease in value of the fund's securities.

EFFECT OF DISTRIBUTIONS ON A FUND'S NAV

The NAV has been analyzed from a number of different aspects— what it means, the effect of various types of changes, etc. However, one factor has not been completely explained—the actual and apparent effects of fund distributions. For example, you may see a sudden drop in the NAV for a particular fund, even when the stock market posted a sizable gain for the day. This appears contrary to what one would expect; the explanation is simple. The fund, in all likelihood, declared and/or made distributions—either dividends or capital gains, or both.

For example, a fund may have made a year-end capital gain distribution of $.50 per share. If you own 1,000 shares, it would be great to receive a $500 distribution check. *Resist temptation, and have the distribution reinvested in your fund instead!* On the ex-dividend date (distribution date), the NAV will automatically decrease by $.50 per share. If the NAV was $8.75 before the ex-dividend date, it will fall to $8.25 right after the ex-dividend date, but you will have experienced no loss because the difference between the two NAVs will be exactly the same as the amount of the distribution. If you had reinvested the distribution, as suggested, your $500 distribution would buy you 60.606 additional shares at the lower NAV price of $8.25.

STUDY GUIDE FOR CHAPTER 2

1. Name the two kinds of mutual funds.
2. What are the characteristics of an open-end fund?
3. How do closed-end mutual funds differ from open-end funds?
4. How and where are closed-end funds purchased?
5. Why are some closed-end funds sold at a discount to their NAV?
6. Why are some closed-end funds sold at a premium in relation to their NAV?
7. Where are open-end funds listed?
8. Where are closed-end funds listed?
9. Why does the NAV, as well as the number of shares that comprise an open-end mutual fund, vary?
10. True or false: The number of shares in a closed-end fund varies from time to time.
11. What kinds of funds should a novice investor consider for purchase?

POSTSCRIPT 2–1

THE "X" DIVIDEND DATE'S EFFECT ON A FUND'S NET ASSET VALUE

When a mutual fund makes a distribution, be it for dividends, capital gains, or both, the money required to pay shareholders for the distribution is taken from the fund's net assets, thereby reducing its NAV by an amount equal to the distribution. For example, if a fund's NAV was $28.00 per share before the distribution, and the distribution amounted to $1.50 per share, the NAV would fall to $26.50 ($28 − $1.50 = $26.50, assuming there were no other changes for the day).

Normally, mutual funds' NAVs reflect the changes in the stock market indices: Dow Jones Industrial, S&P 500, AMEX, NASDAQ. When these indices show gains, mutual funds' NAVs will generally show gains as well. (The reverse, of course, is also true.)

Occasionally, however, the indices will show *substantial gains*, yet certain well-performing funds will show *large losses*. This is contrary to what one would expect. The reason for this contradiction is generally found by noting a small *x* following the name of the fund. The *x* indicates that the fund has made a distribution. Thus, the reason for the decline in the fund's NAV was actually due to the distribution. Generally, the amount of the loss is exactly the same as the amount of the distribution.

See Figure 2–1 on page 15 for examples of the "distribution effect" on a fund's NAV when stock market indices showed substantial gains. You will note that funds with the *x* all showed losses despite the large gains in the stock market indices for the day.

FIGURE 2-1

DOW JONES INDUSTRIAL AVERAGES
for the last 30 trading days
in 1997

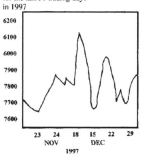

Sun-Sentinel, Tuesday, December 30, 1997

Stocks rise on hopes for a strong January

The Dow Jones industrial average rose 113.10 to 7,792.41 pushing the 1997 gain back above 20percent with just two sessions to go.

The Stand & Poor's 500-stock index rose 16.89 to 953.35 bringing the 1997 gain to 28.7 percent. The technology-laden Nasdaq composite index rose 26.07 to 1,537.45, putting 1997's gain at 19.1 percent.

	1-Yr Ret	NAV	NAV Chg
AAL Mutual A			
Bond m	+8.4	10.02	...
CGrowth	+28.7	25.46	+.48
EqInc	+19.9	13.06	+.18
Intl m	+1.5	10.45	+.03
MidCap b	+15.8	14.06	+.22
MuniBd m	+9.9	11.56	...
AARP Invst			
BalS&B x	+19.9	20.35	-.99
CaGr x	+29.8	50.99	-3.89
GinvM	+7.2	15.20	...
GiblGr x	+14.8	17.90	-.47
Gthinc x	+27.9	52.20	-4.64
HQ Bd	+7.1	16.27	-.01
TxFBd	+8.4	16.60	-.05
JANUS			
→ Balanced x	+19.6	15.05	-1.41
Entrprs	+8.5	29.38	-1.29
EqInc x	+27.9	13.15	-.63
FixInc x	NA	9.87	-.21
Fund x	+19.0	24.30	-4.31
GrInc x	+30.2	22.72	-1.89
HiYld x	NA	11.38	-.56
→ Mercury x	+9.4	16.16	-1.46
Olympus x	+22.11	7.12	-.33
Ovrseas x	+18.9	17.31	-.30
SplStu x	NA	13.54	-.40
Twen x	+24.0	30.47	-3.80
Ventur x	+10.8	48.31	-8.29
WrldW x	+20.4	37.54	-1.93
JapanFd	-14.6	6.72	+.04

Price Funds			
Balan x	+16.9	16.37	-.08
BluChip x	+23.7	23.68	+.26
CapAp x	+14.8	14.54	-1.99
DivGro x	+28.6	19.91	-.52
EmMktS d	-0.4	11.42	+.11
EmgMktB	+16.3	13.70	-.07
EqIdx x	+27.8	25.91	+.22
EquIn x	+25.7	25.76	-1.62
Europ x	+19.3	19.41	-.95
FEF x	+4.2	15.81	-.46
FLInsInf	+6.8	10.73	...
FinSvcs x	+38.4	15.33	-.24
GNMA	+8.7	9.57	+.01
→ Grwth x	+23.6	28.48	-3.44
Gthinc x	+20.1	25.93	-.82
HelSci	+18.3	13.36	-.82
HiYld d	+14.6	8.74	+.01
Incom	+8.7	9.07	-.04
IntDis d	-4.9	15.00	-.16
IntlBd	-1.4	9.68	+.04
ThriStk x	+3.8	13.37	-.56
Japan	-23.2	6.75	+.02
LatAm d x	+28.9	10.49	+.21
McapGro	+16.7	27.83	+.08
McapVal x	+25.9	14.24	-.07
MdSht	+4.2	5.12	...
MediaTel	+5.0	17.11	-1.89
N AmGr	+18.3	42.74	-1.49
N Asia x	-37.8	5.64	-.01
N Era x	+8.4	25.45	-2.58
N Horz	+8.0	22.60	+.20
NJ TF	+8.9	11.49	-.01
NYTF	+9.3	11.24	-.01
PSBal x	+16.1	14.68	-.14
PSInc x	+13.9	12.37	-.34
ST Bd	+6.1	4.88	...
SciTc	-2.5	26.45	-2.08
ShtUSG	+6.2	4.85	...
SmCapStk x	+26.9	21.66	-.82
SmCapVal x	+26.4	22.96	-1.46
SpcGr x	+15.3	15.85	-1.56
Specinc	+11.5	11.64	-.14
TFInsI	+7.2	11.04	-.03
TxFHi	+10.1	12.82	...
TxFrI	+9.0	9.93	-.01
TxFrSI	+5.3	5.36	-.01
US Int	+7.7	5.28	...
USLng	+13.5	11.28	-.02
Value x	+26.9	17.94	-1.51

Scudder Funds			
Balanced	+20.0	16.63	+.20
Devel	+6.1	37.42	-3.11
EmgMktGr x	+2.9	13.99	+.19
EmMkt	+12.4	11.24	+.11
GNMA	+7.5	14.80	...
GibBd	+0.9	9.88	+.01
GlbDis x	+9.0	19.41	-1.75
Glbl x	+17.6	28.15	-5.00
Gold x	-41.1	7.26	-.28
GrEuGro x	+26.3	20.60	-1.61
Grwin x	+27.2	26.90	-1.59
HiYldBd	+14.8	12.29	...
Incom	+8.3	13.48	-.01
Thrt Fd x	+9.3	45.69	-4.98
IntBd	-3.0	10.24	-.02
LaAme x	+28.3	25.97	-.48
LgCoGro	+28.2	24.57	-.91
LgCoVal x	+28.4	26.73	-1.73
LtdTrTF	+6.0	12.15	...
MAT x	+8.6	14.36	...
MMB	+9.2	9.12	...
MedTF	+7.5	11.40	...
MicrCap	+34.0	17.19	+.08
NYTax	+9.2	11.31	...
PacOpps x	-38.2	10.01	-.26
PwyBal	+12.5	13.13	+.10
ST Bond	+5.8	11.03	-.01
SmCoVal d x	+35.9	20.53	-.17
TxFHi	+12.1	12.77	...
→ Value x	+31.6	21.76	-1.55

POSTSCRIPT 2–2

EFFECT OF PURCHASING AND REDEEMING SHARES ON FUND'S NAV

A little understood concept is the effect that purchasing and redeeming a fund's shares has on its NAV. Although it would seem that such changes should affect the fund's NAV, usually they do not have *any effect whatsoever.* The example below will help explain why. Minimum amounts are used in order to simplify the arithmetic, and it is assumed that *no other changes* occurred, other than the buying and redeeming of shares.

Say the XYZ Mutual Fund has assets of $60 million, and there are 500,000 shares outstanding: $60 million divided by 500,000 shares equals a NAV of $120.

On a particular day, the fund received deposits from investors totaling $40,000. The fund's assets now amount to $60,040,000. At the NAV of $120, the fund, therefore, issued 333,333 new shares to cover the deposits. Now, the fund's assets must be divided by the new total of 500,333.33 shares. This equals an NAV of exactly $120. *No change!*

The reverse would be true if depositors had *redeemed* $40,000 worth of shares. The NAV would *not have changed,* because the fund's assets would have been reduced by $40,000 and at the NAV of $120 there would be 333.333 fewer shares outstanding. Thus, the NAV would still be $120. Do the arithmetic, and see for yourself.

CHAPTER 3

Types of Mutual Funds

Not too many years ago, mutual funds were simply broad-based investment instruments created to simplify the intricacies involved in investing in separate securities. They also provided a greater measure of safety through broad diversification and the kind of top-notch professional management that is usually out of reach for the small investor.

Today, however, mutual funds are highly specialized and offer almost unlimited diversity. The types of mutual fund portfolios available run the gamut from conservative to aggressive, from stocks to bonds, from domestic to international portfolios, from taxable to tax-free, and from virtually no-risk money market funds to high-risk options funds. The great variety of mutual funds available makes it possible to select a fund, or several funds, which precisely match any investor's specific objectives and investment goals. The various types of funds and their primary objectives are described below. (They are arranged in order of increasing risk factors, except for the tax-free listing.) All of the fund types described in this chapter are available as *no-load* funds.

MONEY MARKET FUNDS

We begin with a discussion of money market funds for several reasons:

1. They are the safest for the novice investor;
2. They are the easiest, least complicated to follow and understand;
3. Almost without exception, every mutual fund investment company offers money market funds;
4. Money market funds represent an indispensable investment tool for the beginning investor (see "telephone switching" strategy in Chapter 12);
5. They are the most basic and conservative of all the mutual funds available; and
6. All offer free check writing.

Money market funds should be considered by investors seeking stability of principal, total liquidity, check-writing features, and earnings that are as high, or higher, than those available through bank certificates of deposit. And unlike bank CDs, money market funds have no early withdrawal penalties.

Specifically, a money market fund is a mutual fund that invests its assets only in the most liquid of money instruments. The portfolio seeks stability by investing in very short-term, interest-bearing instruments issued by the United States Treasury, state and local governments, banks, and large corporations. The money invested is a loan to these agencies, and the length of the loan might range from overnight to one week or, in some cases, as long as 90 days. These debt certificates are called "money market instruments"; because they can be converted into cash so readily, they are considered the equivalent of cash.

Note: There are also tax-free, municipal bond money market funds that have all the excellent features described above, plus earnings that are federally tax-free, and in some cases free of state taxes as well. (See Chapter 4 for examples.)

Although it seemed almost impossible to improve upon the safety features of money market funds, the Securities and Exchange Commission (SEC) did so just recently. It ruled that:

1. A minimum of 95% of a money market fund's assets must be invested in *top-rated securities only.*
2. No more than 1% of a money market fund's assets may be

invested in the securities of *any one issuer* whose rating is *below the top rating*.

3. The maximum maturity of any fund's holdings was reduced from 120 days to 90 days.

These new regulations have further improved the safety, liquidity, and portfolio diversification of all money market funds.

Lastly, since the investments made by money market funds are so stable, they are able to maintain a *fixed share price*—usually valued at a dollar per share. Because the NAV is fixed and does not fluctuate, an investor will always own one share for each dollar invested in a money market fund. Thus, if you were to invest $1,000 in such a fund, you would own 1,000 shares. While the NAV would not change, the *interest rate* paid on your investment is adjusted daily to reflect changing market conditions.

If the fund succeeded in paying 8% interest over the course of the year on your $1,000 investment, you would have accumulated 80 or more additional shares, assuming you had reinvested your dividends each time the fund made a dividend distribution. This is due to the fact that most money market funds distribute dividends monthly, and by reinvesting them monthly, they too would begin earning interest (compounding) as of the date they were credited to your account. Of course, you could take your monthly dividends in cash, but then you lose the valuable benefit of interest compounding.

To understand why I recommend money market mutual funds as an ideal investment, let me reemphasize just seven of the advantages they offer:

1. *Safety of principal,* through diversification and stability of the short-term portfolio investments
2. *Total and immediate liquidity,* by telephone or letter
3. *Better yields than offered by banks,* 1% to 3% higher
4. *Low minimum investment,* some as low as $100
5. *Professional management,* proven expertise
6. *No purchase or redemption fees,* no-load funds
7. *Free check-writing privileges,* checks continue to earn interest until cleared

Money Market Update

Americans have a big chunk of cash stowed away in money market funds. As of January 1, 1999, a total of about *$1.4 trillion* was invested in money market mutual funds. Deposits have been increasing steadily over the years. In 1998 alone, *$290 billion* was deposited in money market mutual funds. Money market mutual funds avoid fluctuations because they do not invest in stocks. They invest in more stable, short-term investments such as U.S. Treasury bills, short-term bank certificates of deposit, letters of credit, and commercial paper. As a result, money market funds are able to maintain a constant $1.00 NAV and pay at least 1.5% to 2.5% more interest than *bank* money market accounts. For example, the average taxable money market mutual fund was yielding *5.64%* in March 2000. Bank money market accounts yielded 2.6% or less at that time.

INCOME FUNDS

The objective of income mutual funds is to seek a high level of current income commensurate with each portfolio's risk potential. In other words, the greater the risk, the greater the potential for generous income yields; but the greater the risk of principal loss as well.

The risk/reward potential is low to high, depending upon the type of securities that make up the fund's portfolio. The risk is very low when the fund is invested in U.S. government obligations, blue-chip corporations, and short-term agency securities. The risk is high when a fund seeks higher yields by investing in long-term corporate bonds, or so-called junk bonds offered by new, undercapitalized, risky companies.

Who should invest in income funds?

- Investors seeking current income higher than money market rates, who are willing to accept moderate price fluctuations
- Investors willing to "balance" their equity (stock) portfolios with a fixed income investment
- Investors who want a portfolio of taxable bonds with differing maturity dates

- Investors interested in receiving periodic income on a regular basis

It should be noted that tax-free municipal bond income funds are also available. The same objectives and risk/reward potentials pertain to these funds as were noted for the taxable income funds; however, yields are somewhat lower, but they are not federally taxed.

INCOME AND GROWTH FUNDS

The primary purposes of income and growth funds are to provide a steady source of income and moderate growth. Such funds are ideal for retirees needing a supplemental source of income without forsaking growth entirely.

GROWTH AND INCOME FUNDS

The primary objectives of growth and income funds are to seek long-term growth of principal and reasonable current income. By investing in a portfolio of stocks believed to offer growth potential plus market or above-market dividend income, the fund expects to realize these objectives. Risk is moderate, as are the rewards. Investors seeking growth of capital and moderate income over the long term (at least five years) should consider growth and income funds. Such funds require that the investor be willing to accept some share-price volatility, but less than found in pure growth funds.

BALANCED FUNDS

The basic objectives of balanced funds are to generate income as well as long-term growth of principal. These funds generally have portfolios consisting of bonds, preferred stocks, and common stocks. They have fairly limited price rise potential, but do have a high degree of safety, and moderate to high income potential.

Investors who desire a fund with a combination of securities in a single portfolio, and who seek some current income and moderate growth with low-level risk, would do well to invest in balanced mutual funds. Balanced funds, by and large, do not differ greatly from the growth and income funds described above.

GROWTH FUNDS

Growth funds are offered by every investment company. The primary objective of such funds is to seek long-term appreciation (growth of capital). The secondary objective is to make one's capital investment grow faster than the rate of inflation. Dividend income is considered an incidental objective of growth funds.

Growth funds are best suited for investors interested primarily in seeing their principal grow and are therefore to be considered as *long-term* investments—held for at least three to five years. Jumping in and out of growth funds tends to defeat their purpose. However, if the fund has not shown substantial growth over a three- to five-year period, sell it (redeem your shares) and seek a growth fund with another investment company.

Candidates likely to participate in growth funds are those willing to accept moderate to high risk in order to attain growth of their capital and those investors who characterize their investment temperament as "fairly aggressive."

INDEX FUNDS

The intent of an index fund is basically to track the performance of the stock market. If the overall market advances, a good index fund follows the rise. When the market declines, so will the index fund. Index funds' portfolios consist of securities listed on the popular stock market indices, mainly the Standard and Poor's 500 Stock Index and the Dow Jones Industrial Average Index. The former index tracks 500 widely held stocks, and the latter tracks 30 actively traded blue-chip stocks.

It is also the intent of an index fund to materially reduce expenses by eliminating the fund portfolio manager. Instead, the fund merely purchases a group of stocks that make up the particular index it deems the best to follow—either the Dow Jones or the S&P index. The stocks in an index fund portfolio rarely change and are weighted the same way as its particular market index. Thus, there is no need for a portfolio manager. The securities in an index mutual fund are identical to those listed by the index it tracks, thus, there is little or no need for any great turnover of the portfolio of securities. The funds are "passively managed" in a fairly static portfolio. An index fund is always fully invested in the securities of the index it tracks.

An index mutual fund may never *outperform* the market but it should not lag far behind it either. The reduction of administrative cost in the management of an index fund also adds to its profitability.

By way of illustration, the Vanguard Index Trust, which uses the S&P 500 Index, has advanced and declined according to the index very accurately, never having finished a year more than 1% to 3% below the index average. In 1980, for example, the S&P 500 Index advanced 33%, and the Vanguard Trust Index Fund advanced 32%. Again in 1985, the same results were achieved. However, in 1981 the index declined 36% from its 1980 high, and Vanguard's Index Trust declined 37%.

In short, if you are willing to have a fund that follows the swings of the stock market, an index mutual fund is the one for you. Knowing when to switch in and out of an index fund is the key to high profits. (Fund switching is covered in Chapter 12.)

Exhibit 3–1 (at the end of this chapter) illustrates a stock market index.

SECTOR FUNDS

As was noted earlier, most mutual funds have fairly broad-based, diversified portfolios. In the case of *sector funds*, however, the portfolios consist of investments from *only one* sector of the economy. Sector funds concentrate in one specific market segment; for example, energy, transportation, precious metals, health sciences, utilities, leisure industries, etc. In other words, they are very narrowly based. (Invesco Funds are good examples.)

Investors in sector funds must be prepared to accept the rather high level of risk inherent in funds that are not particularly diversified. Any measure of diversification that may exist in sector funds is attained through a variety of securities, albeit in the same market sector. Substantial profits are attainable by investors astute enough to identify which market sector is ripe for growth—not always an easy task!

SPECIALIZED FUNDS

Specialized funds resemble sector funds in most respects. The major difference is the type of securities that make up the fund's portfolio. For example, the portfolio may consist of common stocks only, foreign securities only, bonds only, new stock issues only, over-the-counter securities only, and so on.

Those who are still novices in the investment arena should avoid both specialized and sector funds for the time being and concentrate on the more traditional, diversified mutual funds instead.

INTERNATIONAL FUNDS

International funds are not, as the name seems to suggest, funds developed and sold in foreign countries (although such funds do exist). International funds are generally put together by various investment companies in the United States. The portfolios consist largely or entirely of the securities of one or more foreign nations—European and/or Asian. Be aware, however, that such funds can be risk ventures, for they depend largely upon the economy of the country or countries whose securities make up their portfolios, and foreign economies are not always stable.

Some diversification is achieved, however, as the securities of a number of different countries generally make up the portfolios of international funds.

TAX-FREE FUNDS

Tax-free funds, in the strictest sense, are not another *type* of fund, for they are available in connection with a number of the fund types discussed above. They are a subdivision of other types or categories of mutual funds. They do, however, warrant a full explanation of their nature and use.

As the name suggests, tax-free mutual funds have portfolios consisting of municipal bonds or other bonds whose income is free of federal income tax liability (many may be free of state and local income taxes as well). Investors in such funds generally receive less in the way of yields; however, the after-tax features frequently make them better investments, especially for higher bracket taxpayers. Investors seeking current income that is tax-free would profit by investing in such funds.

Tax-free funds also provide "balance" to investors' equity portfolios or taxable funds. Furthermore, tax-free funds serve well those investors seeking to reduce their total tax liability. Understand that tax-free funds (other than money market funds) may fluctuate in NAV, and if the fund has produced capital gains, you may be subject to a tax on the amount of the capital gain. The fund is required to notify you and the IRS at year-end as to whether the fund had paid such gains. It would also advise you of the amount of accrued dividends it paid for the year. However, there would be no federal tax due on the dividends.

How can you tell whether you would fare better in a taxable or a tax-free fund? Table 3–1 below compares equivalent yields for each type of investment. The computations are simple. Keep in mind that the table refers to federal income taxes only. If your state has an income tax, there are funds that are free of both federal *and* state taxes. In this case, your yield would be even higher. Most double tax-free funds may be secured through any of the larger investment companies—Vanguard, Fidelity, Dreyfus, Prudential Funds, to name a few. Check their prospectuses carefully, however, because

TABLE 3–1

Tax-Free Means More

Tax-free Investing Can Increase Your Return				
Tax-free yield of:	28% bracket	31% bracket	36% bracket	36.9% bracket
4%	5.56%	5.8%	6.25%	6.33%
5%	6.94%	7.25%	7.81%	7.92%
6%	8.33%	8.70%	9.38%	9.51%
7%	9.72%	10.14%	10.94%	11.09%

T A B L E 3–1 (continued)

Can a 6.0% tax-free investment earn you more income than an 8.9% taxable one?

The answer is yes!
A lower yield from a tax-free fund can earn you more income than a comparable taxable investment paying a higher yield!

Take one minute to see how the tax-free advantage can pay off for you.

To find out which investment can earn more for you –
a Tax-Free General Bond Fund or a
comparable taxable one:

1. Enter the yield of any Tax-Free
   Mutual Fund.
2. Subtract your income tax bracket from 100.
3. Divide that number into the Fund's yield to find
   your equivalent taxable yield.

The One-Minute Worksheet

	_____6%_____ (yield of fund)
$\div$	100 – 31% = 69 (100 minus your tax rate)
=	6% $\div$ 69 = 8.7% (your equivalent taxable yield)

If your tax bracket is 31% and the
yield for the Fund is 6.00%, the
formula would look like this: **6**

So after tax you would have to $\div$ **69**
have 8.7% on a taxable invest-   ―――――――
ment to equal a 6.00% yield.   = **8.70%**

they are not all no-load funds, and for the time being you want to stay with no-load funds exclusively.

STOCK MARKET INDICES

The Dow Jones Average and Index Mutual Funds

The Dow Jones Industrial Average is the oldest stock index. As a means of tracking movement of the stock market, it was begun in 1884 by Charles Dow and consisted of 11 stocks. Their closing prices were totaled each day and divided by 11 to determine a simple mean, or average (much like a fever chart).

Many changes in the composition of the stocks included in the Dow, as it is called today, have occurred since 1884, as well as in the number of stocks in the list and the way in which the average is determined.

Today, there are 30 stocks included in the index. The criteria used to determine which stocks are included in the magic 30 remains undisclosed; however, they are all very large corporations. Presumably, the selection is intended to be representative of the market as a whole. (See Exhibit 3–1.)

As time passed, it became more and more difficult to maintain continuity in the validity of the averages due to corporation mergers, stock splits, and dividend changes. As a consequence, the divisor has been modified, until today it is down to slightly over 1. The continuity of *relative value* remains one of the major strengths of the Dow. Yet, the DJIA is still criticized as being unrepresentative, because it includes only 30 of the over 1,700 stocks traded on the NYSE. However, since the 30 stocks include about 35% of the total capitalization (a combination of equity and debt) of the stocks on the NYSE, they carry a lot of weight in showing what's happening in the overall market. The movement of the Dow directly affects the NAV of index mutual funds. It has a comparable effect on mutual funds in general.

During the year 2000, the Dow rose to above 11,000. Compare that total with the highest level reached in the years 1993–94 (3,650). In just six years the Dow gained over 7,400 points! (See Exhibit 3–2.)

E X H I B I T   3–1

Dow Jones Industrial Index

Composition of the Index, 1996

Alcoa	Dupont	Minnesota Mining & Manufacturing
Allied Signal	Eastman Kodak	J.P. Morgan
American Express	Exxon	Phillip Morris
AT & T	General Electric	Proctor & Gamble
Bethlehem Steel	General Motors	Sears Roebuck
Boeing	Goodyear Tire	Texaco
Caterpillar	I B M	Union Carbide
Chevron	International Paper	United Technologies
Coca-Cola	McDonald's	Westinghouse
Disney	Merck	Woolworth

1997 Changes: What's Out: Bethlehem Steel, Texaco, Westinghouse, Woolworth
What's In: Hewlett Packard, Johnson & Johnson, Travelers Insurance, Wal-Mart

Composition of the Index, 2001

Alcoa	Hewlett Packard	*SBC Communications*
Allied Signal	*Home Depot*	United Technologies
American Express	I B M	Wal-Mart
AT & T	Intel	Walt Disney
Boeing	International Paper	
Caterpillar	J.P. Morgan	*Removed from previous index:*
Citicorp	Johnson & Johnson	Chevron
Coca-Cola	McDonald's	Goodyear Tire
Dupont	Merck	Sears Roebuck
Eastman Kodak	*Microsoft*	Union Carbide
Exxon	Minnesota Mining (3 M)	
General Electric	Phillip Morris	*Replaced by:*
General Motors	Proctor & Gamble	Home Depot
		Intel
		Microsoft
		SBC Communications

Companies that are no longer representative of the overall stock market are re-moved from the Dow Jones Industrial Index periodically and are replaced by companies more representative of the general stock market's composition. Thus, the Dow continues to remain one of the most viable barometers of the country's economy.

EXHIBIT 3–2

Dow Jones Industrial Average Daily closes for the 1993–'94 year (right) compared to 1999 (left)

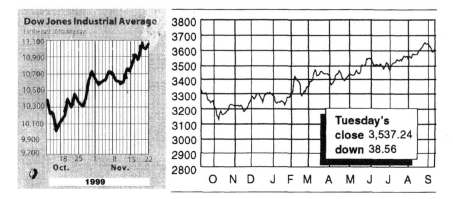

Standard & Poor's 500 Composite Stock Price Index

This consists of 400 industrials, 40 utilities, 20 transportation, and 40 financial stocks.

Wilshire 5,000 Index

This includes 75% of all U.S. securities traded on the New York Stock Exchange, the American Stock Exchange, and NASDAQ (National Association of Security Dealers Automated Quotation System), an over-the-counter exchange. This is the broadest index available in the United States.

Other Indices

The *Wilshire 4,500 Index* of small and medium-sized companies represents the remaining influential 25% of the U.S. stock market.

The *International Equity Index* tracks 300 companies in Australia, Hong Kong, Japan, Malaysia, New Zealand, and Singapore. This is a lesser used index; however, Vanguard has a mutual fund based on it.

STUDY GUIDE FOR CHAPTER 3

1. Which is the least risky of all the mutual funds? Give three reasons to support your choice.
2. Why would you invest in an income fund?
3. What types of securities make up a growth and income fund?
4. Why should an investor commit to holding a growth fund for the long run?
5. What type of return should you expect from an index fund?
6. Why are sector and specialized funds considered risky?
7. Would you buy an international fund? Why?
8. Would you invest in tax-free funds even though their yields are lower than taxable funds? Why?

P O S T S C R I P T   3–1

HOW TO DEAL WITH GYRATING STOCK MARKET INDICES

We all know that there are two *inevitable* events we must face in life: death and taxes. For the investor, add a third inevitability: *The stock market goes up, and the stock market goes down.* Here are some important lessons to help you cope with the severe market fluctuations, be they in the Dow, the S&P 500, the NASDAQ, etc.

- Pay no attention to the stock market gurus, because *no one* knows where the stock market is headed *short-term.*

- Don't try to time the market. With no *reliable way* to predict which way the market will move, you are just as likely to be invested in equities when you should be out, and vice versa.

- Frequent trading can *wreak havoc with your returns.* Each time you switch from one investment to another, you incur expenses. In the case of stocks it's stockbrokers' commissions, and in the case of mutual funds it could be new loads to pay and/or capital gains taxes to pay, or both.

- Stocks and equity-based mutual funds are no place to be for *short-term money.* The recent (July and August 2000) steep market declines serve as reminders of just how risky a place the stock market can be. Many stocks and mutual funds have lost *10% to 20% of their recent highs.* History shows that stocks can go down much more than that and stay down for years. Therefore, you should not invest in equities with money you will need in the *next few years.*

- *Short-term risk* mandates that investors plan to sell equities and/or equity-based mutual funds well in advance of the time the money will actually be needed. A long lead time is necessary so you don't risk selling during a prolonged slump.

- *Diversify,* because you obviously run a greater risk of major losses when you have no backup investments to offset poorly performing ones.

- *Bull markets do not last forever.* The spectacular performance of the stock market in recent years has led many investors to expect stocks to provide returns that far exceeded historical averages. The *15% to 18%* average returns that stocks have delivered for the past decade are unrealistic over the long term. A more realistic expectation is a *10% range,* which is the historical average for the previous 100 years.

POSTSCRIPT 3-2

UNDERSTANDING THE DOW JONES INDUSTRIAL AVERAGE INDEX

First, you need to know that the Dow Jones Industrial Average consists of only 30 of more than the almost 10,000 stocks regularly traded in the United States. The 30 stocks in the Dow Index are the very large so-called blue-chip companies. They are selected by the editors of the *Wall Street Journal* to represent different sectors of the economy.

The 30 stocks currently listed on the Dow are named in this chapter. However, in order to keep abreast of any changes that comprise the DOW, check page 3C of the *Wall Street Journal*. This where the current Dow Index is shown regularly. Changes do occur from time to time.

The Dow average is calculated as follows: The price of each of the 30 stocks listed on the index is added daily, and the result is then divided by the divisor. The divisor changes from time to time. It too is published daily in the *Wall Street Journal* on page 3C. As of November 27, 1998, the divisor was 0.24275214. Dividing that number is the same as multiplying by 4.12. Therefore, the Dow Jones Industrial Average is 4.12 times the combined price of the 30 Dow stocks.

Generally, the Dow goes up four points every time any stock goes up a dollar, and down four points every time a listed stock goes down a dollar. Therefore, if the Dow goes down 100 points in one day it could be because 25 stocks of the 30 listed stocks each went down one dollar and the other five did not change. Or maybe, just 10 of the stocks fell $2.50 each, and the others did not change. Or any combination you can think of. In other words, just because the Dow went down 100 points, it may not have been such a terrible day in the overall market.

There is still another factor that must be kept in mind concerning the point changes in the Dow. The same percentage move in different stocks can have a greater or lesser impact on the Dow. The following examples will illustrate this point. If IBM goes up from $155 to $156, it has moved only 0.75%, and it causes the Dow to go up more than four points. For Disney to have the same impact on the Dow, it would have to go from $28 to $29—a 3.56% jump. A big move in the Dow can occur simply because of modest percentage changes in the biggest-priced stocks.

That said, the Dow still provides a fairly accurate gauge of market returns in general. It is for this reason that the Dow is so carefully monitored by investors. However, the Dow is not the only index you should follow. There is the Standard & Poor's 500 Index, among others, which are significant indicators of the market's daily performance.

One last word. Do not jump to conclusions based on *one day's move* in the market. Stay invested for the long term. Historically, this has proved to be the best course to follow in up *and* down markets.

P O S T S C R I P T 3–3

TEN REASONS TO INDEX
(EXCERPTED FROM VANGUARD BOOKLET)

Indexing as an investing approach has begun to capture the attention of individual investors who are placing increasing amounts of their assets in index funds. What is indexing? And why is it attracting so much attention?

Simply put, indexing is an investment strategy that seeks to match the performance of a group of securities that form a market measure, known as an index. Among the broad stock indices are the Standard & Poor's 500 Corporate Stock Price Index and the Wilshire 5,000.

The index approach is gaining favor with investors for a number of reasons, including the following ten:

Simplicity: Indexing is a "market matching" strategy. An index mutual fund simply seeks to match the performance of a group of stocks or bonds. There are some 4,000 equity mutual funds in the marketplace today. Most of these funds are "actively managed" in an attempt to achieve their stated objectives. The aim of actively managed funds is to beat the market and may involve very complex policies. Whereas index funds are managed for very specific objectives and follow straightforward investment policies. The fund is invested in the securities of the index upon which the fund is based.

Broad Diversification: As a general rule, index funds are broadly diversified. For instance, an index fund that seeks to match the S&P 500 Index may own all 500 stocks contained in the index. Some actively managed funds hold far fewer securities, and may be highly concentrated, and therefore may be exposed to a greater degree of risk.

Competitive Performance: Conventional wisdom would lead you to believe that most professional investment managers—who typically are highly educated, employ sophisticated computer technologies, and have access to the latest market research— deliver performances consistently better than market average. Actual results, however, defy this "wisdom." Over a 10-year period (ending 12/31/94), the S&P 500 Index outpaced the annual return of the average general equity fund by 1.6%. In dollar terms, this return differential equates to a $5,690 difference on a hypothetical $10,000 investment made at the beginning of the period. Similar results were evident in index funds tracking other indices such as the Lehman and Wilshire indices.

Low Cost: The primary reason index mutual funds offer such competitive investment performance is that their costs are consistently lower than those of actively managed funds. For instance the average expense ratio of a stock index fund runs around 0.2%—Average expense ratio for an average managed stock fund is about 1.5%. The impact of these costs on a fund's returns can be clearly demonstrated. A 2% expense ratio of a conventional stock mutual fund reduces a hypothetical 10% return to 8%, whereas an index fund with expenses of 0.2% would offer a net return of 9.8%.

Relative Performance Consistency: Research shows that in each of the 12 years following 1984, the index funds outperformed more than half of all general equity mutual funds. Further, even in its worst year, the index still outperformed four out of ten general equity funds.

Relative Performance Predictability: Index funds can be expected to perform more predictably relative to general market trends than actively managed funds. The performance of an index fund can be expected to closely parallel the performance of the specific target index. Whether the stock or bond markets go up or down, the value of an index investment should go up or down by approximately the same magnitude. The returns of actively managed funds may vary widely from those of a representative market index.

Potentially Lower Taxes: Mutual funds must distribute annually all interest and realized capital gains. The impact of taxes on fund distribution has the potential to substantially reduce long-term investment returns. Since index funds largely follow a buy and hold approach, most index funds distribute only modest capital gains to shareholders. For this reason, index funds are considered the most "tax efficient" funds available. For tax-averse investors then, index funds may provide a meaningful way to limit current tax liability.

An Easy-to Implement Investment Strategy: Index funds are suitable vehicles for any investment goal. An "All-Index" approach portfolio could consist solely of index funds. A "Market Participation" approach is a simple way to complement or diversify your existing investment program. A portfolio consisting of U.S. stock funds may be diversified by an international index fund. This might be a cost-efficient, convenient way to participate in international equity markets.

A Time-Tested Strategy: The indexing concept derives from the "efficient market" theory developed by a team of Nobel prize–winning academicians in the early 1960s. It was first put into practice by large institutional pension managers in the early 1970s. Today Vanguard is the recognized leader in index fund investing and manages more than $35 billion in index assets. Note that there are other index funds available from other mutual fund companies.

POSTSCRIPT 3–4

NEED TAX RELIEF? TRY MUNIS

Frequently, investors who are in the higher federal tax brackets (28%, 31%, 36%, 39.6%) are able to benefit by investing in tax-free municipal bond mutual funds (commonly referred to as "munis") rather than investing in taxable bond funds—even though the taxable bond fund may provide a better yield than the "muni."

Here's how it works. Say you are considering a tax-free muni that yields 6% (not too difficult to find), and your combined federal and state tax liability puts you in the 28% tax bracket. (Florida does not have a state tax, true; but it does have an intangible tax that has to be factored into your overall tax liability.)

The formula to determine your equivalent tax-free yield is calculated as follows:

TAX-FREE YIELD

Here's how it works for someone in the *28%* tax bracket:

$$\frac{6\%}{(100\% - 28\%)} = \frac{.06}{.72} = \textit{8.33\%}$$

Here's how it works for some one in the *36%* tax bracket:

$$\frac{6\%}{(100\% - 36\%)} = \frac{.06}{.64} = \textit{9.37\%}$$

The higher your federal tax bracket, the worse off you are. For example, an individual in the 36% tax bracket (as shown above) would have to find a taxable bond fund yielding *9.37%* to equal the yield of a "muni" earning *6%*. Consider, also, that being able to *exclude all the income derived from "munis"* could possibly lower one's income tax bracket, resulting in *considerable* tax savings.

CHAPTER 4

Load Versus No-Load Mutual Funds

WHAT ARE LOAD FUNDS?

A load fund is sold to investors at net asset value plus a sales commission (load). Most load funds are sold by brokerage firms and other sales organizations. Loads vary considerably in amount. Load funds permit stockbrokers to collect commissions on their sales. The commissions frequently are as high as 8.5% of the investor's total purchase price. Even when the buyer deals *directly* with a load fund, thus bypassing the broker, the load is still collected. The load is an "up front" charge that the investor *must pay* when buying shares of any load fund.

WHAT ARE NO-LOAD FUNDS?

Funds that sell their shares directly to the public strictly at net asset value with no sales charge are known as no-load mutual funds. Since there are no salespeople involved in the transaction, such funds are not marked up in price. When buying a no-load fund, the investor deals directly with the investment company that offers the fund. There are no middlemen; therefore, no commission is added to the NAV to pay salaries. (See also "How to Obtain a Prospectus," in Chapter 8.)

WHICH SHOULD YOU CHOOSE?

There is no question in my mind that the novice investor should avoid load funds entirely, the bottom-line reason being that 100% of your investment capital is at work for you in a no-load fund, rather than only about 90%, as is the case in many load funds.

Numerous research studies have proved beyond any doubt that there is no significant correlation between sales charges and performance. For example, two studies, one conducted by the Securities and Exchange Commission, "Institutional Investor Report," and the other by Irwin Fried, et al., concluded that: "If there is any relationship between sales charges and performance, it appears to be negative."

The fact is, when you invest in a load fund your investment suffers an instant loss. For example, $10,000 invested in an 8.5% load fund puts only $9,150 into your account. The $850 difference is in the account of the *brokerage firm* through which the fund was purchased. By contrast, when you invest $10,000 in a no-load fund the entire $10,000 is credited to *your* account. Since you start with less in the load fund, your investment naturally earns less in the way of interest or dividends. Add to that the compounding effect of the interest you receive on your reinvested dividends, and the difference between the two investments becomes greater and greater each year.

To quickly determine the actual load charged on a particular fund without having access to its prospectus, merely consult the mutual fund listings in the daily newspapers. (See the exhibit in Appendix B and Figure 4–2.) The daily table will show the *bid* and *asked* prices, sometimes called *buy* and *sell* prices. Use these figures to calculate the difference between the two prices. The difference represents the load per share. For example, if the difference between the two is $.85, then the fund carries an 8.5% load. On the other hand, when the two prices are the same, you are looking at a no-load fund listing. Be certain you are checking the *daily* fund listings in the newspaper, not the *weekly* summary listing. No-load funds are usually designated by an n or NL following the listing. The weekly mutual fund table in the newspaper will show each fund's NAV at the beginning of the week, its NAV at the end of the week, and the amount of change; a gain will be shown by a plus sign, a loss by a minus sign. (Refer to the discussion of NAV in Chapter 2.)

Figure 4–1 graphically illustrates the effect of an 8.5% load on a $10,000 investment versus the same investment in a no-load fund.

FIGURE 4–1

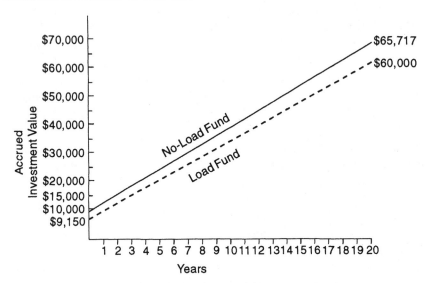

Twenty-Year Investment of $10,000 in a Load and a No-Load Mutual Fund
(10% annual return compounded)

It assumes an annual compound interest rate of 10% for both investments. The chart shows the two lines diverging further the longer the investment is held. Using this example, after 20 years, other things being equal, there would be a difference of $5,717 between the two accounts. Obviously, giving up $850 at the outset becomes increasingly more costly as time goes by. Again, the prudent investor, seeking to maximize the return on his or her investment, should avoid load funds.

STUDY GUIDE FOR CHAPTER 4

1. Why should you avoid buying load funds?
2. How high a load may be charged legally?
3. True or false: the real load may amount to as much as 9.3%.
4. What are no-load funds?
5. What has research proved about load versus no-load funds?

6. Why do the differences between the value of load and no-load funds grow greater the longer they are held?

7. What is a quick way to determine which funds are load funds and which are no-load funds?

8. What reason could you give as to why you might wish to purchase a load fund?

FIGURE 4–2

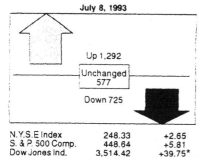

MARKET PROFILE
N.Y.S.E. ISSUES TRADED
July 8, 1993

Up 1,292

Unchanged
577

Down 725

N.Y.S.E Index	248.33	+2.65	
S. & P. 500 Comp.	448.64	+5.81	
Dow Jones Ind.	3,514.42	+39.75*	

DOW JONES INDUSTRIALS

Over the past 30 trading days

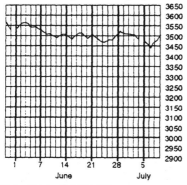

			3650
			3600
			3550
			3500
			3450
			3400
			3350
			3300
			3250
			3200
			3150
			3100
			3050
			3000
			2950
			2900

1   7   14   21   28   5
June   July

	Sell	Buy	Chg.
Delaware Group			
Trend p	13.93	14.78	+ 0.03
Value p	19.03	20.19	+ 0.02
Delcp p	23.90	25.36	+ 0.01
Dectrl	17.68	19.32	+ 0.15
Dectll p	14.00	14.85	+ 0.11
→ Delaw p	18.94	20.10	+ 0.10 ←
IntlEq p	10.56	11.20	+ 0.02
Delch p	7.07	7.42	
USGvl p	9.06	9.51	+ 0.01
Treas p	10.06	10.37	...
TxUS p	12.53	13.15	...
Txlns p	11.57	12.15	...
Vanguard Group			
Admi T	10.66	NL	+ 0.02
Admi_T	10.90	NL	+ 0.02
AdmST	10.27	NL	+ 0.01
AssetA	14.49	NL	+ 0.12
Convrt	12.14	NL	− 0.02
Eqinc	13.97	NL	+ 0.15
Expir	44.17	NL	+ 0.18
Morg	12.75	NL	+ 0.14
Prmcp	17.04	NL	+ 0.16
Prefd	9.56	NL	+ 0.04
Quant	17.43	NL	+ 0.26
STAR	13.42	NL	+ 0.10
Trlntl	28.23	NL	− 0.11
TrUS	30.72	NL	+ 0.29
GNMA	10.53	NL	
HYCorp	7.91	NL	+ 0.01
IGCorp	9.42	NL	+ 0.01
STCorp	11.01	NL	.+ 0.01
StFed	10.46	NL	+ 0.01
STTsry	10.48	NL	
ITTsry	11.17	NL	+ 0.02
LTTrsy	10.61	NL	+ 0.02
IdxBnd	10.23	NL	+ 0.01
IdxBal	10.70	NL	+ 0.06
→Idx 500	42.29	NL	+ 0.54 ←

Determining a Fund's Load
(See Delaware Fund.)
Sell price is $18.94; Buy price is $20.10; the difference is $1.16. This represents a load of 5.77% ($1.16−$20.10 = 5.77%), of $1.16 on every share purchased. On 100 shares: costing $2,010, the salesman takes $116. Therefore, only $1,894 goes into your account.

Comparing performance of load vs. no-load funds
On this day the Dow Jones Average gained 39.75* points. The Delaware Fund gained $.10, while the *no-load* Vanguard Windsor II Fund gained $.22. (This may not hold true *every* time, but more often than not, it does. Therefore, why pay a load at all?) Also take a look at Vanguard's Index 500 Fund!

---

*These two charts reinforce the way to (1) calculate a fund's load and (2) that load funds are not superior to no-load funds. In fact, the no-loads often prove to be the superior performers.

NO-LOAD MUTUAL FUNDS VS. BANK CDS

Certificates of Deposit Advantages
1. FDIC Insured to 100,000
2. Face value of CD protected

No-Load Mutual Fund Advantages
1. Yields considerable higher
2. Instant liquidity
3. No penalty for early withdrawal
4. Appreciation potential
5. Check writing available on certain funds
6. Automatic investment programs available
7. Reinvestment of distributions available
8. Automatic withdrawals available
9. Wire transfers offered
10. Toll-free calls permissible at all times
11. Telephone exchanges between funds allowable at any time
12. Wide variety of funds available to choose from
13. Funds are professionally managed
14. Any investment style may be accommodated, from conservative to aggressive
15. Smaller investments may be made vis-à-vis CDs
16. Capital gains are taxed at 20% if the security was held for one year or more

CD Disadvantages
1. Low yield
2. Penalty for early withdrawal
3. Principal does not grow

No-Load Fund Disadvantages
1. Not FDIC insured
2. Value of fund shares subject to fluctuations
3. Nominal expenses are incurred

4. Illiquid if penalty is to be avoided
5. May suffer loss of principal if rate of inflation exceeds interest rate
6. To earn higher interest rates, large sums required, from $5,000 to $100,000
7. Interest rate is locked in until maturity even if interest rates rise
8. Earnings are taxed at regular tax rates from 28% to 39.6%

LOAD FUNDS VS. NO-LOAD FUNDS

For years, the argument has raged: Which are better, no-load funds or load funds? Several studies, limited in scope, have provided tentative evidence that paying sales commissions (loads) does not produce superior performance. Until now, comprehensive evidence has not been available.

The Institute for Econometric Research conducted a 25-year study that provides definite proof that no-load funds reward their shareholders with superior returns, and that superiority exists *before* adjusting for sales charges. In other words, the performance gap widens even further in favor of no-load funds when sales loads are charged against the performance of load funds. Put another way, sales charges do not buy superior performance, they just buy a salesman.

The first analysis compared the performance of growth no-load funds against the performance of all growth funds from 1971 to 1996. Over the 25 years, the no-loads provided an average annual return of 12.1%. On a $10,000 investment, that growth resulted in a return of $173,800. Meanwhile, all growth funds together returned only 10.6% per annum. Thus, a $10,000 initial investment returned only $124,100—a difference of $49,700 in favor of the no-load funds. A second study analyzed growth and income funds on the same basis as the growth fund analysis. The results *further* confirmed the original findings.

Sales commissions *did not* buy superior performance. All other factors being equal, "no-load funds are certainly preferable to load funds." This is your author's credo. It is my practice, therefore, not to recommend load funds for the portfolios I prepare for my clients. I can always find no-load funds that have performance records equal to and, in most cases, better than comparable load funds.

P O S T S C R I P T 4–3

CALCULATING A FUND'S LOAD USING MUTUAL FUND LISTINGS

1. The "Sell" column is the price you pay when you sell (redeem) any of your shares.
2. The "Buy" price is the price you pay when buying shares.
3. The difference between the two prices is the load (commission) you pay on each share.

EXAMPLE:

Check the Seligman Group in the first column of Figure 4–3, then find Frontier A Fund (first fund listed). The "Sell" price is $11.16 and the

F I G U R E 4–3

Mutual Funds

MUTUAL FUNDS

	Sell	Buy	Chg.
Seligman Group*			
Frontier A	11.16	11.72	+4.05
Cap. Apprec	16.83	17.47	+6.85
FL tx-free	8.44	8.44	+4.01
GA tx-Free	8.14	8.57	
Strong Funds*			
Opportunity	24.58	NL	+.85
Total Inc.	22.85	NL	+.08
T N E Funds*			
Gv Sc	12.09	12.66	+.02
Long Term	12.71	13.10	+.04
Vanguard Group*			
Asset Alloc.	15.02	NL	+.07
Balanced	.14.78	NL	+.09
Windsor	32.15	NL	+09

* Brief selection of fund offerings

NOTE: The NL
following the fund's
buy price means its a
No-load fund. Both
Vanguard and Strong
offer nothing but NL
(No-Load Funds)

"Buy" price is $11.72, a difference of $.56. To find the *load*, divide the $.56 by $11.16. The result is 5%. This is the load you pay on every dollar invested.

Assuming that your initial purchase was $2,500 (a typical initial minimum requirement), it will purchase exactly 213.310 shares at the buy price of $11.72. If there were no load on this purchase, your $2,500 would have purchased 224.014 shares at the sell price of $11.16.

The bottom line is: you gave away $125 in commissions (5% of $2,500) and lost 10.704 shares in the bargain. This is what the $125 would have bought in additional shares, representing a loss of another $119.46. This amounts to an *immediate loss of $244.46* on just the initial purchase, and you will go on losing 5% of *every* subsequent purchase you make. *Wow! Listen to me and don't buy load funds.*

Because the print in the funds column is small, it has been enlarged below for clarity.

Seligman Group	Sell	Buy
Frontier A	11.16	11.72

CHAPTER 5

Advantages of Mutual Fund Investing

The tremendous growth of the mutual fund industry as noted in Chapter 1 attests to its popularity and success. This chapter examines the many reasons for its broad acceptance by millions of investors worldwide.

Mutual funds offer many features for the novice that are just not attainable through other investment vehicles, unless, of course, you have a million dollars or so to invest. Assuming you are not fortunate enough to be in that position, it will be necessary to examine the advantages of mutual fund investing as a means to wealth-building. Descriptions follow of some of the more important advantages of mutual fund investing for any investor—but especially for the novice.

PORTFOLIO DIVERSIFICATION

Simply put, diversification means not placing all your eggs in one basket. Put another way, it means spreading investments among many different securities in order to reduce risk.

A mutual fund automatically provides this diversity because mutual funds are required by law (Investment Act of 1940) to diversify their assets among a number of security issuers. Not only is it prudent for a mutual fund to have a well-diversified portfolio, but it is equally astute for novice investors to diversify their own mutual fund portfolios by investing in funds from among several different investment companies.

In the investment world it is often said that you have to risk more in order to gain more. Though this has become somewhat of a truism, it is still possible to reduce risk to a comfortable level and still earn more by the simple technique of diversification. Fund managers diversify when they plan a fund's portfolio. You must diversify your portfolio of mutual funds in order to reduce risk also.

Figure 5–1 shows how diversification serves to reduce risk. The chart assumes that your portfolio of funds will represent a variety of fund types (see Chapter 3). If all your funds were aggressive growth funds, the benefits of diversification would be minimal as far as risk reduction is concerned. If, on the other hand, all your funds were money market funds with a stable $1.00 per share NAV, the risk would be almost nil. However, by diversifying your portfolio, it is possible to minimize risk and still earn the greatest return on your investments.

FIGURE 5–1

Reduction of Risk Through Diversification

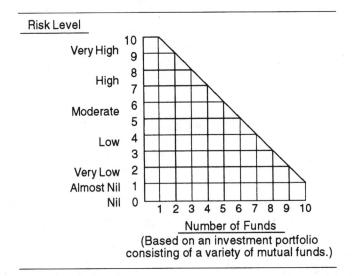

Number of Funds
(Based on an investment portfolio
consisting of a variety of mutual funds.)

PROFESSIONAL MANAGEMENT

As important as diversification is in the makeup of every mutual fund's portfolio, perhaps even more important is the expertise of the professional management team that controls the buying and selling of the securities that comprise the fund. Mutual fund companies generally hire their own financial advisers (managers) for the funds within their family. The success of a mutual fund is largely attributable to the skill of the fund's professional management. Most funds engage full-time investment managers who are responsible for obtaining and conducting the needed research and financial analyses required to select the securities to be included in the fund's portfolio.

Fund managers are responsible for all facets of the fund's portfolio—diversification of securities, buying and selling decisions, risk versus return, and investment performance are but a few of the manager's major responsibilities. Understandably, fund managers receive very large salaries. However, the performance of fund managers is evaluated on an ongoing basis. Positive results are *all* that count; not the manager's credentials, his or her reputation, or past performance. The manager's current performance must be consistently *superior.* Good managers are the real key to the success of any fund! (See Chapter 7 for more on this topic.)

REDUCTION OF RISK

A third major advantage of investing in mutual funds is the wide variety of funds available. Whatever your risk level may be, there will be any number of excellent funds that will be compatible with your degree of risk tolerance. The risk factors and objectives of mutual funds are spelled out in their respective prospectuses. Risk factors will range from very low for money market funds, to moderate for balanced and income funds, to high for aggressive growth funds and many specialized funds. Investors must determine for themselves just how much risk they are willing to take in order to profit from their investments (see Chapter 6).

As pointed out earlier, the large diversity of funds available today makes it possible for investors to find funds that suit their acceptable level of risk. It is foolish to chase after high profits if the risk

involved prevents you from sleeping at night because you fear losing all or part of your investment.

Your anxiety may be further alleviated by knowing that fairly
broad diversification is achieved through the ownership of even *one*
good mutual fund. Exhibit 5–1, taken from Vanguard Windsor II
Fund's Annual Report, clearly shows that this one fund consists of
a portfolio of 104 different securities from 29 varied industries!

REDUCTION OF TRANSACTION COSTS

Another important advantage inherent in mutual fund investing is
the reduction, or elimination entirely, of the cost of buying and selling individual securities to build a portfolio. Of course, you could
build a diversified portfolio on your own, but a stockbroker's commission would have to be paid for each individual security purchased and/or sold for your portfolio. Commission costs can be
considerable, especially if frequent trading is involved in maintaining your own portfolio. This is true even if you choose to use the services of a discount broker, in which case you are *entirely* on your
own. They do not provide research materials, advice, or tracking
service. On the other hand, as the owner of a mutual fund, you have
all these very important things done for you by a well-paid, knowledgeable, qualified expert—the fund's manager.

In addition to the dollars and cents cost involved in going it
alone, there are the time costs (and time is money). In order to do
the job right, you would have to conduct your own time-consum-
ing research and maintain detailed records. If your portfolio turned
over frequently, record keeping alone could cause severe migraines.
Unless you are willing to engage your own account and investment
adviser, the whole process can become extremely frustrating as well
as very costly. These are jobs for the professionals, not the average
investor.

Suffice it to say, not one of these headaches is involved when
investing in mutual funds. The fund manager, the transfer bank,
and the fund's large staff handle everything, down to the final detail of providing you with end-of-the-year tax data, as well as periodic account statements for your records. Thus, individual investor
costs and headaches become minimal.

Vanguard Windsor II Fund Portfolio

(Observe broad diversification provided in just a single fund.)

	Shares	Market Value (000)†
COMMON STOCKS (91.0%)		
Appliances (.3%)		
General Electric Co.	205,000	$ 15,708
Automotive (3.3%)		
Chrysler Corp.	1,464,600	39,727
Ford Motor Co.	413,000	15,075
*General Motors Corp.	3,397,500	104,473
Group Total		159,275
Banks (10.1%)		
BankAmerica Corp.	1,107,323	46,231
Bankers Trust New York Corp.	1,520,872	97,336
The Chase Manhattan Corp.	2,758,674	66,208
*Chemical Banking Corp.	4,636,916	159,394
First American Bank Corp.	133,900	4,553
First Chicago Corp.	3,177,565	101,285
First Fidelity Bancorp	111,464	4,347
J.P. Morgan & Co. Inc.	175,000	11,025
Group Total		490,379
Beverages (1.1%)		
Anheuser-Busch Co., Inc.	967,400	54,900
Broadcasting (1.7%)		
CBS, Inc.	81,300	16,545
Capital Cities ABC, Inc.	151,700	66,748
Group Total		83,293
Building & Construction (.1%)		
Kaufman & Broad Home Corp.	410,000	5,996
Chemicals (.2%)		
Dow Chemical Co.	143,400	8,012
Computers (.1%)		
Intel Corp.	102,000	6,834
Drugs (4.1%)		
Allergan, Inc.	1,990,450	45,283
American Home Products Corp.	1,233,400	83,563
Baxter International, Inc.	488,000	16,348
Bristol-Myers Squibb Co.	249,000	16,932
Humana, Inc.	154,000	3,484
Imcera Corp.	468,000	16,673
Eli Lilly and Co.	249,100	15,351
Group Total		197,634

E X H I B I T   5 – 1   (continued)

	Shares	Market Value (000)†
Electronic Data Processing (.2%)		
International Business Machines Corp.	164,000	$ 10,968
Entertainment (.2%)		
General Cinema Corp.	327,000	9,647
Financial Services (4.6%)		
*American Express Co.	4,908,200	104,913
Beneficial Corp.	70,700	4,101
*The Dun & Bradstreet Corp.	1,865,200	107,715
PaineWebber Group, Inc.	239,900	4,858
Group Total		221,587
Food Processing (3.5%)		
Borden, Inc.	567,000	15,522
H.J. Heinz Co.	1,078,300	42,458
Sara Lee Corp.	269,400	16,130
Unilever NV	875,200	95,397
Group Total		169,507
Insurance (9.8%)		
Aetna Life & Casualty Co.	1,953,000	82,270
American General Corp.	1,189,400	61,403
American International Group	506,500	56,032
*Chubb Corp.	1,340,100	116,254
Geico Corp.	865,900	50,763
Lincoln National Corp.	809,400	54,230
Old Republic International Corp.	265,000	6,890
Provident Life & Accident Insurance Co.	185,400	4,797
St. Paul Companies, Inc.	85,745	6,066
Travelers Corp.	1,745,526	40,365
Group Total		479,070
Leisure and Recreation (.9%)		
Brunswick Corp.	3,299,800	46,197
Manufacturing (4.5%)		
Aluminum Co. of America	117,500	8,196
Armstrong World Industries, Inc.	208,000	5,850
B.F. Goodrich Co.	378,600	16,374
Johnson Controls, Inc.	199,800	8,442
Lockheed Corp.	75,000	3,450
Northrop Corp.	232,800	5,966
Raytheon Co.	2,211,500	95,924

EXHIBIT 5–1 (continued)

	Shares	Market Value (000)†
TRW, Inc.	112,000	$ 5,838
Westinghouse Electric Corp.	5,397,500	69,493
Group Total		219,533
Natural Gas Diversified (1.0%)		
Panhandle Eastern Corp.	2,508,518	49,230
Office Equipment (1.7%)		
Xerox Corp.	1,112,807	82,626
Oil (10.8%)		
Amoco Co.	1,299,400	68,706
Atlantic Richfield Co.	765,900	88,653
British Petroleum Co. ADR	342,000	15,176
Chevron Corp.	137,500	9,762
Exxon Corp.	1,635,900	100,199
Mobil Corp.	207,800	13,091
Phillips Petroleum Co.	3,122,300	78,057
Texaco Inc.	1,538,100	92,286
USX-Marathon Group	3,645,800	62,434
Group Total		528,364
Oil Services and Equipment (3.5%)		
Burlington Northern, Inc.	425,000	16,203
Halliburton Co.	1,686,900	51,872
*Schlumberger Ltd.	1,603,400	101,816
Group Total		169,891
Paper (.4%)		
Federal Paper Board Co., Inc.	214,000	5,698
International Paper Co.	251,000	16,252
Group Total		21,950
Photography & Optical (1.7%)		
Eastman Kodak Co.	1,951,100	79,751
Polaroid Corp.	166,600	5,206
Group Total		84,957
Publishing (.5%)		
Gannett Co. Inc.	442,600	22,960
Retail (10.2%)		
Dayton Hudson Corp.	227,000	17,394
Fleming Companies, Inc.	146,627	4,252
*K Mart Corp.	4,992,600	131,680
*J. C. Penney Co., Inc.	1,654,700	124,930
*May Department Stores Co.	1,701,200	120,360
Sears, Roebuck and Co.	2,328,800	97,810
Group Total		496,426

E X H I B I T 5 – 1 (continued)

	Shares	Market Value (000)†
Savings and Loan (.1%)		
H. F. Ahmanson & Co.	262,200	$ 3,933
Telephone (4.3%)		
Ameritech Corp.	65,700	4,385
American Telephone & Telegraph Co.	367,000	16,010
Bell Atlantic Corp.	204,500	9,739
GTE Corp.	1,988,600	67,861
Pacific Telesis Group	213,200	8,741
Sprint Corp.	3,920,300	100,458
Group Total		207,194
Tobacco (6.5%)		
American Brands, Inc.	1,992,100	85,162
*Philip Morris Cos., Inc.	2,151,900	163,544
(1)RJR Nabisco Inc.	3,033,200	25,782
RJR Nabisco PERC	4,402,300	43,473
Group Total		317,961
Transportation (.2%)		
CSX Corp.	53,800	3,524
(1)UAL Corp.	49,000	5,953
Group Total		9,477
Utilities (5.4%)		
Commonwealth Edison Co.	2,235,100	51,966
Entergy Corp.	2,129,000	68,394
General Public Utilities Corp.	586,000	15,602
Long Island Lighting Co.	184,900	4,599
Ohio Edison Co.	3,693,700	82,185
Oklahoma Gas & Electric Co.	107,700	3,554
Pacific Gas & Electric Co.	247,500	7,827
Pennsylvania Power & Light Co.	168,400	4,568
Public Service Enterprise Group, Inc.	241,800	6,891
San Diego Gas & Electric Co.	249,000	5,945
Southern Co.	202,000	7,449
Union Electric Corp.	161,100	5,920
Group Total		264,900

TOTAL COMMON STOCKS
(Cost $3,995,524)   4,438,409

NOTE: MUTUAL FUND ACCOUNTS ARE PROTECTED UP TO $2.5 MILLION.

Mutual Fund Companies are members of the Securities Investor Protection Corporation (SIPC), which insures investors' accounts up to $2.5 million against company bankruptcy, fraud, and so on.

Banks, on the other hand, are generally insured by the Federal Deposit Insurance Corporation (FDIC), but only up to $100,000 per account.

STUDY GUIDE FOR CHAPTER 5

1. What are the advantages of mutual fund investing over individual purchases of stocks?
2. What are the benefits of diversification?
3. What type of fund assures the highest level of safety?
4. If you can afford and / or tolerate some level of financial risk, what types of funds are appropriate?

During 1999 the Dow was up 400 points one month and down 500 points the next month. However, the reassuring facts are these: For the year, the Dow advanced 20%, the S&P 500 was ahead 14%, and the NASDAQ shot up 52%, with all its technology stocks. Had you invested $10,000, you could have been $5,200 richer for the year.

POSTSCRIPT 5–1

DO YOU BUY LOTTERY TICKETS?

If an investment company promised its investors a chance to turn a nominal sum into millions of dollars, its executives *could wind up in jail.*

Every day, however, millions of Americans make an investment in state lotteries with a very high probability of total loss of principal. The odds of winning some state drawings have been as high as 200 million to one.

If someone who spent a dollar a day ($30 a month) on lottery tickets for the past 20 years had instead systematically invested the same amount of money in stock mutual funds that tracked the Standard & Poor's Index, he or she would have a nest egg of $56,550 as of June 28, 2000. This would be enough for a down payment on a new home.

The $56,550 nest egg would have the potential to generate more than enough in annual *dividends* to buy a lottery ticket *every day* for the rest of this person's life. (Incidentally, the principal would never have to be touched.) This calculation is based solely on the current S&P yield of just 1.5% and assuming a moderate level of long-term corporate earnings growth—a very conservative assumption.

If the same dollar a day allocated to a state lottery were invested in state and/or local governments in a different way—through *municipal bond funds*—our hypothetical ticket buyer would still have a nest egg of $19,122 as of June 28, 2000. That's enough to buy a new car. In addition, the dividends earned on municipal bond funds are *totally free of federal income taxes.*

Investing will never make you *suddenly rich,* as if you had "hit" the lottery jackpot, but prudent financial planning offers a *far* better chance to *attain* one's financial goals.

CHAPTER 6

Risks in Mutual Fund Investing

The preceding chapter, though it promotes the reduction of risk as one of the advantages of mutual fund investing, does not imply that the element of risk can be *entirely* eliminated in every instance. There is some degree of risk in *every* investment, although it is reduced considerably in mutual fund investing. Do not let the specter of risk stop you from becoming a mutual fund investor. However, it behooves all investors to determine for themselves the degree of risk they are willing to accept in order to meet their objectives *before* making a purchase. Knowing of potential risks in advance will help you avoid situations in which you would not be comfortable. Understanding the risk levels of the various types of mutual funds at the outset will help you avoid the stress that might result from a thoughtless or a hasty purchase.

Let us now *examine* the risk levels of the various types of mutual funds described previously.

LOW-LEVEL RISKS

Mutual funds characterized as low-level risks fall into three categories:

1. Money market funds
2. U.S. Treasury bill funds
3. Insured bond funds

MODERATE-LEVEL RISKS

Mutual funds considered moderate-risk investments may be found in at least the nine types categorized below.

1. Income funds
2. Balanced funds
3. Growth and income funds
4. Growth funds
5. Short-term bond funds (taxable and tax-free)
6. Intermediate bond funds (taxable and tax-free)
7. Insured municipal bond funds
8. Index funds
9. GNMA funds

HIGH-LEVEL RISKS

The types of funds listed below have the potential for high gain, but all have high risk levels as well.

1. Aggressive growth funds
2. International funds
3. Sector funds
4. Specialized funds
5. Precious metals funds
6. High-yield bond funds (taxable and tax-free)
7. Commodity funds
8. Option funds

Figure 6–1 depicts three types of mutual fund portfolios structured according to risk level. You may wish to use this as a guide to building a portfolio based on your level of risk tolerance. The percentages of each type of fund recommended in the portfolios reflect a reasonable degree of diversification, balance, and risk level as indicated.

F I G U R E   6–1

Portfolio Allocations Based on Risk Levels

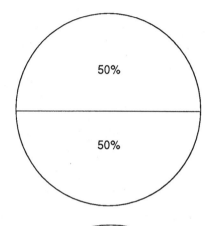

LOW-LEVEL RISK
CONSERVATIVE PORTFOLIO

50% U.S. Gov't. Treasury Bill Funds
50% Money Market Funds

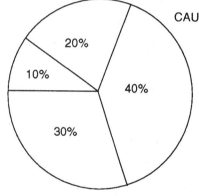

MODERATE-LEVEL RISK
CAUTIOUSLY AGGRESSIVE PORTFOLIO

40% Growth & Income Funds
30% Gov't. Bond Funds
20% Growth Funds
10% Index Funds

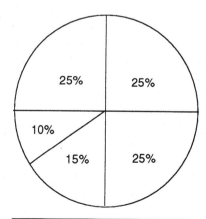

HIGH-LEVEL RISK
AGGRESSIVE PORTFOLIO

25% Aggressive Growth Funds
25% International Funds
25% Sector Funds
15% High Yield Bond Funds
10% Gold Funds

MEASURING RISK

As you become a more experienced investor, you may want to examine other, more technical, measures to determine risk factors in your choice of funds.

Beta coefficient is a measure of the fund's risk relative to the overall market, i.e., the S&P 500. For example, a fund with a beta coefficient of 2.0 means that it is likely to move twice as fast as the general market—both up and down. High beta coefficients and high risk go hand in hand.

Alpha coefficient is a comparison of a fund's risk (beta) to its performance. A positive alpha is good. For example, an alpha of 10.5 means that the fund manager earned an average of 10.5% more each year than might be expected, given the fund's beta.

Interest rates and *inflation rates* are other factors that can be used to measure investment risks. For instance, when interest rates are going up, bond funds will usually be declining, and vice versa. The rate of inflation has a decided effect on funds that are sensitive to inflation factors; for example, funds that have large holdings in automaker stocks, real estate securities, and the like will be adversely affected by inflationary cycles.

R-Square factor is a measure of the fund's risk as related to its degree of diversification.

However, at this stage of your venture, you needn't employ these ultrasophisticated risk factor measurements in order to achieve success as a mutual fund investor. The majority of *seasoned* investors probably have never used beta coefficients, alpha coefficients, or R-Square factors either. The information is supplied here merely to acquaint you with the terminology in the event you should wish to delve more deeply into complex risk factors. The more common risk factors previously described are all you really need to know for now, and perhaps for years to come.

One caveat is in order, however. There is no such thing as an absolutely 100% risk-free investment. Even funds with excellent 10-year past performance records must include in their literature and prospectuses the following disclaimer: "Past performance is no guarantee of future results." However, by not exceeding your risk tolerance level, you can achieve a wide safety and comfort zone with mutual fund portfolios such as those shown in Figure 6–1.

According to the Investment Company Institute, a list of fund types arranged according to increasing risk level consists of the following categories of funds:

- Money market funds
- Insured municipal bond funds
- Corporate bond funds (investment grade)
- GNMA funds (Government National Mortgage Association)
- Government bond funds
- Index funds
- Balanced funds
- Growth and income funds
- International funds
- Precious metals funds
- Growth funds
- Aggressive funds

FIND YOUR RISK TOLERANCE LEVEL

You are the sole judge of your own risk level. By answering the following questions, you may be able to arrive at a clearer understanding of the level of risk you are able to accept.

1. Does the thought of a bear market worry you?
2. Would you lose sleep if your mutual fund portfolio showed a steady decline?
3. Are you naturally the worrisome type?
4. Would you rush to redeem shares of a fund that had declined in value?
5. Would suffering a loss discourage you from continuing a long-term investment program?
6. Would you be angry with yourself if you sold too soon and the price continued to rise?

If you answered no to almost every question, consider yourself able to handle virtually any market situation that might confront

Types of Funds by Objectives and Risk Levels

Type of Fund	Money Market	Fixed Income	Income	Growth & Income	Growth	Aggressive
Fund Example*	U.S. Treas. Money Mkt.	Short-term Bond Fund	Wellesley Fund	Wellington Fund	U.S. Growth Portfolio	Explorer Fund
Risk Level	None to Very Low	Low	Low to Moderate	Moderate	High	Very High
Main Objective	Liquidity	Yield	Income	Growth	Capital Gains	Maximum Capital Gains
Concommitant Objectives	Preservation of Principal & Income	Yield & Stability	Growth	Income	Price Appreciation	Price Appreciation

*All Funds named are from the Vanguard family of funds.
Note. Other investment companies offer similar types of funds.

you. If you answered yes to most of the questions, you had better stay with money market funds and U.S. government bond funds until you have the confidence and knowledge needed to invest in riskier alternatives.

Figure 6–2 depicts another way to evaluate risk, by using investment objectives as the criteria for selecting your mutual funds.

STUDY GUIDE FOR CHAPTER 6

1. What do you estimate your risk level to be?
2. List the type of funds that would fit your risk level.
3. How do interest rates affect bond mutual funds?
4. How does the rate of inflation affect mutual funds?
5. How can you be sure you are not investing in mutual funds that will exceed your risk level?

POSTSCRIPT 6-1

Check Your Risk Tolerance

RISK TOLERANCE QUIZ

1. What is your age?
20-29 years of age	= 5 points	
30-39 years of age	= 4 points	
40-49 years of age	= 3 points	
50-59 years of age	= 2 points	
60 years of age or older	= 1 point	Your score_____

2. When do you expect to retire?
5 years	= 1 point	
10 years	= 2 points	
15 years	= 3 points	
20 years	= 4 points	
25 years or more	= 5 points	Your score_____

3. Many types of investments can go up or down greatly, especially **short term.** How willing are you stay the course given the following levels of **decline** in the value of your account?
Down 5% (would hold)	= 1 point	
Down 10% (would hold)	= 2 points	
Down 15% (would hold)	= 3 points	
Down 20% or more (would hold)	= 4 points	Your score_____

4. Do you believe that at least a portion of your long-term investments should be in stocks and/or stock mutual funds?
Strongly agree	= 5 points	
Agree	= 4 points	
Neutral	= 3 points	
Disagree	= 2 points	
Strongly disagree	= 1 point	Your score_____

5. Would you accept more risk in order to **possibly** achieve higher returns?
Absolutely	= 5 points	
Yes	= 4 points	
Maybe	= 3 points	
No	= 2 points	
Never	= 1 point	Your score_____

6. I would be able to retire comfortably given my present salary, savings, investments, and living expenses.
Strongly agree	= 5 points	
Agree	= 4 points	
Possibly	= 3 points	
Disagree	= 2 points	
Strongly disagree	= 1 point	Your score_____

TOTAL SCORE _____

YOUR RISK TOLERANCE LEVEL & INVESTMENY APPROACH

Aggressive (high risk)	**26-29 points**
Growth oriented	**21-25 points**
Balanced	**15-20 points**
Moderate	**10-14 points**
Conservative (low risk)	**6-9 points**

POSTSCRIPT 6-2

RISK CONTROL TECHNIQUES

1. It is important to determine *your own risk tolerance level.*
2. Never take more risk than you are able to live with comfortably. It's not worth it! You've only yourself to blame if you *exceed* your risk tolerance level.
3. Remember, however, there is no reward without taking *some* risk. Establish your own risk comfort zone and *stay within it.*
4. Always externalize; do not internalize.
   a. Externalizers blame the *fund* for poor performance, not themselves. They unload poor performers using the guidelines shown in the examples below.
   b. Internalizers blame *themselves* when they pick a poorly performing fund. They feel guilty and are loath to unload it—always waiting for it to come back. Meanwhile they are losing valuable income they could be earning in a better fund, to say nothing of the loss of principal while waiting for a loser to become a winner again. A true loser *rarely* comes back.
5. A fund that has shown *steady declines* during any *three month period,* under the following conditions, needs to be carefully reevaluated. For example:
   a. The general market indices have been advancing (Dow, S&P 500, etc.).
   b. Other *similar type funds* are registering gains.
   c. Interest rates have not fluctuated to any *significant degree.*
   d. The economy and state of the nation are *stable.*
6. Establish cut-off percentages for all funds exhibiting the following returns:
   a. Funds that have shown *consistent losses* amounting to 12% *during any three month period* should be placed on *hold*— make no further deposits and continue to monitor daily.
   b. Funds that have shown an overall loss of 15% or more during any *six month period are sell candidates.* Do not wait for them to rebound. The likelihood that they will is *minimal* at best. Look for other funds, ones that will meet your expectations. They are out there!

Example of 6a. above:	Example of 6b. above
Fund's NAV: $37.50	Fund's NAV: $37.50
2% of NAV = $4.50	15% of NAV = $5.63
Alert point: $33.00	*Sell point:* $31.87

P O S T S C R I P T   6–3

MARKET TIMING: SHOULD YOU OR SHOULDN'T YOU? A Hypothetical Look at Two Investors' Reactions to Market Fluctuations: Terry Truehart and Tommy Timer

Terry had $10,000 invested in an S&P 500 fund on January 1, 1987. While concerned about the volatility in the market toward the latter part of the year (the Dow fell over 500 points in one day: October 19, 1987), she stayed committed to her investment plan. By staying invested, Terry was rewarded with a two-year annualized return of *10.9%* by the end of 1988, and her $10,000 investment was then worth *$12,290.*

Terry's friend Tommy also had $10,000 invested in an S&P 500 fund on January 1, 1987. However, in early November 1987, after the market lost over 500 points or 21.5% of its value in October, he took his investment out of stocks and put it in a money market fund. After watching the market lose value off and on during 1988, Tommy decided to stay invested in the money market fund until July 1988, when he put his assets back into the S&P 500 fund. When the market dropped for two consecutive months, he went back to the money market fund. By moving in and out of the market versus staying completely invested as Terry had, Tommy's annualized return for the two years was only *4.6%*, and his $10,000 investment was worth only $10,944 by December 31, 1988.

As, you can see Tommy's decisions were not based on his lifestyle or financial objectives, but rather, on an emotional response to the inevitable movement of the market. Terry, on the other hand, while disturbed by the market plunge, stayed committed to her plan and was rewarded in the end by *$1,346* more than Tommy had earned in just two short years.

The above scenarios do not negate my advice regarding the 12% hold and the 15% sell strategies. These both apply to a *steadily declining* market, over a period of three or more months, not to a catastrophic *one day loss* such as occurred in 1987.

CHAPTER 7

Investment Companies

CONCEPT AND DEFINITION

Despite the fact that most people think investment companies represent a fairly recent investment concept, such companies have been operating in Europe since the early part of the 19th century, where they originated. By the latter part of that century the idea had spread to the United States. Today, investment companies constitute a large and vital segment of the investment milieu in the United States as well as internationally.

The complexities of managing an investment company notwithstanding, the concept is not complicated at all. Simply put, investors interested in common investment objectives place their money with a company that invests it for them. The investors' pooled money is managed by an experienced investment manager and a team of advisers who are hired by the investment company to manage the portfolio of one or more of its funds. The investment manager and his or her team of analysts use the best research available to study industry forecasts, economic conditions, the latest trading data, and which companies are likely to prosper under the prevailing conditions. This intense process is conducted before (and after) committing investors' money to make purchases for the fund that they are responsible for managing. The investment manager, as head of the fund's team, is also responsible for determining the best strategy for meeting the fund's objectives. He likewise controls the trading (buying and selling) of the securities that make up the fund's portfolio. Last, and most important, he is charged with the ultimate responsibility for producing maximum returns on the investors' money while protecting the principal value of the shareholders' investments.

Figure 7–1 on page 69 depicts the organization of a typical investment company. Generally, an investment company establishes a number of separate funds to meet the objectives of various groups of investors. The group of diverse mutual funds sponsored by a single investment company is also referred to as a "fund family." Such a fund family is diagramed on the bottom line of Figure 7–1.

EXAMPLES IN TODAY'S MARKET

Investment companies with very large fund families include Fidelity Investments, the Dreyfus Corporation, the Vanguard Group, and Prudential Funds, to name but four of the over 100 such large investment companies doing business today.

The companies noted above, as well as many others, offer a wide variety of funds to meet the varied objectives of novice and experienced investors alike: income funds, growth funds, balanced funds, tax-free funds, and so on, as previously described.

The Vanguard Group, for example, offers over 80 mutual funds, all of which are open-end/no-load funds. The Fidelity Investment Corporation, for another example, has over 250 different mutual funds in its family of funds. All its funds are open-ended, but some are loaded funds and some are no-load funds. A prospectus will tell you which are which (see Chapter 8). Table 7–1 shows a partial listing of Fidelity's extensive family of funds and the objectives of each of its categories of funds.

Whatever type of fund you seek—low-risk or speculative, conservative or aggressive, domestic or foreign, income or growth, broad-based or specialized, load or no-load—be assured that there are mutual funds available to meet your individual objectives and financial means.

At this point it will be helpful to familiarize yourself with the offerings of some major fund families—their objectives and their special features. Table 7–2 shows the portfolio of a fund from another mutual fund family. Table 7–3 gives a partial listing of Vanguard's family of mutual funds. Two such fund families, USAA and Vanguard, are shown in Tables 7–2 and 7–3. Examine each to determine

FIGURE 7–1

Investment Company Organization Chart

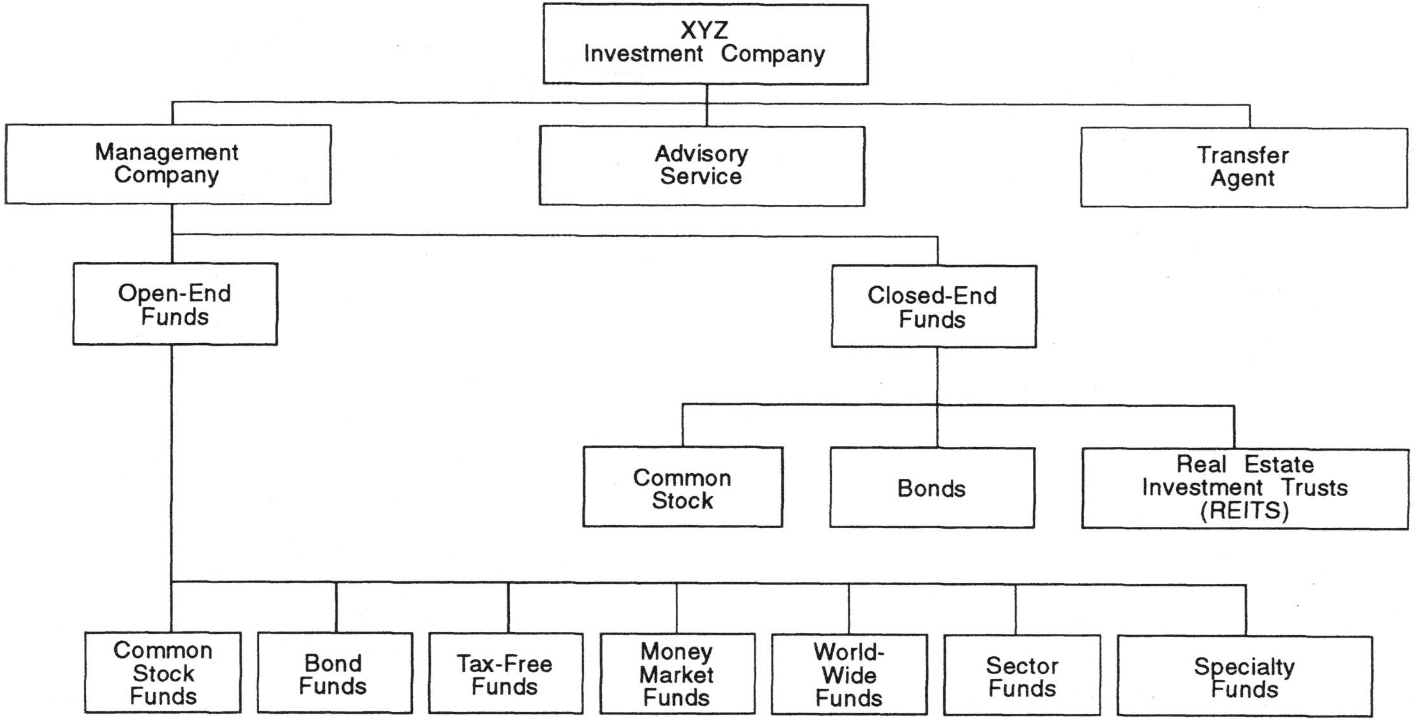

whether you are able to extract from the charts answers to questions you may have. If the charts are not meaningful to you at this point in your orientation, be assured that you will be able to understand and utilize any mutual fund listing by the time you completed this book.

STUDY GUIDE FOR CHAPTER 7

1. Explain the concepts upon which investment companies are built.
2. What is meant by the fund portfolio?
3. What are the responsibilities of the fund's investment manager?
4. Why are the funds called mutual funds?
5. Describe a fund family.
6. Why does a fund family offer multifund choices?
7. True or false: Most fund families offer a large number of funds from which to choose.
8. Name three factors to consider in selecting a fund in which to invest.
9. Using the Vanguard Group as an example, name two funds that stress capital appreciation; three funds that aim to provide current income; and two funds that seek to generate income and growth (see Table 7–3).

TABLE 7–1

Fidelity Investments: Family of Funds*

Money Market Funds: For current income and preservation of capital.
Fund Name (commencement date)
Fidelity Cash Reserves (5/79)
Fidelity Daily Income Trust (5/74)
Fidelity Select Money Market Portfolio (8/85)
Fidelity U.S. Gov't. Reserves (11/81)
SPARTAN MONEY MARKET FUNDS
Spartan Money Market Fund (1/89)
Spartan U.S. Gov't. Money Market Fund (2/90)
Spartan U.S. Treasury Money Market Fund (1/88)

Fidelity Select Money Market Portfolio has a 3% sales charge.

Tax-free Money Market Funds:
For current income exempt from federal (and, in some cases state and local) taxes and preservation of capital.
Fidelity California Tax-Free Fund: Money Market Portfolio (7/84)
Fidelity Connecticut Municipal Money Market Portfolio (8/89)
Fidelity Massachusetts Tax-Free Fund: Money Market Portfolio (11/83)
Fidelity Michigan Municipal Money Market Portfolio (1/90)

TABLE 7–1 (continued)

Fidelity New Jersey Tax-Free
   Money Market Portfolio (3/88)
Fidelity New York Tax-Free Fund:
   Money Market Portfolio (7/84)
Fidelity Ohio Municipal Money
   Market Portfolio (8/89)
Fidelity Tax-Exempt Money Market Trust
   (1/80)
SPARTAN TAX-FREE MONEY MARKET
   FUNDS
Spartan California Municipal
   Money Market Portfolio (11/89)
Spartan Municipal Money Fund (1/91)
Spartan New Jersey Municipal
   Money Market Portfolio (5/90)
Spartan New York Municipal Money
   Market Portfolio (2/90)
Spartan Pennsylvania Municipal
   Money Market Portfolio (8/86)

Income Funds: For current income from
   bonds.
   Fund Name (commencement date)
Fidelity Capital & Income Fund
   (11/77)
Fidelity Flexible Bond Portfolio (8/71)
Fidelity Ginnie Mae Portfolio (11/85)
Fidelity Global Bond Fund (12/86)
Fidelity Government Securities Fund
   (4/79)
Fidelity Intermediate Bond Fund (5/75)
Fidelity Mortgage Sec. Portfolio (12/84)
Fidelity Short-Term Bond Portfolio
   (9/86)
Fidelity Capital & Income Fund has a 1.5%
   redemption fee on share:
SPARTAN INCOME FUNDS
Spartan Government Income Fund
   (12/88)
Spartan High Income Fund (8/90)
Spartan Limited Maturity Government
   Bond Fund (5/88)
Spartan Long-Term Government Bond
   Fund (9/90)

Growth and Income Funds: For current
   income and potential long-term
   growth.
   Fund Name (commencement date)
Fidelity Balanced Fund (11/86)
Fidelity Convertible Sec. Portfolio
   (1/87)
Fidelity Equity-Income Fund (5/66)
Fidelity Equity-Income II Fund (8/90)
Fidelity Fund (4/30)

Fidelity Growth & Income Portfolio
   (12/85)
Fidelity Puritan Fund (4/47)
Fidelity Real Estate Investment Portfolio
   (11/86)
Fidelity Utilities Income Fund (11/87)

Growth Funds: For long-term growth of
   capital.
Fund Name
Fidelity Blue Chip Growth Fund (12/87)
Fidelity Capital Appreciation Fund
   (11/86)
Fidelity Contrafund (5/67)
Fidelity Disciplined Equity Fund (12/88)
Fidelity Emerging Growth Fund (12/90)
Fidelity Growth Company Fund (1/83)
Fidelity Low-Priced Stock Fund (12/89)
Fidelity Magellan Fund (5/63)
Fidelity OTC Portfolio (12/84)
Fidelity Retirement Growth Fund (3/83)
Fidelity Stock Selector Fund (9/90)
Fidelity Trend Fund (6/58)
Fidelity Value Fund (12/78)

Other Funds: An asset allocation fund
   for one-fund diversification across
   equities, bonds, and money market
   instruments, and an index fund
   managed to replicate the performance
   of the S&P 500.
   Fund Name (commencement date)
Fidelity Asset Manager (12/88)
Spartan Market Index Fund (3/90)

Federally Tax-free Income Funds:
   For current income exempt from
   federal (and, in some cases, state)
   taxes.
   Fund Name (commencement date)
Fidelity Aggressive Tax-Free Portfolio
   (9/85)
Fidelity High Yield Tax-Free Portfolio
   (12/77)
Fidelity Insured Tax-Free Portfolio
   (11/85)
Fidelity Limited Term Municipals
   (4/77)
Fidelity Municipal Bond Portfolio (8/76)
SPARTAN FEDERALLY TAX-FREE
   INCOME FUNDS
Spartan Municipal Income Portfolio
   (6/90)
Spartan Short-Intermediate Municipal
   Fund (12/86)

TABLE 7-1 (continued)

State Tax-free Income Funds: For current income exempt from federal and state (and, in some cases, local) taxes.
Fund Name (commencement date)
Fidelity California Tax-Free Fund: High Yield Portfolio (7/84)
Fidelity California Tax-Free Fund: Insured Portfolio (9/86)
Fidelity Massachusetts Tax-Free Fund: High Yield Portfolio (11/83)
Fidelity Michigan Tax-Free High Yield Portfolio (11/85)
Fidelity Minnesota Tax-Free Portfolio (11/85)
Fidelity New York Tax-Free Fund: High Yield Portfolio (7/84)
Fidelity New York Tax-Free Fund: Insured Portfolio (10/85)
Fidelity Ohio Tax-Free High Yield Portfolio (11/85)
SPARTAN STATE TAX-FREE INCOME FUNDS
Spartan California Municipal High Yield Portfolio (11/89)
Spartan Connecticut Municipal High Yield Portfolio (10/87)
Spartan New Jersey Municipal High Yield Portfolio (1/88)
Spartan New York Municipal High Yield Portfolio (2/90)
Spartan Pennsylvania Municipal High Yield Portfolio (8/86)

International Growth Funds: For long-term growth of capital from investments in foreign securities.
Fund Name (commencement date)
Fidelity Canada Fund (11/87)
Fidelity Europe Fund (10/86)
Fidelity Int'l. Growth & Income Fund (12/86)
Fidelity Int'l. Opportunities Fund (11/90)
Fidelity Overseas Fund (12/84)
Fidelity Pacific Basin Fund (10/86)
Fidelity Worldwide Fund (5/90)
EAFE Index (*valid for comparison only with Fidelity Overseas Fund*)

Foreign Currency Portfolios: To approximate the performance of foreign currencies against the U.S. dollar.
Fund Name (commencement date)
Fidelity Deutsche Mark Performance Portfolio, L.P. (11/89)

Fidelity Sterling Performance Portfolio L.P. (11/89)
Fidelity Yen Performance Portfolio, L.P. (11/89)

Fidelity Select Portfolios: For long-term growth of capital by means of sector investing.
Fund Name (commencement date)
Air Transportation (12/85)
American Gold (12/85)
Automotive (6/86)
Biotechnology (12/86)
Broadcast and Media (6/86)
Brokerage and Investment Management (7/85)
Chemicals (7/85)
Computers (7/85)
Construction and Housing (9/86)
Consumer Products (6/90)
Defense and Aerospace (5/84)
Developing Communications (6/90)
Electric Utilities (6/86)
Electronics (7/85)
Energy (7/81)
Energy Service (12/85)
Environmental Services (6/89)
Financial Services (12/81)
Food and Agriculture (7/85)
Health Care (7/81)
Industrial Materials (9/86)
Industrial Technology (9/86)
Insurance (12/85)
Leisure (5/84)
Medical Delivery (6/86)
Paper and Forest Products (6/86)
Precious Metals and Minerals (7/81)
Regional Banks (6/86)
Retailing (12/85)
Savings and Loan (12/85)
Software and Computer Services (7/85)
Technology (7/81)
Telecommunications (7/85)
Transportation (9/86)
Utilities (12/81)

Fidelity's Annuity Portfolios: For long-term tax-deferred investing.
Fund Name (commencement date)
Money Market Portfolio (4/82)
High Income Portfolio (9/85)
Equity-Income Portfolio (10/86)
Growth Portfolio (10/86)
Overseas Portfolio (1/87)
Short-Term Portfolio (12/88)
Asset Manager Portfolio (9/89)

TABLE 7–2

USAA Growth Fund Portfolio of Investments

July 31, 1998

Number of Shares	Security	Market Value (000)
	COMMON STOCKS (99.8%)	
	Advertising/Marketing (0.1%)	
41,000	Nielsen Media Research, Inc.	$ 169
	Aerospace/Defense (0.8%)	
289,100	Boeing Co.	11,220
	Agricultural Products (0.1%)	
60,000	Pioneer Hi-Bred International, Inc.	1,898
	Air Freight (0.4%)	
97,080	FDX Corp. *	5,892
	Airlines (0.9%)	
400,000	Southwest Airlines Co.	13,175
	Banks - Major Regional (2.9%)	
151,910	Banc One Corp.	7,852
74,000	Fleet Financial Group, Inc.	6,359
129,000	National City Corp.	8,627
172,300	Norwest Corp.	6,192
86,000	PNC Bank Corp.	4,638
19,700	Wells Fargo & Co.	7,011
		40,679
	Banks - Money Center (4.3%)	
166,200	BankAmerica Corp.	14,916
33,000	Bankers Trust Corp.	3,698
101,300	Citicorp	17,221
167,000	First Union Corp.	10,062
185,800	NationsBank Corp.	14,818
		60,715
	Beverages - Alcoholic (1.1%)	
293,400	Anheuser-Busch Companies, Inc.	15,165
	Beverages - Nonalcoholic (7.9%)	
1,721,704	Cadbury Schweppes plc ADR	95,447
400,000	PepsiCo, Inc.	15,525

T A B L E   7–2 (continued)

July 31, 1998

Number of Shares	Security	Market Value (000)
	Foods (2.6%)	
85,000	Campbell Soup Co.	$ 4,590
200,000	ConAgra, Inc.	5,175
170,000	General Mills, Inc.	10,529
100,000	Kellogg Co.	3,312
92,300	Sara Lee Corp.	4,627
124.000	Unilever N V	8,618
		36,851
	Gaming Companies (0.5%)	
280,000	International Game Technology	6,860
	Healthcare - Diversified (4.2%)	
120,000	Abbott Laboratories	4,988
350,000	American Home Products Corp.	18,025
100,000	Bristol-Myers Squibb Co.	11,394
125,000	Johnson & Johnson, Inc.	9,656
200,000	Warner-Lambert Co.	15,112
		59,175
	Healthcare - HMOs (2.9%)	
392,900	Pacificare Health Systems, Inc. "A" *	26,815
238,000	United Healthcare Corp.	13,447
		40,262
	Healthcare - Specialized Services (0.5%)	
41,000	IMS Healthcare, Inc.	2,575
500,000	PhyCor, Inc. *	4,563
		7,138
	Household Products (2.3%)	
33,600	Colgate-Palmolive Co.	3,106

* The above table represents only a partial listing.

T A B L E 7–3

The Vanguard Group

Growth & Income Funds

Index 500
Convertible Securities
Equity Income
Growth & Income
REIT Index
Selected Value
Tax Managed Growth & Income
Total Stock Market Index
Utilities Income
Value Index
Windsor
Windsor II

Growth Funds

Extended Market Index
Growth Index
Mid-Cap Index
Morgan Growth
PRIMECAP
Tax-Managed Capital Appreciation
U.S. Growth

Aggressive Growth Funds

Aggressive Growth
Capital Opportunity
Energy
Explorer
Gold & Precious Metals
Health Care
Small-Cap Growth
Small-Cap Index
Small-Cap Value Index
Tax-Managed Small-Cap

International Funds

Emerging Markets Stock Index
European Stock Index
Global Asset Allocation
Global Equity
International Growth
International Value
Pacific Stock Index
Tax-Managed International
Total International Stock Index

Comparative Indexes
S & P 500
Wilshire 4500
Russell 2000

Balanced Funds

Asset Allocation
Balanced Index
LifeStrategy Conservative Growth
LifeStrategy Income
LifeStrategy Moderate Growth
Tax Managed Balanced
Wellesley Income
Wellington

Bond Funds

Admiral Intermediate –Term Treasury
Admiral Long-Term Treasury
Admiral Short Term Treasury
GNMA
High Yield Corporate
Intermediate-Term Bond Index
Intermediate-Term Corporate
Intermediate Treasury
Preferred Stock
Short-Term Bond
Short-Term Federal

Tax-exempt Funds

California Insured Intermediate Term
California Insured Long-Term Tax Exempt
FL Insured Long-Term Tax Exempt
High-Yield Tax Exempt
NJ Insured Long-Term Tax Exempt
NY Insured Long-Term Tax Exempt
OH Insured Long-Term Tax Exempt
PA Insured Long-Term Tax Exempt
Short-Term Tax Exempt

CHAPTER 8

The Prospectus

A prospectus is a formal, printed document offering to sell a security. The Securities Act of 1933 requires delivery of a prospectus prior to, or with, any solicitation of an order for mutual funds. All prospectuses must contain certain specific information required by law. They may look complicated, but in reality they are fairly simple; and once you become familiar with one mutual fund prospectus, you will have no difficulty in understanding them all.

At times a prospectus may be a bare-bones, three- or four-page document that provides little more than the information required by the federal Securities and Exchange Commission (SEC). Other prospectuses provide not only the SEC required disclosures, but in addition furnish detailed, comprehensive data about the fund. Such prospectuses may be 15 or more pages long.

INFORMATION CONTAINED IN A PROSPECTUS

The prospectus is required to disclose important information about the security. A mutual fund prospectus, for instance, must disclose (as a minimum) the fund's financial history, investment objectives, and management data. A typical mutual fund prospectus will also contain most if not all of the following information.

The front page of the prospectus will always show the date of its publication, the name of the fund, the type of fund, and its major objective(s). There is generally a table of contents on the first page, which will include nearly all of the following:

Description of the fund	How to redeem shares
Objectives of the fund	Shareholder services
Management of the fund	Distributions and taxes
Performance history	Yield information
Operating expenses	Schedule of investments
Schedule of fees	Financial statements
How to buy shares	General information

Do not be concerned if the first page of the prospectus contains the statement, "These shares have not been approved or disapproved by the SEC." No publicly offered mutual fund may be sold in the United States unless it is registered with the SEC. This requires strict adherence to SEC regulations as stipulated in the Investment Company Act of 1940. (Figure 8–1 shows the first page of the prospectus for the Vanguard Morgan Growth Fund.)

WHY IS A PROSPECTUS NECESSARY?

As previously noted, neither an investment company nor a broker may legally offer a mutual fund for sale unless a prospectus has been provided to the investor. The SEC *requires* it! Unfortunately, the SEC cannot make you *read* it. It is, however, the *key* source of information regarding a mutual fund, and I strongly urge you to read it carefully.

While a prospectus may be rather dry reading, it does provide you with vital information, especially the Investment Summary and the Summary of Fees and Expenses. Be sure to read these two parts even if you choose to skip the rest. From the first, you will learn whether the fund's objectives and your goals are compatible. The second can be used to compare expenses charged by various funds. (See also Chapter 15.)

Finally, the prospectus is necessary for your own protection and that of the fund. It protects you against any misrepresentation by the fund and protects the fund against lawsuits resulting from failures to provide "full and honest disclosure."

FIGURE 8-1

Vanguard Morgan Growth Fund

Prospectus
April 30, 1999
A Growth Stock Mutual Fund

Contents

1 Fund Profile	10 Financial Highlights
2 Additional Information	11 Investing with Vanguard
3 A Word About Risk	11 Services and Account Features
3 Who Should Invest	12 Types of Accounts
3 Primary Investment Strategies	12 Buying Shares
6 The Fund and Vanguard	14 Redeeming Shares
7 Investment Advisers	17 Transferring Registration
8 Year 2000 Challenge	17 Fund and Account Updates
8 Dividends, Capital Gains, and Taxes	Glossary *(inside back cover)*
9 Share Price	

Why Reading This Prospectus Is Important

This prospectus explains the objective, risks, and strategies of Vanguard Morgan Growth Fund.

Note: The statement in the prospectus, "Neither the Securities and Exchange Commission nor any state securities commission has approved or disapproved these securities," is not to be taken as a reflection of the worth or value of the fund. This caveat appears in every prospectus. It merely means that the SEC takes a neutral position with respect to the fund's worth. It neither approves nor disapproves the purchase of the fund by investors.

HOW TO OBTAIN A PROSPECTUS

A prospectus may be secured (1) through stockbrokers (bear in mind that stockbrokers usually handle load funds only, since this is how they earn their commissions—see Chapter 4), (2) by writing to the investment company that sells the fund, or (3) by calling the fund's toll-free 800 number. Virtually every fund has an 800 number. Fund addresses and telephone numbers may also be secured by checking investment magazines such as *Money,* and financial newspapers such as the *Wall Street Journal* and *Barron's.* Of course, public libraries offer a number of comprehensive references that provide complete information on any mutual fund. One such publication is the *Individual Investor's Guide to No-Load Mutual Funds* (annual editions published by American Association of Individual Investors, Chicago, Illinois), a directory of no-load funds. It also provides investment objectives for each fund as well as addresses and telephone numbers. (Appendix C provides a listing of 15 well-known, reputable mutual fund companies. All of the information needed to secure their prospectuses is provided. Of course, there are many more equally fine mutual fund companies, but this is a good list with which to start.)

A prospectus is provided free of charge to anyone who requests it. Investment companies are happy to mail them. Included with the prospectus will be an application and a postage paid return envelope in which to forward your check and completed application, should you decide to invest. Often, you will receive the fund's latest annual report and other informative literature as well.

The prospectus will also help you decide whether that particular fund is one in which you should invest. Here, you will find whether it matches your objectives, if it provides the services you need, how expensive it is to own (management and advisory fees), whether it has sales and/or redemption charges, and, perhaps most important, what its current annual rate of return is and what it has been over the years.

Most prospectuses (and/or the fund's periodic reports) will provide detailed, statistical data regarding the fund's year-by-year financial activity and will be somewhat similar to the table shown in Table 8–1, which is from the Vanguard Star Fund Prospectus of April 27, 1993.

CALCULATING A FUND'S RETURN OR YIELD

If the prospectus or period reports fail to spell out the fund's annual return (profitability) or yield (distributions compared to cost), it is a simple matter to calculate both. To find a fund's annual return, take the fund's ending NAV for the year, plus all distributions for the year, minus the fund's beginning NAV for the year, times 100; divide the answer by the year's beginning NAV. The result equals the fund's *annual return percentage.*

TABLE 8–1

Vanguard Star Fund

	Year Ended December 31,						
	1992	**1991**	**1990**	**1989**	**1988**	**1987**	**1986**
Net Asset Value, Beginning of Period	$12.30	$10.73	$12.05	$11.12	$9.98	$11.34	$11.45
Investment Activities Total Income and Net Investment Income	.69	.97	.91	1.18	.80	1.31	1.15
Net Unrealized Gain (Loss) on Investments	.59	1.59	(1.34)	.90	1.06	(1.07)	.31
Total from Investment Activities	1.28	2.56	(.43)	2.08	1.86	.24	1.46
Distributions Net Investment Income	(.51)	(.62)	(.73)	(.77)	(.69)	(.85)	(.86)
Realized Net Gain	(.18)	(.37)	(.16)	(.38)	(.03)	(.75)	(.71)
Total Distributions	(.69)	(.99)	(.89)	(1.15)	(.72)	(1.60)	(1.57)
Net Asset Value, End of Period	$12.89	$12.30	$10.73	$12.05	$11.12	$9.98	$11.34
Ratio of Expenses to Average Net Assets	0%	0%	0%	0%	0%	0%	0%
Ratio of Net Investments Income to Average Net Assets	4.36%	5.48%	6.65%	6.42%	5.87%	6.08%	5.44%
Portfolio Turnover Rate	3%	11%	12%	7%	21%	17%	0%
Number of Shares Outstanding, End of Period (thousands)	193,192	128,036	96,807	78,807	61,283	56,883	40,091

Table 8–1 applies the following data for the Vanguard Star Fund:

Ending NAV	$12.89
Distributions + unrealized gains	$ 1.28
Beginning NAV	$12.30

($12.89 + $1.28 − $12.30) = $1.87 × 100 = $187 ÷ $12.30 = 15.20%

Using the formula described above, the profitability for the Star Fund amounted to a very respectable 15.20% for the 1992 year.

To determine a fund's *yield* for the year, divide the total distributions paid for the year by the beginning NAV for the year (assuming you were a shareholder for the year). The formula below is applied to Figure 8–1.

Determining Annual Yield Percentages from a Prospectus

$$\$.69 \div \$12.30 = 5.6\%$$

STUDY GUIDE FOR CHAPTER 8

1. List the three required elements of a prospectus.
2. Name five things you can learn about a fund by reading the prospectus.
3. List three ways to secure a prospectus.
4. What are some of the financial data that can be found in a prospectus?
5. How can you ascertain a particular fund's profitability even if the prospectus does not give it?
6. Where can you find the data to calculate any fund's annual return?

82   CHAPTER 8

P O S T S C R I P T   8–1

PROFILE PROSPECTUS DEBUTS (From <u>Mutual Funds</u> Magazine, October 1995)

The next time you call a mutual fund company to request a prospectus, ask whether they have the new Profile Prospectus. If they do, ask to receive a copy of it in addition to the *complete* prospectus. Eight mutual fund companies working in cooperation with the SEC (Securities and Exchange Commission) have devised pamphlets that highlight seven key points about a particular fund without the obfuscating legalese of the full prospectus.

The SEC has approved the new fund profiles to be *used as a supplement to, but not as a replacement for the longer versions.* However, if the results of an industry survey reflect investor acceptance, that may change. The seven points covered by the abbreviated profile include the following:

1. The fund's goals   5. Fees
2. Investment strategies   6. Expenses
3. Risks   7. Past performance history
4. Investor suitability   (other points may eventually be
                                  added)

Participating fund families are American, Dreyfus, Fidelity, IDS, Pacific Horizon, T. Rowe Price, Scudder, and Vanguard. NOTE: Some of the fund families listed offer only load funds, some offer load and no-load funds, others are true no-load companies, namely the last three listed.

While the formal test effort to provide investors with the profiles involves only the above sponsors, the SEC has given the green light to *all* funds to adopt the new format.

Update
The number of mutual funds currently using the new profile-type prospectus has grown by leaps and bounds. Virtually all new prospectuses published by major mutual fund companies use the profile prospectus. Investors have expressed great satisfaction with the new format, because it is far more readable and much more informative.

POSTSCRIPT 8-2

CALCULATING THE ROI (RETURN ON INVESTMENT) Annualized One-Year Return

FORMULA AND EXAMPLE*

Note the ending NAV ($12.89) in Table 8–1.

Add the total from investment activity (includes unrealized and realized gains) ($1.28) (realized capital gains amounted to $.69 of the above $1.28, the rest was from unrealized capital gains).

Subtract the beginning NAV ($12.30).

Multiply the result by 100 (to obtain a percentage).

Divide the result from the above calculations by the beginning NAV.

Final result equals the ROI or annualized one-year return.

EXAMPLE

$$\$12.89 + \$1.28 = \$14.17 - \$12.30 = \$1.87 \times 100 =$$
$$\$187 \div \$12.30 = 15.20\%$$

In the above example the ROI for the fund in question = 15.20%.

TO CALCULATE A FUND'S YIELD

Divide the fund's distributions, dividends, and *realized* capital gains by the ending NAV.

$$\$.69 \text{ divided by } \$12.98 = 5.4\%$$

(The yield formula excludes *unrealized* capital gains.)

REMINDER: *Realized capital gains* result from the manager's *sale* of securities from the fund's portfolio at a price higher than the price at which the securities were purchased originally. *Unrealized capital gains* result from the increase in the value of securities in the fund's portfolio. However, these appreciated funds have *not been sold*. They remain in the portfolio.

*Based on Vanguard's STAR Fund (see page 80).

CHAPTER 9

How to Open a Mutual Fund Account

INITIAL CONTACTS—SURVEYING THE MARKET

Chapter 8 identified sources of information about mutual funds for which you might wish to receive prospectuses. It was noted that newspapers, financial publications, magazines, and mutual fund reference sources found in public libraries are good starting points for gleaning information about some of the many hundreds of mutual funds on the market.

However, if you want a quick, comprehensive, and bare-bones reference source for *every* mutual fund, consult an up-to-date copy of *Standard and Poor's Security Owner's Stock Guide,* a monthly publication available in libraries, from stockbrokers, and through subscription (call 1-800-221-5277—subscription rate is $124 per year). This publication provides a brief, "all-you-need-to-get-started" mutual fund summary containing an alphabetical listing of just about every mutual fund. Everything you initially need to know about a particular fund will be found here:

- Year the fund was formed
- Principal objective
- Total net assets
- IRA and Keogh information
- Net assets per share % change (NAV beginning of period compared to NAV at end of period)

- Minimum unit (minimum initial purchase amount)
- Distributions (dividends and capital gains)*
- Maximum sales charge (for load funds)
- $10,000 invested 12/31/96—now worth* (covers six-year period)
- Price record (based on NAV per share)*
- Percent yield from investment income*

By using such a summary, you can narrow your fund selections down to just those that meet your objectives and have respectable performance records.

If you are looking for more detailed information and are willing to limit your selections to no-load mutual funds, as recommended throughout this book, an excellent, comprehensive reference source is *The Dow-Jones Irwin Mutual Fund Yearbook,* William G. Droms, editor (Homewood, Illinois). The yearbook provides detailed descriptions of all no-load funds quoted in the *Wall Street Journal.* Information includes names and addresses, fund managers and their fees, and a detailed description of the fund's investment philosophy. Each entry also includes a performance summary giving the rate of return for the past 10 years. It also notes asset size, year first offered, fund advisers, portfolio turnover, minimum initial investment, minimum subsequent investment, total expense ratio, shareholder services, dividend payment dates (income and capital gains), investment performance summary data, and total annual return summary.

Chapter 6 detailed how to go about selecting funds that are both compatible with your risk tolerance level and still meet your investment objectives. Assuming you have made your choices, you are now ready to start the process for opening a mutual fund account.

If you have chosen a load fund (heaven forbid!), contact a stockbroker who sells that particular fund; the broker will take it from there, but it will cost you a hefty commission of up to 8.5% of

---

*Remember the caveat: "Past performance does not guarantee future results." Consult the prospectus for full disclosure.

your initial investment and 8.5% on each succeeding investment you make (see Chapter 4).

With very little extra effort, you can open accounts in no-load funds that will offer the identical objectives, risk factors, and yields as the load funds and save you up to 8.5% commission in the bargain. On a no-load fund investment of $2,500, a fairly typical minimum investment amount, you will have saved $212.50, the commission on an 8.5% load fund.

OPENING AN ACCOUNT— APPLICATION PREPARATION

Now let's see exactly what is involved in opening a no-load mutual fund account. By way of illustration, suppose you have decided on the Vanguard Group as your investment company and have found two or three of their funds that interest you. Now, follow the steps outlined below. (The process would be the same for any other investment company's no-load funds.)

1. Call Vanguard's toll-free number (see Appendix C).
2. Having called the 800 number, you will be answered by a Vanguard representative (a live person, not a recorded message).
3. Request prospectuses for each of the funds in which you are interested. Expect to receive them in two to three weeks.
4. Carefully read the prospectuses, and make sure you understand them. If you don't, call the representative and ask for answers to any of the questions you may have.
5. For each fund in which you wish to invest, complete the application that comes with the prospectus.
6. Determine what the prospectus indicates is the minimum initial investment required to open an account in the fund(s) you have chosen. (You may invest more than the initial minimum, but not less.)
7. Send a check and an application for each fund in which you are investing. Sometimes you may invest in more

than one fund using the same application, as long as the accounts are registered in the same way and your check covers the minimum investment required for each account.

8. On your application, you must indicate exactly how you wish to have the account registered. (More about this in Chapter 10.) You should also indicate on the application how you want to have your dividend and capital gains distributions handled. You may elect to receive them in cash or have them reinvested. (By reinvesting them, you will enjoy the growth-building power of compounding; see Figure 9–1.)

9. All parties whose names appear on the application must sign and date it.

10. Shortly thereafter, you will receive in the mail a confirmation of your investment(s) and your account number(s). The confirmation form will also have a tear-off deposit slip to be used for making your next deposit. In the case of Vanguard, a postage-paid return envelope is also included. This process will be repeated each time you make another deposit. Save all your confirmation slips until you receive your annual, year-end cumulative confirmation slip, at which time you may discard the intervening slips. (If you invest regularly, these do have a tendency to pile up and stretch the limits of your file.)

The process described above appears graphically in Figure 9–2.

F I G U R E   9–1

The Power of Compounding

Monthly Investments	Number of Years				
	5	10	15	20	25
$100	$7,348	$18,295	$34,604	$58,902	$95,103
$300	$22,043	$54,884	$103,811	$176,706	$285,308
$500	$36,738	$91,473	$173,019	$294,510	$475,513

This chart illustrates the future value of different regular monthly investments for different periods of time and assumes an annual fixed investment return of 8%.

Starting a Mutual Fund Investment Program

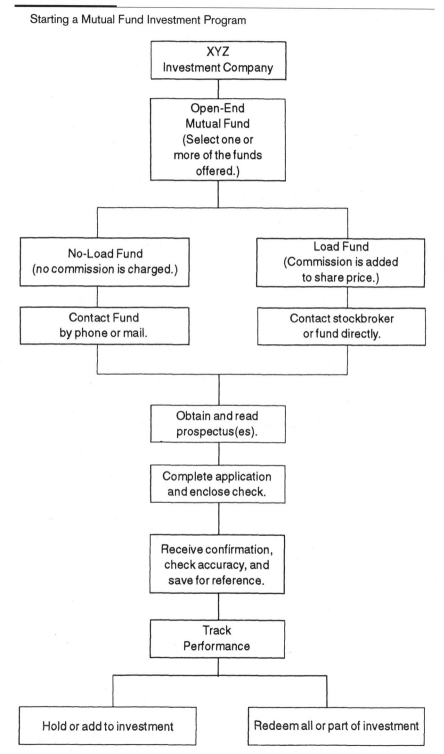

Finally, it should be noted that most mutual funds may be used to establish an IRA (individual retirement account). However, opening an IRA mutual fund account requires a slightly different type of application form. Therefore, should you decide that you want your mutual fund to go into an IRA, indicate that you wish to have the special IRA application form and IRA information when you request the prospectus.

Bear in mind that not *all* mutual funds are suitable for IRAs. For example, it is not a good idea to establish an IRA using a tax-free municipal bond fund, since you are not subject to Internal Revenue Service taxes on an IRA account until such time as you begin to make withdrawals (redemptions). Therefore, why take the lower yields usually paid on tax-free municipal bonds when you do not need tax relief for an IRA? Also, since an IRA is meant to be a nest egg for your retirement years, avoid high-risk mutual funds. Instead, select a fund with a record of *proven growth* over a long period of time. Incidentally, minimum initial investment amounts are usually lower for IRAs than for regular mutual fund accounts.

Lastly, unlike regular mutual fund account applications, IRA application forms do contain provisions for naming both primary and secondary beneficiaries. Thus, in addition to all the advantages noted for regular mutual fund accounts, IRAs offer special tax benefits allowed by the IRS—as long as you abide by the rules. All the rules regarding IRAs are spelled out in IRS publication No. 590, which may be obtained free of charge by calling 1-800-829-3676.

STUDY GUIDE FOR CHAPTER 9

1. What steps should you take before investing in any mutual fund?
2. What caveat applies to every mutual fund?
3. What is the first step in investing in any mutual fund?
4. Why is it always a good idea to reinvest your fund's distributions?
5. Other than reinvesting distributions, in what other ways may you receive fund distributions?
6. What is the simplest way to open a load fund account?

P O S T S C R I P T   9–1

INSTRUCTIONS FOR OPENING AN INDIVIDUAL RETIREMENT ACCOUNT

The instructions for establishing an IRA are the same as noted on the instructions for implementing a regular mutual fund account with the following differences:

1. When requesting the prospectus and annual report, specify that you wish to receive an IRA application. (See number 4 below.)

2. The IRA application will permit the registered shareholder(s) to name beneficiaries.

3. Often, an IRA account may be opened with an initial deposit that is considerably less than required to open a non-IRA account. (The application will indicate the amount.)

4. Now that there are three different types of IRAs; you will have to specify which type of application you wish to have.
   a. Traditional IRA
   b. Roth IRA
   c. Education IRA

   There are significant differences among the three IRAs. If you wish to have more help in deciding which IRA would be most suitable for your retirement needs, refer to Chapter 14 as well as the special IRA pages included in the postscripts to Chapter 14 (14–2 through 14–4).

CHAPTER 10

Registering a Mutual Fund Account

Each mutual fund account you open may be registered in the manner designated by the owner(s). Several options are provided.

INDIVIDUAL OWNERSHIP

You may desire to register your mutual fund accounts in your name only. Doing so permits you alone to make deposits, exchange funds (switching), initiate redemptions, write checks against the account (where such a feature is offered), request information about your account, and close an account. However, you are responsible for making separate provisions for the disposition of the fund's assets in the event of your death. Unlike insurance, mutual funds do not provide for the naming of beneficiaries on accounts registered in one name. Therefore, you must provide for the disposition of your fund's assets in your will.

JOINT ACCOUNT

An account may be registered jointly. Such an account is called a "tenancy in common" account. Each owner retains absolute control over his or her share of the account. Again, provision must be made in a will for the disposition of each owner's share of the assets in the account upon the death of one or both owners.

JOINT ACCOUNT WITH RIGHTS OF SURVIVORSHIP

Married persons may establish a joint account with rights of survivorship. This type of account is known as "tenancy by the entirety." With such an account in force, the surviving spouse automatically has full rights to the entire account upon the death of the other spouse.

What, if any, benefits are there in registering an account in this manner? As you probably know, at death an individual's property (estate) normally goes through probate (the court procedure that validates the will and supervises the execution of the terms of the will). Court fees, accountant's fees, attorney's fees, and other costs associated with probate can be substantial. Joint tenancy with rights of survivorship (JTWROS) is an ownership arrangement that allows property held in joint tenancy to pass to the surviving owner without the need for probate. It is important that you realize that a joint ownership account *does not* take the place of a will.

TRUSTS

A mutual fund account registered as a trust creates a fiduciary relationship in which one person (the trustee) holds title to the account (the trust property) for the benefit of the other (the beneficiary). Trust accounts are generally created for the purpose of estate planning and to minimize the tax consequences upon the death of the trustee.

Due to the complexity of establishing trusts, it is best to seek the help of an attorney or other legal adviser.

Other than setting up trusts, the whole process of registering a mutual fund account sounds much more complicated than it really is. You certainly can do it on your own, or you may seek the help of a fund representative.

Figure 10–1 is a sample application form showing the various registration options.

STUDY GUIDE FOR CHAPTER 10

1. Who determines how a new mutual fund account is registered?

Pennsylvania Mutual Fund Account Application and Registration Form

APPLICATION TO OPEN A PMF INVESTOR ACCOUNT

REGISTRATION INSTRUCTIONS:

☐ Individual _____
Name

☐☐☐ — ☐☐ — ☐☐☐☐
OR

☐ Joint Tenant _____
(if any) Name

☐☐☐ — ☐☐ — ☐☐☐☐
(List One Social Security No. If Joint Ownership)

Gift/Transfer to
☐ Minors Act _____
Custodian's Name (Only One Permitted)

As Custodian for _____
Minor's Name (Only One Permitted)

Under the _____
State

Uniform Gift/Transfer to Minors Act.

☐☐☐ — ☐☐ — ☐☐☐☐
Minor's Social Security No.

☐ Trust— _____
(Including Trustee(s)
Corporate
Retirement _____
Plans) Name of Trust

Under Agreement Dated _____

☐☐☐ — ☐☐ — ☐☐☐☐   OR   ☐☐ — ☐☐☐☐☐☐☐
Social Security No.   Tax Identification No.

Corporation,
☐ Partnership, etc. _____
Name of Entity

☐☐ — ☐☐☐☐☐☐☐
Tax Identification No.

MAILING ADDRESS:

_____
Street

Residence Telephone _____
Area Code   Number

_____
City   State   Zip Code

Business Telephone _____
Area Code   Number

The attached check for $_____ is in payment of ☐ initial order   ☐ initial telephone order, previously
submitted, telephone order #_____.

☐ Please send duplicate account
statements to: _____
Name

_____
Address   State   Zip Code

DISTRIBUTION OPTION:

If no box is checked, you will have income dividends and capital gain distributions reinvested.

A. ☐ Reinvest capital gain distributions, pay dividends in cash.   B. ☐ Pay capital gain distributions and dividends in cash.

I (We) am (are) of legal age and capacity in my (our) state of residence and have received and read a copy of Pennsylvania Mutual Fund, Inc.'s current prospectus and agree to its terms and hereby certify, under the penalties of perjury, (1) that the Social Security or Taxpayer Identification number provided above is correct and (2) that the IRS *has not* notified me (us) that I (we) am (are) subject to 20% back-up withholding. Cross out (2) only if you *have been* notified by the IRS that you are subject to back-up withholding.

Check One: ☐ **U.S. Citizen**   ☐ **Resident Alien**   ☐ **Non-Resident Alien**

_____
Signature   Date

_____
Signature   Date

2. What, if any, restrictions are placed on mutual fund accounts registered to one individual?

3. Compare mutual fund individual ownership with an insurance policy, as to the disposition of assets upon the demise of the owner.

4. Explain the features of jointly registered mutual fund accounts.

5. What are the provisions of mutual fund accounts registered as joint accounts with rights of survivorship?

6. Why is it advantageous for married couples to register an account as "tenancy by the entirety"?

7. What is the main reason for registering a mutual fund account as a trust?

WHAT'S IN A NAME: REGISTERING AN ACCOUNT

The account registration essentially denotes who owns the assets. How the account is registered determines who can access and make decisions about your account while you're living. It also determines how ownership of the assets will be transferred when you die. Here are some of the most common registration options.

Individual Account   Your investment assets are registered in your name only, meaning you're the only person who can access the account or obtain information about it. It might surprise you, but not even your spouse is legally allowed access to or information on an individual account registered in your name. At your death, the account goes either to your estate or to beneficiaries designated in your will, according to the laws of the state where you live.

Generally, property being passed on via a will is subject to a legal proceeding known as probate. This process includes having the will filed with and validated by a local court; inventorying the deceased's property and having that property appraised; paying off all debts; and distributing remaining assets. Depending on the state you live in, the probate process may take a year or more to complete, according to Dennis Clifford, coauthor of the consumer-oriented book, *Plan Your Estate* (Nolo Press). Probate legal fees on an uncomplicated estate valued at $400,000 can easily amount to $10,000, Clifford says.

Joint Tenant with Right of Survivorship   The account is registered in the name of more than one owner. Typically you and your spouse may be joint tenants, but ownership may be shared by others as well. All owners listed on the account have access to it and can make buying and selling decisions. What does "right of survivorship" mean? When one owner dies, the account passes to the other owner or owners without having to go through the probate process. In nearly all states, all owners must share an equal stake in the account.

"Some people choose this option to do an end run around probate," says David Rhine, national director of family wealth planning at the New York City office of BDO Seidman, a nationwide accounting firm. He says a joint tenant account may be a good choice if you live in a state where probate is expensive. (Check with your attorney to get an estimate of costs where you live.)

You might also consider this registration if your assets are not great enough to make you subject to federal estate tax. Estate tax is levied on assets valued at more than $675,000 currently. Assets include the appreciated value of your home or other real estate as well as retirement savings and investments. "The bottom line is that if you have substantial assets, you don't want all assets jointly held, because you could end up paying higher taxes," says Rhine.

Tenants in Common   This registration is established by two or more account owners. The shares can be divided between the owners any way they choose. (This is different from joint tenants with rights of survivorship, who must share equally.) When an owner dies, that portion of the assets does not automatically pass to the surviving tenant(s). It generally goes to the deceased's estate and is subject to probate.

Transfer on Death   This option is available in all states except Louisiana, New York, and North Carolina. You retain sole ownership and decision-making ability for your account while you're alive. But you designate one or more beneficiaries on the application; so at your death, the account passes directly to them without being subject to probate.

Uniform Transfers to Minors   This option allows you to provide an irrevocable gift to a minor by establishing an account in his or her name. You or someone you choose serves as custodian for the account until the child reaches a specified age. In most states, custodianship terminates, and the account passes directly to the minor, when he or she reaches age 21. For tax purposes, income in the account is reported as income for the minor.

Making Changes   What if you want to change the form of registration on your account? You are required to supply written instructions indicating the change you want, signed by all registered owners of the account, along with a completed new account form. In addition, when you change an account registration due to an event such as marriage or death, a supporting document such as a death or marriage certificate is required.

DETAILS OF VARIOUS TYPES OF MUTUAL FUND REGISTRATIONS

Individual Ownership   The individual in whose name the account is registered is the sole owner and is responsible for the tax liabilities as well as making provision for the disposition of the assets of the fund(s) upon his/her demise by means of a will. Beneficiaries may not be named in such an account registration only by means of the will. (The account is subject to probate as are most wills.)

Multiple Ownership and Beneficiaries   There are different types of multiple ownership registrations, namely *Joint Tenants with Rights of Survivorship, Joint Tenants in Common,* and *Tenancy by the Entirety.* Joint Tenancy with Rights of Survivorship provides co-owners with rights of survivorship. In other words, the survivor receives total right of ownership to the property so registered at the death of the other co-owner. Mutual fund accounts are considered property. Joint Tenancy by the Entirety is limited to joint ownership by husband and wife. In some states this is limited to real estate only. Upon the demise of one spouse, the entire account goes to the surviving spouse without probate. Tenancy in Common permits two or more persons to own undivided shares in real or personal property; co-owners' shares pass to their heirs or beneficiaries (by means of a will), *not* to the surviving co-owners. (wills are subject to probate.)

Trusts   Trusts serve many worthwhile purposes, but they are somewhat complex; therefore, which type is best for you should be left to an attorney or arranged by the trust department of a bank. Trusts can be expensive to establish and maintain, especially if they need to be changed or modified at any time after being established.

Changing the Way a Mutual Fund Account Is Registered
Send a letter of instructions including the account number(s), the names and addresses, and the signatures of all shareholders in whose names the account(s) is currently registered; a signature of all the shareholders and a new updated completed Enrollment Form to the Program. The Enrollment Form may be obtained by calling the fund(s) representative.

When you change your account registration, the shares in the current account will be transferred to a new account under a new account number. The old account will be closed. Any previously elected privileges will become void. You must reapply for such privileges as check writing, Telephone Transactions, Automatic Investing, Automatic Distributions, etc., on the new Enrollment Form.

Summary of Multiple Owner Registrations and Recent Changes Joint Tenants with Rights of Survivorship   You may have a spouse and other owners named in such an account. With this type of registration, each named owner has an equal number of shares. Upon the demise of one owner, his/her shares are divided equally among the surviving owners. Probate is avoided in this type of registration.

Tenants in Common   (There is a difference of opinion here.) For example, Scudder says it is possible to have multiple ownership in a mutual fund account. It is necessary, however, for a letter to be attached to the account application indicating what percentage of the total shares each named owner is to own. Upon the demise of one of the owners, his/her shares go to the estate of the demised owner. The deceased owner's estate must go through probate. Vanguard, on the other hand says it is not permissible to have as a joint tenant anyone other than a spouse in this type of registration.

Conclusion   If you wish to register an account naming multiple owners, it is imperative that you check with the mutual fund company in which you are investing and request specific information regarding its policy regarding multiple registrations.

CHAPTER 11

Making Subsequent Investment Purchases

AMOUNT REQUIRED FOR ADDITIONAL PURCHASES

The minimum amount required for additional investment purchases varies with your particular mutual fund accounts and may range from $25 to $100 or more. The most common minimum additional investment is $100. You are not obligated to make additional purchases; this is entirely up to you. When you do make additional investments in your account, however, the number of shares that your investment will purchase varies with the NAV at the time your investment reaches the fund. For example, an investment of $100 into a no-load fund whose NAV is $5 will add 20 additional shares to your account ($100 divided by $5). When your fund declares a dividend or capital gain, and you have elected to have all distributions reinvested, they will be treated exactly as if you had made an additional cash purchase. (Minimum amount requirements are waived in this instance.) If you are not reinvesting distributions, you will receive a check for the amount of the dividend and/or capital gain declared by the fund. However, you will lose the benefits of compounding by not reinvesting your distributions. If possible, it is always best to have all distributions reinvested.

BY MAIL

You may add to your mutual fund account by mailing a check or money order along with the deposit slip that comes with each purchase confirmation.

Routinely, each time you make an investment in your mutual fund, or the fund declares a dividend or capital gain, you will receive an Investment Account Statement (confirmation statement) showing:

1. The trade date (usually the date your purchase or distribution was added to your account).
2. The dollar amount of your investment or distribution.
3. The NAV (share price) when your investment or distribution was credited to your account.
4. The number of new shares your investment or distribution added to your account.
5. The total number of shares you now own.
6. Some funds may also show the total dollar value of your account as of the date the statement was issued.

Most, if not all, mutual funds have a detachable investment form on the Investment Account Statement, which should be used for your next investment. Usually the investment slip will indicate the minimum amount required for additional purchases. Of course, you may always invest more than the minimum. It will also include:

- Fund name
- Name(s) in which the account is registered
- Account number
- Your address
- Your Social Security number (Tax ID number)
- Space to show the amount of your investment

A self-addressed envelope in which to mail your new remittance is also provided with your Investment Account Statement. Some funds (among others, Vanguard, USAA Funds, and Strong Funds) will provide *postage-paid* return envelopes for your subsequent remittances. Others will merely provide an envelope in which

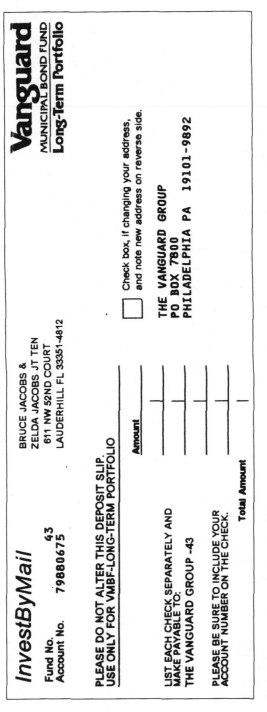

InvestByMail

Fund No. 43
Account No. 79880675

BRUCE JACOBS &
ZELDA JACOBS JT TEN
611 NW 52ND COURT
LAUDERHILL FL 33351-4812

PLEASE DO NOT ALTER THIS DEPOSIT SLIP.
USE ONLY FOR VMBF-LONG-TERM PORTFOLIO

Amount

LIST EACH CHECK SEPARATELY AND
MAKE PAYABLE TO:
THE VANGUARD GROUP -43

PLEASE BE SURE TO INCLUDE YOUR
ACCOUNT NUMBER ON THE CHECK.

Total Amount

☐ Check box, if changing your address,
and note new address on reverse side.

THE VANGUARD GROUP
PO BOX 7800
PHILADELPHIA PA 19101-9892

Vanguard
MUNICIPAL BOND FUND
Long-Term Portfolio

Reprinted with permission of The Vanguard Group.

THE Vanguard GROUP
OF INVESTMENT COMPANIES℠

POST OFFICE BOX 7800 • PHILADELPHIA, PA 19101-9892

BUSINESS REPLY MAIL

FIRST CLASS MAIL   PERMIT NO. 14   SOUTHEASTERN, PA

POSTAGE WILL BE PAID BY ADDRESSEE

**PLEASE SEND ONLY
ADDITIONAL PURCHASES
IN THIS ENVELOPE**

NO POSTAGE
NECESSARY
IF MAILED IN
THE UNITED STATES

Reprinted with permission of The Vanguard Group.

to mail your next remittance. Be sure to write your account number on all remittances. (See Exhibit 11–1.)

BY WIRE

The new account application provides several options for the manner in which additional investments may be made other than by mailing them. One of them permits you to purchase additional shares by wire. If you choose this option, you are required to supply the fund with the name of your bank, your account number, the bank's address, and a voided blank check. Your mutual fund will make the other necessary arrangements with your bank without any further action on your part. Then you can authorize your bank to transfer funds from your checking account to your mutual fund account. You need only advise your bank when and how much to wire to your fund. The transaction is executed by electronic transfer of funds. Your bank must be a member of the Federal Reserve System if this option is to be used. Your mutual fund will mail you a deposit confirmation each time an electronic transfer of funds is executed.

The benefit of this option is that there are occasions when you want to make sure that the fund receives your investment on the *same day* in order to take advantage of a favorable turn in the market. It is possible that the advantage could be lost if the investment were to be delayed even for a day—as it certainly would if it were to be sent by ordinary mail.

AUTOMATIC PURCHASE OPTION

By selecting this option, you authorize your bank, in a manner similar to sending funds by wire, to transfer a set amount (determined by you) from your checking account on a periodic basis (also determined by you—monthly, quarterly, etc.) to your fund account. Each such transfer will purchase additional shares in your name at the current NAV. A confirmation statement will be sent to you by the fund each time a deposit from your bank checking account is made to your mutual fund account.

Exhibit 11–1 shows samples of a tear-off Reinvestment Form and a postage-paid return envelope from the Vanguard Investment

Group. (Not all mutual fund companies provide postage-paid return envelopes, however, they will all supply reinvestment slips and self-addressed return envelopes.)

STUDY GUIDE FOR CHAPTER 11

1. What determines the number of additional shares that will be purchased by each deposit that is made to your fund?
2. How may additional investments be made to your mutual fund account(s)?
3. What does the fund send you after each deposit or distribution made to your account?
4. What information is recorded on Investment Account Statements?
5. What are the advantages of having funds wired to your account?
6. What is meant by an automatic purchase option?

THE MOST IMPORTANT INVESTING PRINCIPLE OF ALL (Based on an excerpt from a recent Louis Rukeyser's Mutual Funds newsletter.)

The principle is illustrated by the following story.

It all starts back in the early 1960s with Ralph, the single *unluckiest* guy in the entire world. (We all feel that way sometimes, don't we?) Starting in 1963, he put $2,000 once a year into stocks that comprise the Standard and Poor's 500 Index—but his timing was so terrible that he chose the worst day of the year every time! Incredibly, he invested at the exact *top* of the market every year—and kept it up for 10 years. (After that he let it ride.)

As of March 1, 1999, his total of $20,000 would have grown to *$810,901*.

But Ralph's brother-in-law, Darth, started investing $2,000 a year in 1973, right after Ralph quit. To everyone's astonishment, especially Ralph's, Darth turned out to be the world's *luckiest* investor. Every year he picked the absolute *bottom* of the market to plunk down his $2,000. And to stack the odds in Darth's favor even more, he kept up his stupendous performance for 20 years, investing *twice as long* as Ralph.

Guess what? As of that same March 1, 1999, Darth's 40 grand would be worth $25,074 *less* than Ralph's stake—$785,074 vs. $810,901. Imagine! Darth put in *twice* the money, and his annual return was far higher, yet Ralph licked him fair and square. Moral: Forget market timing! Timing and luck are nice, but you can make more money just by starting now, investing regularly, and staying the course.

THE MORAL IS . . .

Establish a comfortable, affordable, ongoing investment plan, and stay with it through all the market's ups and downs. You can't control the market, but you can use it to your advantage. The market's volatility should not be a deterrent to your investment program, but an incentive to stay with the plan. Don't try to time the market. It is an exercise in futility!

CHAPTER 12

Strategies to Maximize Return on Investment

BUY AND HOLD

Probably the most common mistake committed by inexperienced investors is the "buy and hold" fallacy. They fall in love with their funds and hate to part with them, or they are too lazy to track their funds' progress and eliminate the losers. There is nothing sinful about "buy and hold" as long as you check on your funds and liquidate or switch out of the poor performers. If you hold onto a poor fund hoping it will recover, you have lost the opportunity to move your investment to a profitable fund. You are, therefore, losing money while you wait. (See "Telephone Switching" in this chapter.) Don't coddle losers; there are plenty of winners out there. By now you've learned how to find them!

DOLLAR-COST AVERAGING

Sometimes you can improve your position in a sluggish fund by utilizing a simple system known as dollar-cost averaging. You must invest the same amount of dollars at regular intervals; thus, your dollars will buy more shares when the NAV is low and fewer when the price is high. Over a period of time, the average per share price will *always* be less than trying to guess the highs and lows. But you must use no-load funds, or the system will not be effective. In reality, dollar-cost averaging offers only a minor improvement over buy-and-hold. The major disadvantage inherent in dollar-cost averaging is that it fails to tell you when to buy, sell, or switch. Thus, the valuable benefit of the switch strategy is completely lost, and with it the larger profits it generates.

Nevertheless, dollar-cost averaging does provide you with positive gains over lump-sum investing, because it relies on the inevitable rise and fall in stock and bond prices as well as in other types of investments found in fund portfolios.

Refer to Figure 12–1, and let's see how dollar-cost averaging works out. Suppose you have $1,200 to invest over the course of the year, and you plan to invest $300 quarterly. In January you purchase a no-load equity fund whose NAV is $10. Your $300 will buy 30 shares. In April, you invest another $300, but now your fund is selling at $7.50 a share. Your $300 now buys you 40 shares. In July your fund has recovered somewhat and shares are now $9.00. Now, your $300 buys 33.33 shares. When October rolls around, you find that your fund has really rebounded and is selling for $10 a share. Now, your $300 buys 30 shares, again.

If you had invested the entire $1,200 in January when the NAV was $10, you would have bought exactly 120 shares. However, by dollar-cost averaging, you now own 133.33 shares. At October's $10 per share price your $1,200 dollar-cost averaging investment is now worth $1,333.33. Figure 12–2 shows how you might set up a dollar-cost averaging account with USAA Management Company, which has a number of fine, no-load equity funds available. (Other investment companies have similar plans.)

FIGURE 12–1

Dollar-Cost Averaging ($300 per quarter chart)

Month	Invest Amt.	NAV	Shares purchased
Jan.	$300	$10	30
Apr.	$300	$7.50	40
July	$300	$9	33.33
Oct.	$300	$10	30
TOTALS	$1,200		133.33 shares

FIGURE 12-2

Establishing a Dollar-Cost Averaging Program

USAA
INVESTMENT
MANAGEMENT
COMPANY

You can invest a specific amount each month in any of your accounts, including IRAs. Choose either the 1st or 15th of the month or both dates. Here's all you do: fill in the date, fund name and account number, and amount (minimum $50). Select either the 1st and/or the 15th of the month you wish the amount invested, and indicate your preferred date to start this service. **Please include a blank voided check or deposit slip from the bank account from which your investment will be made to give us your bank's address and routing number. Each listed account owner's signature must appear on the authorization form for this service.**

INVESTRONIC INVESTMENT PLAN AUTHORIZATION

This authorization form must be accompanied or preceded by your fund application.

I authorize USAA Investment Management Company to draw on my bank account for an investment in the following fund accounts:

Fund Name _____   Fund Name _____

Fund Account No. _____   Fund Account No. _____

Amount $ _____   Amount $ _____

Debit my account on: ❏ 1st   ❏ 15th   ❏ 1st & 15th   Debit my account on: ❏ 1st   ❏ 15th   ❏ 1st & 15th

Effective Date _____   Effective Date _____

Minimum investment per debit is $50 for each fund account. You may use this form to authorize additional investments to a regular fund account or an IRA. (For IRAs, make sure your total annual contribution doesn't exceed $2,000).

Signature _____   USAA Number _____

Social Security Number _____   Date _____

Signature of Joint Tenant (if any) _____   USAA Number (if any) _____

Social Security Number _____   Date _____

Assuming you are going to make additional deposits in your fund, dollar-cost averaging is a certain method of improving your position in a fund with no additional cost to you. To take advantage of the process, you must make certain that you establish a means whereby you can consistently and regularly add to your investment. One way is to *pay yourself first.* Set aside 10% (more if you can) of your weekly or monthly income for your dollar-cost averaging plan. Set aside from each paycheck the amount needed to cover the budgeted item and place it in the respective envelopes. Make the disbursements monthly.

Reprinted with permission of the USAA Investment Management Company.

VALUE AVERAGING

Value averaging is a more sophisticated yet still relatively easy means of increasing the value of your investments. For example, if you want your investments to increase in value by $100 a month: (1) Look at the market value of your investments, and if they have risen

$100 by the end of the month, invest nothing that month; (2) if they have fallen by $100, invest $200 that month (buying the shares at the lower price); and (3) if they have risen $150 in market value, sell $50 worth. This is buying low and selling high. Every investor's dream! Value averaging disciplines you to do just that.

THE COMBINED METHOD

By combining dollar-cost averaging and value averaging, it is possible to increase the impact of both. Any aggressive growth fund and the money market fund of the same family may be used to implement the system. Let's use 20th Century Investors' Cash Reserves and 20th Century Select Funds in our example. Because they have no minimum investment requirement, everyone can do this. For example, invest $100 every month in the Cash Reserves Money Market Fund. You have met your budgeted investment, and your savings program fits your need for a fixed amount every month. Now add value averaging to your strategy. Base your decisions on the value of your 20th Century Select Investment Fund, and the following month transfer money into or out of the Cash Reserves Fund to meet the strategic requirement. For example, invest $100 in Cash Reserves, a money market fund with a constant $1.00 per share price. Then check the value of your Select Investment Fund. If the value has declined by $100, shift $100 from the Cash Reserve Fund account into the 20th Century Fund. All it takes is a phone call. If the value has risen $100, do nothing. If the value has risen $200, shift $100 of the gain back into the Cash Reserve Fund. There is nothing wrong with taking a profit! Continue the system on a regular basis. It does require a bit more effort, but it does pay handsomely in a rising (bull) market.

TELEPHONE SWITCHING

Telephone switching is undoubtedly the most effective method for increasing profits on your investments. Some market timing systems almost guarantee a 20% annual profit by following their telephone switching systems. See Chapter 14 for a detailed analysis of this technique.

CASH BENEFITS OF DOLLAR-COST AVERAGING

Without dollar-cost averaging: $1,200 bought 120 shares at $10 per share, representing an account value of $1,200 (120 shares × $10 per share). *With* dollar-cost averaging: 133.33 shares would have accumulated over the course of the year, versus the 120 shares by the lump-sum deposit. Thus, 133.33 shares at $10 per share equals an account value of $1,333.30, or $133.30 *more* than the $1,200 lump-sum account value. (The above example does not take into account distributions which may have been made.)

See Exhibits 12–1 and 12–2.

E X H I B I T 12–1

Dollar-Cost Averaging

The question is often raised, "Don't you lose money (dividends) by not having the $1,200 on deposit for the full year?" The answer is "Yes" and "No." You lose *some* dividends, but you *make* money in the long run (see below).

Lump-sum deposit: a $1,200 deposit for the full year earns $72 on a 6% yield.

Dollar-cost averaging: a $1,200 investment @ $300 quarterly using the same 6% yield earns the following:

Jan. $300 deposited for 12 months = $18.00 in dividends
Apr. $300 deposited for 9 months = $13.50 in dividends
Jul. $300 deposited for 6 months = $ 9.00 in dividends
Oct. $300 deposited for 3 months = $ 4.50 in dividends

TOTAL $45.00 in dividends

$72.00 in dividends earned on the $1,200 lump-sum deposit in 1 year.
$45.00 in dividends earned by dollar-cost averaging over 1 year.

$27.00 loss in dividends by dollar-cost averaging for 1 year.

However, @ $10.00/share, you will have $133.30 *more* in your account at the end of the year by dollar-cost averaging (120 shares vs. 133.33 shares @ $10.00/share)

$133.30 extra account value
− 27.00 loss in dividends

$106.30 overall gain by dollar-cost averaging

Note: An additional benefit is realized, because you would pay IRS income taxes on the $45 dividend, rather than on the $72 dividend.

E X H I B I T   12–2

Dollar-Cost Averaging

Dollar-cost averaging of $1,200 @ 6% yield on $100 monthly investments:

Jan. $100 on deposit for 12 months = $6.00 dividend
Feb. $100 on deposit for 11 months = $5.50 dividend
Mar. $100 on deposit for 10 months = $5.00 dividend
Apr. $100 on deposit for 9 months = $4.50 dividend
May $100 on deposit for 8 months = $4.00 dividend
Jun. $100 on deposit for 7 months = $3.50 dividend
Jul. $100 on deposit for 6 months = $3.00 dividend
Aug. $100 on deposit for 5 months = $2.50 dividend
Sep. $100 on deposit for 4 months = $2.00 dividend
Oct. $100 on deposit for 3 months = $1.50 dividend
Nov. $100 on deposit for 2 months = $1.00 dividend
Dec. $100 on deposit for 1 month = $0.50 dividend

TOTAL DIVIDENDS $39.00

$72.00 dividend earned from lump-sum deposit in 1 year
$39.00 dividend earned by dollar-cost averaging for 1 year

$33.00 loss in dividends by dollar-cost averaging for the year

However, @ $10.00/share, you will end up with $133.30 *more* in your account by dollar-cost averaging than by a lump-sum deposit of $1,200. (120 shares vs. 133.33 shares @ $10/share). (Refer to Fig. 12.1.)

$133.30 extra share value in the account
− 33.00 loss in dividends

$100.30 gain by dollar-cost averaging

Note: An additional benefit is realized, because you would pay IRS income taxes on the $39 dividend, rather than on the $72 dividend.

STUDY GUIDE FOR CHAPTER 12

1. What is wrong with the "buy and hold" method of investing?

2. How does dollar-cost averaging fall short of being a sound investment method, and what are its good features?

3. Value averaging is a newer method of investing. How does it operate?

4. How do dollar-cost averaging and value averaging combine to give the best method of investing?
5. How may telephone switching be employed to maximize profits?

QUICK MONEY FORMULAS

The following formulas can help you evaluate your return on an investment—assuming you know the rate of return and assuming that rate is fixed.

Rule of 72: Doubling Your Money

To find out when you'll double your money, divide 72 by the yield you make on an investment. Earn nine percent yearly and your money doubles in eight years. A higher yield means a shorter wait.

Examples

9% return: 72 ÷ 9 = 8 years
11% return: 72 ÷ 11 = 6½ years

POSTSCRIPT 12–1

WHAT IS DOLLAR-COST AVERAGING?

Dollar-cost averaging takes advantage of Wall Street's only certainty: stock and bond prices fluctuate. With dollar-cost averaging you are making the market's natural volatility work for you by lowering the average price you pay for your shares.

TABLE 12–1

MARKET GOES UP . . .		
Monthly Investment	**Share Price**	**Shares Acquired**
$ 400	$ 5	80
$ 400	$ 8	50
$ 400	$ 10	40
$ 400	$ 10	40
$ 400	$ 16	25
Total $ 2,000	$ 8.51*	235

*Your Average Share Cost: $8.51 ($2,000 ÷ 235 shares)
The Average Share Price: $9.80 ($49 ÷ 5 months)

MARKET GOES DOWN . . .		
Monthly Investment	**Share Price**	**Shares Acquired**
$ 400	$ 16	25
$ 400	$ 10	40
$ 400	$ 8	50
$ 400	$ 8	50
$ 400	$ 5	80
Total $ 2,000	$ 8.16*	245

*Your Average Share Cost: $8.16 ($2,000 ÷ 245 shares)
The Average Share Price: $9.40 ($47 ÷ 5 months)

MARKET GOES BOTH WAYS . . .		
Monthly Investment	**Share Price**	**Shares Acquired**
$ 400	$ 10	40
$ 400	$ 8	50
$ 400	$ 5	80
$ 400	$ 8	50
$ 400	$ 10	40
Total $ 2,000	$ 7.69*	260

*Your Average Share Cost: $7.69 ($2,000 ÷ 260 shares)
The Average Share Price: $8.20 ($41 ÷ 5 months)

Simply put, when you "dollar-cost average," you invest a fixed amount in a particular investment at regular intervals. Because the amount you invest remains constant, you buy more shares when the price is low, but fewer shares when the price is high. As a result, the average dollar amount you pay (your average cost per share) is always lower than the average market value of your investment (the average price per share). There's no magic to it . . . just simple arithmetic!

Table 12–1 illustrates the effects of a dollar-cost averaging program when the market is performing in three different ways.

POSTSCRIPT 12–2

SELL? HOLD? BUY?

Sell? Hold? Buy?

A Look Back.

In 1987, the Dow Jones Industrial Average dropped 19% between August 25th and October 25th. Let's look at how individuals would have fared over the past 12 years, depending upon the investment decisions they made back then. We'll use the AARP Growth and Income Fund as an example. We'll consider an investment in the Fund valued at $10,000 on 1/1/87. Keep in mind, the Fund's objective is to pursue long-term growth and quarterly income. And all examples are hypothetical and do not reflect the actions of any particular investor(s).

Sell

On October 31, 1987, the $10,000 investment in the **AARP Growth and Income Fund** dropped in value to $9,383. At that time, disappointed investors could have sold all their shares, putting the money into an FDIC-insured, fixed-rate CD with an annual rate of return of 7%. As of May 31, 1999, that investment would have been worth **$20,938**.

Hold

A second option for investors would have been to do nothing, keeping all of their shares invested in the **AARP Growth and Income Fund**. With an average annual return of 14.74% over the past 12 years, this investment would have grown to **$55,126** as of May 31, 1999.

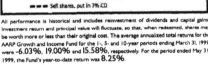

$110,000						
$90,000						
$70,000						
$50,000						
$30,000						
$10,000						
1/87	3/89	3/91	3/93	3/95	3/97	5/99

— With an additional $100 investment per month
— With no additional investments
– – Sell shares, put in 7% CD

All performance is historical and includes reinvestment of dividends and capital gains. Investment return and principal value will fluctuate, so that, when redeemed, shares may be worth more or less than their original cost. The average annualized total returns for the AARP Growth and Income Fund for the 1-, 5- and 10-year periods ending March 31, 1999, were -6.03%, 19.00% and 15.58%, respectively. For the period ended May 31, 1999, the Fund's year-to-date return was 8.25%.

Buy

Investors also had the option of leaving their existing shares invested, while taking advantage of lower share prices by beginning to add $100 a month to the account starting on November 1, 1987. As of May 31, 1999, they would have invested an additional $13,900, and their total investment in the **AARP Growth and Income Fund** would have been worth **$94,035**.

Remember, past performance is no guarantee of future results, and a mutual fund's share price will fluctuate over time, so you should plan to invest for five

Focus On The Long Term.

years or more. Remember also that when you sell fund shares for more than their original cost, the gain is taxable. And of course, the AARP Growth and Income Fund incurs capital gains periodically throughout the year, which are also taxable.

We hope the information in this brochure has helped you put your investment in the AARP Growth and Income Fund into perspective. Generally, we believe that investors who continue to invest regularly in order to meet their long-term goals can come out ahead of those who overreact to market swings. If you have any further questions, or would like to find out about a plan for regular investing,** please call us at 1-800-253-2277. Our knowledgeable AARP Mutual Fund Representatives are here to help you make informed investment decisions, Monday through Friday, 8:00 a.m. to 8:00 p.m., ET.

P O S T S C R I P T 12–3

DOLLAR-COST AVERAGING BUDGET PLAN

Assuming that you are going to be making additional deposits in one or more of your funds, in addition to *reinvesting* all your distributions, which I highly recommend, dollar-cost averaging is another almost certain way to improve your position in a fund at *no additional cost* to you beyond the amount you planned to add to your fund(s) during the year. (See note below.)

To take advantage of the dollar-cost averaging process, you must make certain that you establish a means whereby you can *consistently and regularly* add to your mutual fund investments. A fairly painless method I have found that works well and that I recommend is the *pay yourself first* budget system. To utilize this system effectively, set aside at least 10%, more, if you can, of your weekly or monthly income for the dollar-cost averaging plan.

Use an envelope-type budget system if you wish, but be sure that one budget envelope is marked *ME* along with the other envelopes marked Mortgage, Utilities, Food, etc. Set aside from each paycheck the amounts needed to cover the standard budgeted items after you have taken care of the *ME* envelope. Then place the other amounts in their respective envelopes. If necessary, cut back somewhat on nonessential items like entertainment, vacations, smoking, etc., if necessary, in order to maintain your 10% dollar-cost averaging level. Even if you earn only $250 a week, setting aside $25 (the recommended 10%), you will have $100 a month available to dollar-cost average, the usual amount required for additional deposits in most mutual funds. The way your fund account growth will truly amaze you! I've been doing it for years—and it does work.

Another alternative is to establish a wire transfer plan between your bank and the fund you wish to dollar-cost average. Such a plan permits you to deposit subsequent amounts into the fund that are not as high as the standard required amounts for subsequent deposits. (See Chapters 11 and 14.) Such a plan is ideal for dollar-cost averaging. Just be sure you have enough in the bank account you are using for the plan to cover the transferred amounts you have established.

Note: By *reinvesting all distributions,* you are, in essence, dollar-cost averaging. (Albeit less frequently than you can by starting your own dollar-cost averaging plan.)

VALUE AVERAGING VS. DOLLAR-COST AVERAGING

There are several variations of the familiar dollar-cost averaging strategy. These variations seek to improve the overall benefits of basic dollar-cost averaging. One such popular variation is known as *Value averaging*.

Value averaging is merely a more sophisticated way to dollar-cost average. It involves a little more time, a little more record keeping, and a little more aggressive approach than basic dollar-cost averaging. However, the added benefits tend to make the extra effort worthwhile.

Instead of investing the *same amount* each month or each quarter, you vary the amount invested at each interval so that your *fund's value* increases by a specific amount or percentage. For example, let's say that instead of investing the same amount each time, you plan to have the *value* of the fund *increase* by $300 each month. In month one the value of your investment rose by $100. Following a value-averaging strategy, you would add $200 to the fund to achieve your plan of having the value of your investment increase by $300 a month. If in a particular month the value of your investment rose by $400, and since under the value averaging strategy you want the value of your investment to increase by only $300, you would *sell $100* worth of the investment. On the other hand, suppose the value of your investment *dropped by $100* in a given month, you would have to *contribute $400* for that month in order to offset the loss, plus the $300 to increase the value of your investment by $300 for the month.

If you examine the two plans—dollar-cost averaging and value averaging—you will find:

- With dollar-cost averaging you know exactly how much you are going to invest over the year, but you will not know what the value of your investment will be at the end of the year.

- With value averaging, you know how much your investment will be at the end of the year, but you don't know how much it will cost out of your pocket.

In comparing the two plans, it is easy to see that value averaging is a more aggressive approach to investing than is dollar-cost averaging. In following the value averaging plan, the total amount invested over the year is not *fixed*, as it is in the dollar-cost averaging plan. However, Michael Edelson, in his book *Value Averaging: The Safe and Easy Strategy for Higher Investment Returns,* found that value cost averaging outperformed dollar-cost averaging more than *90% of the time.*

Which plan is appropriate for you depends to a large degree on how much time you want to spend monitoring your investment and how much you can afford to invest to maintain the plan over the course of the year.

If you are investing small amounts each month, dollar-cost averaging is probably preferable. If you are investing $500 to $1,000 or more each month, value averaging may be more advantageous.

P O S T S C R I P T   12–5

PORTFOLIO MANAGEMENT TECHNIQUES

WHEN TO SELL LOSERS

When the *cost basis** of your shares has *steadily* declined over a period of three months or more by 12%, put your fund on *hold*. When the shares have declined by *15%* over the same period of time, *sell* your entire position. Losers of this type rarely come back; move on to a better fund. They are out there. (We all pick losers from time to time—don't hold on to congenital losers.)

WHEN TO SELL WINNERS

Remember, *bulls* make money, *bears* make money, but *pigs* seldom do. When your fund shares are up 25% above their *cost basis** sell one-fourth of your position and stash the money in a money market fund until a new investment opportunity comes along. (You can't go wrong taking a *profit!*)

Note: None of the above *negates* my advice regarding selling losers. The advice is based on a *steady* loss in value over a three or four month period. It does not pertain to the occasional catastrophic one-day loss such as the 500 point loss experienced by the market back in October 1987.

HOW TO MINIMIZE PICKING LOSERS

Choose funds based on the following eight factors:

1. The fund's long-term performance history (return on investment)
2. The fund's expense ratio
3. The fund's management stability and style
4. The fund's tax consequences
5. The fund's cost policy—load or no-load (always select the no-loads)
6. Your goals and objectives
7. Your risk tolerance
8. Your time horizon

---

*Cost basis is the amount of your original investment, plus any subsequent deposits, plus all reinvested distributions.

ANOTHER BIT OF ADVICE ON BUYING INVESTMENTS

Never be rushed into an investment. No really good deal disappears overnight.

HOW MANY FUNDS SHOULD YOU OWN?

The average investor needs no more than five as a general rule:

1. A money market fund
2. An income fund
3. A growth and income fund
4. A growth fund
5. An index fund

And perhaps an international fund, if the time is right.

Tracking a Fund's Performance

DAILY NEWSPAPERS

In an effort to make intelligent decisions regarding the funds you own and those you contemplate buying, you must monitor their performance. When tracking a fund's performance, you should record the NAV of each of the funds you are following on a regular basis, certainly no less than weekly.

Most, if not all, major daily newspapers print stock and mutual fund tables. These are arranged alphabetically by the investment company's name; for example, American Funds, Dreyfus, Financial Funds, etc. Below the fund's family name will be listed the names of all its funds, along with the current price and any change from the previous day's price. The *Wall Street Journal* is probably the best source for this information. If it is not available at your newsstand, you may subscribe for daily delivery. Most public libraries will usually have the current edition, as well as back editions, of the *Wall Street Journal* for you to consult.

If you plan to track the funds on a weekly basis, the Sunday edition of your local newspaper is a suitable, convenient source. There, you will find the same mutual fund listings as appeared in the daily newspaper. The Sunday edition will also show the high and low NAVs for the week, as well as the the amount of change in the NAV from the previous week. An excellent, comprehensive, detailed source of weekly data is to be found in *Barron's*, a weekly national business and financial newspaper. Subscriptions are also available for home delivery. Most libraries will have the current copy on hand.

FINANCIAL MAGAZINES

There are a number of popular, nontechnical financial magazines available by subscription, on the newsstands, and in libraries. *Kiplinger's Personal Finance, Forbes,* and *Money* are excellent for beginning mutual fund investors. In them, you will find funds ranked according to performance and objectives. Other pertinent data about each fund are also provided, e.g., type of fund, risk rating, minimum investment, load (if any), toll-free telephone numbers, total return for various periods of time (one year, five years, 10 years), and price range over a 52 week period. All these data are essential in tracking a fund in which you are interested.

TOLL-FREE CALLS

The vast majority of mutual fund companies provide toll-free 800 numbers. You may call about any of their funds and find out such things as the current NAV, yield, change in price from previous day, latest dividend, and any other information you may desire.

If you have an account in one of the company's funds, you may also find out your account balance, the date of your last investment, the value of your account, the date of your last redemption, number of shares in your account, and so on. This information is available through the fund's toll-free number only if you have requested and received a personal identification number. You must provide this number when calling for account data. The personal identification number is to prevent unauthorized persons from receiving information about your account. Most large investment companies provide this service on a 24 hour basis through their automated, computerized telephone systems.

There are several specialized sources of general information and statistical data about mutual funds that are helpful in tracking performance. One such quarterly publication is *Standard and Poor's/ Lipper Mutual Fund Profiles* (Standard & Poor's Corp., New York, NY 10004). A subscription is rather expensive, so I would suggest that you plan to use it as a reference source in the public library. This comprehensive, easily understood publication provides for every mutual fund:

- The latest NAV and the NAVs for a five-year period
- Fund investment objective
- Performance evaluation
- Yields
- Portfolio composition
- Fund adviser and portfolio manager

A second specialized quarterly source of mutual fund data is available in the *Mutual Fund Source Book* (Mutual Fund Sourcebook, Inc., Chicago, Illinois 60606), which comes in two editions—one for equity funds, and the other for fixed income funds. Both provide:

- Risk factors
- Portfolio makeup
- Performance data
- Fund operations

As these are both expensive volumes too, they also may be consulted in your public library.

An inexpensive source of mutual fund information and financial planning guidance is provided in a publication called *Investment Vision.* It costs only $15 a year. Call 1-800-777-1851 for more information.

An interesting source of tracking information is provided by the Mutual Fund Education Alliance, a nonprofit trade organization for the mutual fund industry. Their materials are provided at cost and include kits, directories, guides, pamphlets, cassettes, and videotapes designed especially for the novice and the intermediate investor. You can call 1-816-471-1454, but since this is not a toll-free number, you may wish to write to this organization at 1900 Erie Street, Suite 120, Kansas City, Missouri 64116.

Lastly, *Donoghue's Mutual Fund Almanac* (1-800-445-5900) provides the track records of over 2,000 mutual funds.

Though there are clearly many sources for tracking just about any fund's performance, history, and operation, it is up to you to *use* the data available and do the necessary research on every fund you may wish to purchase *before* you invest your money.

ANNUAL, SEMIANNUAL, AND QUARTERLY REPORTS

Periodic reports to shareholders are formal financial statements issued by a corporation or a mutual fund investment company. All mutual funds are required to issue annual reports—more frequent financial reports are operational. Shareholders can increase their knowledge of a fund if they take the trouble to read and analyze its annual reports. Most annual reports provide you with enough information to form a good basis for evaluating many aspects of the fund's "health." Though these reports may seem complex and somewhat technical at first glance, they provide excellent insights into, and analyses of, the fund's operation. They often also include a statement regarding the fund's progress, problems, and prognosis prepared by the president of the investment company or chairman of the board. In most cases, it is an optimistic report. Its intention is to reassure the fund's investors (see Figure 13–1).

A fund's annual, semiannual, or quarterly report typically will include most or all of the following items:

- Name of the fund and date of issue
- Period covered by the report—annual (past 12 months), semiannual (past six months), quarterly (past three months)
- Statement of investments (portfolio makeup) as of the date of the report
- Cost of each security in the portfolio and its current value
- Statement of assets and liabilities
- Statement of operations (income and expenses)
- Statement of changes in net assets
- Notes to the financial statements
- Reports of the independent auditors
- Condensed financial information (historical review)
- Report from the fund's president or board chairman

FIGURE 13-1

Chairman's Letter to Shareholders

Fellow Shareholder:

I t was "Wellesley weather" during the six months ended June 30, the first half of Wellesley Income Fund's 1993 fiscal year. With a total return of +10.1%, the Fund nicely outpaced broad measures of performance for both the bond market and the stock market.

The table below compares the Fund's total return (capital change plus income) during the period with the returns of the two unmanaged indexes of the securities markets that we use as our benchmarks: for bonds, the Salomon Brothers High-Grade Bond Index; for stocks, the Standard & Poor's 500 Composite Stock Price Index.

	Total Return Six Months Ended June 30, 1993
Vanguard/Wellesley Income Fund	**+10.1%**
Salomon Brothers Bond Index	**+ 9.3%**
Standard & Poor's 500 Stock Index	**+ 4.9**

The Fund's total return is based on net asset values of $18.16 per share on December 31, 1992, and $19.41 on June 30, 1993, with the latter figure adjusted to take into account the reinvestment of two quarterly dividends totaling $.56 per share from net investment income and a carryover distribution of $.01 per share from net capital gains realized during 1992. At June 30, 1993, Wellesley's dividend yield was 5.9%.

The good news in the bond market was the sharp decline in interest rates, which drove bond prices higher. The yield on the 30-year U.S. Treasury bond fell from 7.4% at the start of the period to 6.7% at its conclusion. This decline resulted in an 8% rise in the price of the long-term Treasury bond, the best-performing sector of the bond market. The rate decline had a less pronounced impact on bonds of shorter maturities, but the entire bond market enjoyed positive returns.

The decline in interest rates also had a positive impact on the stock market, most especially on what we call "interest-rate-sensitive" stocks, which are prized more for their dividend yields than for their capital growth potential. Included in this broad group are public utility stocks and energy stocks, both of which

were among the stock market leaders during the period, contrasting sharply with the drug stocks and the "brand-name" stocks in the consumer staples area. Both of those groups not only lagged the market, but experienced negative returns.

Wellesley's policy, of course, is to emphasize income, and we have consistently maintained a portfolio allocation guideline of about 60% high-quality bonds and 40% stocks with above-average yields. On June 30, the portfolio was balanced as follows: bonds 63% of total net assets, stocks 36%, and cash reserves 1%. The bond position has a maturity averaging about 17 years, with an average quality between Aaa and Aa. More than one-half of the stock position is invested in utility and energy stocks, together representing 21% of total net assets.

We performed well compared to other mutual funds with a comparable income objective. Our return of +10.1% for the period compared with a return of +7.9% for the average income fund. We have outpaced this standard with reasonable consistency over the years, and we are pleased to be staying the course so far in 1993.

Wellesley Income Fund has provided a remarkable combination of solid return and low risk, and we receive much favorable commentary from the mutual fund statistical services and the press. The result has been very substantial growth in our assets, from $495 million at year-end 1987, to $1.9 billion at year-end 1991, to $4.6 billion on June 30, 1993.

We would emphasize to our new shareholders and remind our existing shareholders that the Fund, while carrying a modest risk relative to stocks, carries significant interest-rate risk. That is, rising interest rates would have a negative impact on both our bond and stock components, just the reverse of what has happened so far this year. I look forward to reporting to you in greater detail in our Annual Report six months hence.

Sincerely,

John C. Bogle

John C. Bogle
Chairman of the Board   July 19, 1993

Note: Mutual fund data from Lipper Analytical Services, Inc.

Reprinted with permission of The Vanguard Group.
Figure 13.1 is an example of a typical annual report—in this case, a semi-annual report, from John C. Bogle, Chairman of the Board of the Vanguard Group. This shows his letter to the shareholders of Vanguard's Wellesley Income Fund. Note the favorable, yet factual, nature of the message.

FIGURE 13-2

Excerpts from Semiannual Report

Statement of Assets and Liabilities February 28, 1991 (Unaudited)

ASSETS:

Investments in securities, at value	
(cost $3,522,670,421)—see statement	$3,657,846,298
Interest receivable	71,850,248
Receivable for investment securities sold	30,946,747
Prepaid expenses	646,516
	3,761,289,809

LIABILITIES:

Due to The Dreyfus Corporation	$ 1,841,239	
Payable for investment securities purchased	33,502,079	
Payable for Common Stock redeemed	12,982,228	
Accrued expenses and other liabilities	4,070,687	52,396,233
NET ASSETS		$3,708,893,576

REPRESENTED BY:

Paid-in capital	$3,634,502,889
Accumulated net realized (loss) on investments	(60,785,190)
Accumulated net unrealized appreciation on investments—Note 3	135,175,877
NET ASSETS at value, applicable to 298,193,377 outstanding shares of Common Stock, equivalent to $12.44 per share—Note 4	$3,708,893,576

Statement of Operations six months ended February 28, 1991 (Unaudited)

INVESTMENT INCOME:

Interest Income		$ 145,774,884
Expenses:		
Management fee—Note 2(a)	$10,896,331	
Shareholder servicing costs—Note 2(a)	1,135,435	
Custodian fees	115,785	
Registration fees	60,425	
Prospectus and shareholders' reports	55,612	
Professional fees	46,896	
Directors' fees and expenses—Note 2(b)	25,399	
Miscellaneous	9,746	
Total Expenses		12,345,629
INVESTMENT INCOME–NET		133,429,255
REALIZED AND UNREALIZED GAIN ON INVESTMENTS—Note 3:		
Net realized gain on investments	$22,195,832	
Net unrealized appreciation on investments	38,664,938	
NET REALIZED AND UNREALIZED GAIN ON INVESTMENTS		60,860,770
NET INCREASE IN NET ASSETS RESULTING FROM OPERATIONS		$ 194,290,025

Figure 13–2 contains excerpts from the Dreyfus Tax Exempt Bond Fund's semiannual report of February 28, 1991. Look at the data. What can you learn about this fund from the excerpts presented? Would you invest in this fund, if you wanted a good return of tax-free income? (Figure 13–3 explains some of the unfamiliar ter-

FIGURE 13-2 (continued)

A Very Small Sampling of the Portfolio

Dreyfus Tax Exempt Bond Fund, Inc.
Statement of Investments February 28, 1991 (Unaudited)

Dreyfus
Tax Exempt Bond Fund, Inc. Semi-Annual Report

February 28, 1991

Principal Amount	Municipal Bonds — 93.8%	Value
	Alabama — .3%	
$ 8,000,000	Camden Indl. Dev. Brd., Pollution Ctl. Facs. Rev., Ref. (Macmillian Bloedel Proj.), 7.75%, 5/1/2009	$ 8,120,000
3,800,000	Columbia Indl. Dev. Brd., Pollution Ctl. Rev. (Alabama Pwr. Farley Plt. Proj.), 9.25%, 12/1/2015	4,218,000
	Alaska — 1.5%	
6,000,000	Alaska Energy Auth., Pwr. Rev. (Bradley Lake Proj.), 7.25%, 7/1/2016 (Insd.; BIGI)	6,097,500
6,485,000	Alaska Hsg. Fin. Corp., Rev.: (Collateralized Veterans Mtg. Program), 10%, 12/1/2012	6,711,975
7,500,000	Home Mtg., 8%, 12/1/2013	7,650,000
25,000,000	(Ref.-Insured Mtg. Program), 7.80%, 12/1/2030	25,375,000
9,200,000	Alaska Indl. Dev. and Expt. Auth., Rev., Ref. (Amern. President Lines Proj.), 8%, 11/1/2009	9,269,000
	Arizona — 2.7%	
	Arizona Municipal Fing. Program, Ctfs. Partn.:	
5,000,000	8.10%, 1/5/2008	5,087,500
10,000,000	8.10%, 7/5/2008	10,175,000
4,855,000	8.10%, Ser. C, 7/5/2013	4,939,962
14,000,000	8.10%, Ser. D, 7/5/2013	14,245,000
28,925,000	8.10%, Ser. E, 7/5/2013	29,431,188
28,800,000	8.10%, Ser. F, 7/5/2013	29,304,000
3,220,000	Central Arizona Irr. and Drain. Dist., Unlimited Tax (Pinal Cnty.), 10.50%, 6/1/1999	3,703,000
	California — 1.6%	
14,850,000	California City Fin. Coop. Fing. Auth., Rev., 9%, 10/1/2017 (Invt. Agreement; Citibank)	14,850,000
	California Hsg. Fin. Agy., Home Mtg. Rev.:	
9,800,000	8%, 8/1/2019	9,934,750
17,165,000	8.35%, 8/1/2019	17,615,581
15,000,000	Los Angeles Dept. of Wtr. and Pwr., Elec. Plt. Rev., 7.25%, 9/15/2030	15,206,250
	Colorado — 1.7%	
3,000,000	Colorado Hsg. Fin. Auth., Single Family Residential Hsg. Rev., 8%, 3/1/2017	3,071,250
	City and Cnty. of Denver, Rev.: Arpt.:	
10,000,000	8.25%, 11/15/2012	9,225,000
35,500,000	8.50%, 11/15/2023	33,192,500
8,240,000	Single Family Mtg. (GNMA Mtg.), 8.125%, 12/1/2020	8,312,100
3,340,000	Garfield Cnty., Single Family Mtg. Rev., 9.125%, 8/15/2011	3,419,325
3,810,000	Thornton, Single Family Mtg. Rev., 8%, 12/1/2009 (Insd.; MBIA)	3,886,200

Principal Amount	Municipal Bonds (continued)	Value
	Florida (continued)	
	City of Miami Health Facs. Auth., Hosp. Rev.: (Cedars Med. Ctr.):	
$ 3,265,000	8.20%, 10/1/2002	$ 3,444,575
7,000,000	8.30%, 10/1/2007	7,306,250
12,500,000	8.375%, 10/1/2017	13,093,750
6,500,000	(Ref.–Mercy Hosp.), 8.125%, 8/1/2011	6,825,000
5,935,000	Nassau Cnty., Pollution Ctl. Rev. Ref. (ITT Rayonier Proj.), 7.65%, 6/1/2006	5,994,350
	Orange Cnty. Health Facs. Auth., Pooled Hosp. Ln. Rev., Ref.:	
27,225,000	7.875%, Ser. A, 12/1/2025 (Insd.; FGIC)	28,586,250
16,830,000	7.875%, Ser. B, 12/1/2025 (Insd.; BIGI)	17,671,500
	Georgia — 4.2%	
100,535,000	Atlanta Arpt. Facs., Rev., Zero Coupon, 1/1/2010 (Insd.; MBIA) (a)	27,018,781
	Burke Cnty. Dev. Auth., Pollution Ctl. Rev.: (Georgia Pwr. Co. Vogtle Proj.):	
5,540,000	11.625%, 9/1/2014	6,426,400
5,000,000	12%, 10/1/2014	5,875,000
10,500,000	11.75%, 11/1/2014	12,285,000
6,000,000	10.125%, 6/1/2015	6,780,000
	(Oglethorpe Pwr. Corp. Vogtle Proj.):	
2,000,000	11.25%, 1/1/2008	2,187,500
30,400,000	10%, 1/1/2010	33,174,000
14,155,000	Georgia Municipal Elec. Auth., Pwr. Rev., 8.125%, 1/1/2020	15,269,706
	Monroe Cnty. Dev. Auth., Pollution Ctl. Rev.:	
26,000,000	(Georgia Pwr. Plt. Scherer Proj.), 10.50%, 9/1/2015	29,932,500
3,000,000	(Oglethorpe Pwr. Corp. Scherer Proj.), 11.25%, 1/1/2008	3,281,250
9,000,000	Municipal Elec. Auth. of Georgia, Spl. Oblig. Ref. (Second Crossover Ser.), 8.125%, 1/1/2017	9,641,250

Auditor's Statement

Review Report of Ernst & Young, Independent Accountants

> **Shareholders and Board of Directors**
> **Dreyfus Tax Exempt Bond Fund, Inc.**
>
> We have made a review of the accompanying statement of assets and liabilities of Dreyfus Tax Exempt Bond Fund, Inc., including the statement of investments, as of February 28, 1991, and the related statements of operations and changes in net assets and condensed financial information (see Note 5) for the six months then ended in accordance with standards established by the American Institute of Certified Public Accountants.
>
> A review of interim financial information consists principally of obtaining an understanding of the system for the preparation of interim financial information, applying analytical review procedures to financial data, and making inquiries of persons responsible for financial and accounting matters. It is substantially less in scope than an audit in accordance with generally accepted auditing standards, which will be performed for the full year with the objective of expressing an opinion regarding the financial statements taken as a whole. Accordingly, we do not express such an opinion.
>
> Based on our review, we are not aware of any material modifications that should be made to the interim financial statements referred to above for them to be in conformity with generally accepted accounting principles.
>
> The statement of changes in net assets for the year ended August 31, 1990 and the condensed financial information contained in Note 5 for each of the five years in the period ended August 31, 1990 were previously audited by us and our report dated October 9, 1990 expressed an unqualified opinion on such statement of changes in net assets and condensed financial information. We have not performed any auditing procedures after October 9, 1990 on such statement and condensed financial information.
>
>   ERNST & YOUNG
>
> New York, New York
> March 28, 1991

Reprinted with permission of The Dreyfus Municipal Bond Fund, Inc.

minology used in Figure 13–2). The terms used in annual, semiannual, and quarterly reports (they all follow the same format) are not difficult to understand, and they will help you extract the real meaning and significance from the array of data covered in the periodic reports issued to shareholders. Unlocking and applying the information contained in these reports will help you attain the goal of profitable mutual fund investing. If nothing else, the reports will help you determine the degree of diversification in the fund's portfolio, the major securities contributing to the fund's objective, the size of the fund, and even its risk level—factors that might help you choose one fund over another when investing.

FIGURE   13–3

Report Terminology Definitions

Net Asset Value—Beginning of Period . . . The price per share of the Fund at the beginning of its fiscal period.

OPERATIONS
Investment Income . . . The Fund's total earned income from dividends and interest per share.

Expenses . . . The Fund's total expenses per share, including advisory and transfer agency fees, registration and directors' fees, etc.Net Investment Income . . . Investment income less expenses.

Net Realized and Unrealized Gain (Loss) on Investments . . . The total change in value of portfolio holdings, both those which were sold (realized capital gains and losses) and those which were still held at the end of the period (appreciation or depreciation in value).

Total from Operations . . . Net investment income plus or minus net realized and unrealized gain or loss on investments.

DISTRIBUTIONS
Net Investment Income . . . Dividends paid to shareholders from net investment income.

Net Realized Gain (Loss) . . . Total capital gains paid to shareholders during the period.

Total Distributions . . . Total dividends and capital gains paid to shareholders.

Net Change in Net Asset Value . . . A figure reflecting the Fund's net investment income, realized and unrealized gains or losses.

Net Asset Value—End of Period . . . The price per share of the Fund at the end of the twelve or six-month period.

RATIOS
Ratio of Expenses to Average Net Assets . . . Total Fund expenses divided by the Fund's monthly average net assets. **[This should be low.]**

Ratio of Net Investment Income to Average Net Assets . . . The Fund's net investment income divided by average net assets. **[This should be high.]**

Portfolio Turnover Rate . . . The rate at which holdings are traded by the Fund. An income fund, which may hold its bonds for long periods, might have a modest turnover rate of 25%; a growth equity fund aggressively trading stocks, on the other hand, might have a turnover rate of over 100%. **[This should be moderate.]**

Shares Outstanding at End of Period . . . The total number of shares owned by shareholders, expressed in thousands. (Since shares of open-end mutual funds are continuously bought and sold, this figure varies daily.) **[This should show growth.]**

Having read the performance tracking measures described on the preceding pages, you also need to familiarize yourself with one additional performance criterion, i.e., your fund's Return on Investment. A complete description of this significant performance measure is presented in Appendix E, which also includes three sample ROIs. Study this appendix carefully before going on to Chapter 14.

STUDY GUIDE FOR CHAPTER 13

1. Why is it important to track your fund's performance regularly?
2. Where do you find the data to monitor your funds?
3. How often should you monitor your funds?
4. What kinds of information can you get regarding your fund by calling the fund's toll-free number?
5. What kinds of reports are funds required to provide investors?
6. What are some of the data provided in a fund's regular reports to its investors?

POSTSCRIPT 13–1

FOCUS ON THE LONG TERM

Assuming you have done your homework and found several mutual funds that meet your investment objectives, your risk tolerance level, and your fund performance requirements, you generally should stick with them for the long haul. However, when the market takes a serious dip, as it is *bound* to do from time to time, your resolve is likely to falter and you will start questioning the outcome of your long-term plan.

How do you keep yourself focused on the long-term plan? Here are a few suggestions.

Don't be a slave to the daily mutual fund results posted in the newspapers or analyzed and reported on financial radio programs and TV shows. On certain programs you'll hear a new investment idea every few minutes. Don't act on these ideas and jump from one investment to another. The likelihood that you will improve on your original plan is very low. Market timers and day traders lose more often than they win.

You start out as a long-term investor, but then you get all this short-term information, and if you cash out at the *first sign of trouble*, you are not going to get those *long-term returns*.

What should you do? The best advice is to keep your total financial strategy in focus. Part of the problem is that many people look only at the gains and losses in a *single* investment. That only makes the problem worse, because you are bound to find a loss somewhere. Remember that one snowflake does not a blizzard make.

Never forget that stocks will do what they want when they want. You have no control over the movement of the market. The big question is, how will you react? "People need to separate their psychological needs from their financial needs," says Dr. Hersh Shefrin, a finance professor at Santa Clara University. "Their psychological needs are short-term and their financial needs are long-term." You must learn to face your psychological needs and not let them control your financial needs. You may find it difficult to "buy and hold" an investment in volatile markets, but this is the best strategy.

"People tell themselves they will sell their losses," Professor Shefrin adds, "but what happens is they hold on, because they can't bring themselves to take a loss." For psychological reasons, people sell their winners *too soon*, and hold on to their losses *too long*. Stay focused on your long-term goals and you will improve your chances for success.

Does that mean that you *never* sell any of your underperforming funds? See the next postscript, "Ten Reasons to Sell Your Mutual Fund."

P O S T S C R I P T 13-2

TEN REASONS TO SELL YOUR MUTUAL FUND (Adapted from a Mutual
Funds magazine article, June 1995)

1. *The Fund Manager Changes*
Because you are buying a manager's experience when you invest
in a mutual fund, changes should be monitored closely. A new manager is usually a bad sign for a good fund and a good sign for a bad
fund. There are exceptions, so watch closely after changes.

2. *The Fund Consistently Underperforms Its Peers*
Carefully identify your fund's peers so you are comparing apples
to apples. For example, measure your small-cap growth fund against
other small-cap funds. Consult an index of small-cap funds to determine if your fund's performance is up to par. Your fund should consistently be in the top one-third of its peer group. If it has overper-
formed for three years and underperformed for one, start to monitor
it quarterly.

How long should you hang on to a fund that is underperforming?
Opinions range from six months to five years. It depends on the kind
of fund you have—an aggressive growth fund should be given a
longer probationary period than a bond fund. Sheldon Jacobs, editor
of the *No-Load Fund Investor* newsletter, says he gives a mutual fund
about a year of underperformance before selling. Other pros say three
years is more reasonable. I personally recommend two to three years,
depending on how poorly the fund is performing. The *worst* reason to
sell a fund is that it is doing poorly *short-term*, or you are chasing a
higher return. You must have had a good reason for buying the fund
in the first place, therefore don't be in a hurry to dump it.

3. *The Fund Changes Its Strategy or Doesn't Stick to Its Stated Mission*
If this is the case, you must check its annual and semiannual reports to see that the fund is doing what it says it is doing. Examine
the fund's 10 top holdings. If it's a growth fund, determine whether
it is holding stocks with high growth potential. If the stocks have high
dividends, that's inappropriate. If the fund has added a high percentage of global funds and you are averse to such funds, that might
be a signal to get out.

4. *Your Reason for Buying No Longer Exists*
There are many reasons for buying a mutual fund. A good piece
of advice is to write them down at the time of purchase. Then every
time you review the fund, compare it against your buying checklist.
If it fails to meet your original criteria, there has to be persuasive additional reasons for continuing to hold, or it's time to consider a sale.

5. *Your Goals Have Changed*

Long-term goals become short-term goals at some point. You may have aggressive funds that you bought when you were much younger (good idea then), but now you are in your sixties or seventies, and it's time to think about switching to more conservative funds.

6. *The Grass Is Greener*

Bear in mind that your fund can never be the number one fund at all times, given the cyclical nature of the market. If you think you have found a better fund, consider the cost of paying sales loads, redemption fees, and capital gains taxes before selling your old fund. Hundreds of new funds appear every year, with great promises, don't be swayed by unsubstantiated claims.

7. *Realize a Loss and Get a Tax Refund*

Perhaps you have a big loss, owing to market conditions and not due to the relative performance of your fund. If you sell, the government will in effect reimburse you for a fraction of your loss equal to your capital gains rate. Consider this: You are in the top tax bracket of 39.6% and have a 20% loss in a fund. By selling, you can turn an overnight profit of 8% (two-fifths of the 20% loss). Rather convoluted thinking for the average individual, nevertheless it is true.

8. *The Fund Is Growing Very Large, Very Fast*

If a fund has historically managed $500 million, or $1 billion, and now has to manage $5 billion, can it find a sufficient supply of high quality stocks or bonds to maintain the quality of the portfolio, or will it begin buying poorer quality securities just to be able to spend the influx of money? Wise fund managers usually close the fund to new investors rather than go into poor investments.

9. *Annual Expenses Are Too High*

What are reasonable annual expense ratios. Some pros say anything greater than 1% a year for a bond fund, 1.5% for a domestic stock fund, and 2% for a foreign stock fund is too high. The average annual expense ratios for all stock funds and bond funds are 1.40% and 1.02% respectively. Investors can frequently improve their returns by switching out of funds with higher than average expense ratios.

10. *The Fund Changes Its Name*

It sounds naive, but a name change throws up a red flag. Check into the reasons for the change, and decide if the reasons are likely to affect the fund's performance.

HOW MANY STRIKES?

Bear in mind that no single guideline is usually reason enough to dump a fund; rather, look at a combination of factors. Percy E. Bolton, a financial planner in Los Angeles, uses a "Four Strike" system to judge his funds. Bolton will not dump a fund for strike one alone. If a fund gets two strikes against it, it is put on a watch list. Three strikes and time-out is called: No more money is added to the fund. Four strikes and it's out!

SEVEN QUESTIONS TO ASK BEFORE SELLING A FUND

1. *Am I selling this investment because my long-term goals have changed?*
   If the answer is yes, you may be making a sound decision. Changing goals require a change in your investment program.

2. *Am I selling because other investments have performed better and I feel like I'm missing out on better opportunities?*
   Sometimes this can be a valid reason to sell. On the other hand, it's not unusual for investments to go through periods of underperformance. Not all funds can top the charts at the same time.

3. *How would I feel if I sold this investment and suddenly it outperforms?*
   Determine if it still meets your needs and why it was out of favor. Think twice before exposing yourself to seller's remorse.

4. *Have I considered possible tax implications?*
   Many investments have appreciated considerably over the past several years. Are you willing to sell your mutual funds and possibly pay capital gains taxes only to discover that you want to own them again?

5. *Will selling this investment affect the overall risk profile of my portfolio?*
   Determine how selling this investment will shift your portfolio's reward potential in relation to its higher growth potential.

6. *What will I buy to replace this investment?*
   It's a good idea to know what you're going to buy with your proceeds before you sell. Consider the possibility that your proposed purchase could be a hot purchase nearing the end of its performance cycle. Also, decide whether the investment you plan to buy is really more appropriate than the one you already have.

7. *Would I be better off adding an investment to my portfolio rather than exchanging one for another?*
   This decision lets you adjust your portfolio without incurring tax consequences and without selling an investment at what could be the wrong time. Most people think successful planning depends on choosing the right investments. *Keeping* the right investments can be just as important. Be sure to maintain a long-term perspective and talk to your financial adviser before making any changes to your portfolio.

WHEN TO SELL OR SWITCH GUIDE

Using the 12% benchmark and the 15% benchmark (based on an extended period of time: three to six months)

There are two methods: (1) using the NAV, (2) using the cost basis.

THE 12% EXAMPLES

Method 1: Using the NAV Method

Original investment NAV: $10.00 loss of 12% = $1.20

Original NAV was $10.00 minus $1.20 = Current NAV is now $8.80

Action Required: Put the fund on hold, make no further investments until it has recovered at least 10% in three to six months.

Method 2: Using the Cost Basis Method

Cost basis of the investment: $5,000 loss of 12% = $600

Cost basis $5,000 and current value is $4,400 (represents the $600)

Action Recommended: Put the fund on hold, make no further investments until it has recovered at least 10% in three to six months.

THE 15% EXAMPLES

Method 1: Using the NAV

Original investment NAV was $10.00. A loss of 15% = a loss of $1.50

Current NAV is down to $8.50 (represents a 15% loss)

Action Recommended: Sell the fund, switch to a better performing fund, or park the assets in a money market fund until the stock market or the fund has recovered at least 10% of its downside trend.

Method 2: Using the Cost Basis Method:

Current cost basis $5,000: current loss is 15% = a loss of $750

Current cost basis value of the fund is now $4250

Action Recommended: See above example.

HOW TO READ MUTUAL FUND LISTINGS IN DAILY NEWSPAPERS

(The following is based on the *Sun Sentinel* newspaper mutual fund listings. This publication uses a rotating field system for reporting mutual fund data. Similar systems are found in many other daily newspapers also.)

Monday: No listings are provided since the stock markets are closed over the weekend.

Tuesday: The one-year return is given. This figure shows the total return (ROI) attained for one year and includes distributions plus change in the NAV.

Wednesday: The annual YIELD is given. This figure indicates the percent of return based on dividend distributions over the year.

Thursday: The three-year return is given. This figure represents the average return (ROI) for the past 36 months for each fund listed.

Friday: Note: On Friday, March 21, 1997, the *Sun Sentinel* changed its Friday field listings. See below for new designations.

Saturday: Mutual fund listings are included in the sports section of the newspaper. Current NAVs are reported.

Sunday: Mutual fund summary for the week is shown. The summary shows the high, low, and change in the NAV for the week.

Fund footnotes: b: fee covering marketing costs (12b-1 fee) which are paid out of the fund's assets; d: deferred sales charge or redemption fee; f: front-end load (sales charge); m: multiple fees are charged, usually a 12b-1 fee, and either a sales or redemption fee or both. (A sign to look for another fund!)

New Friday Designations:

FUND OBJECTIVES

These are the new Morningstar fund categories that will be used to classify mutual funds in the *Sun-Sentinel*:

- LG Large-cap growth
- MG Medium or mid-cap growth
- SG Small-cap growth
- LB Large-cap blend
- MB Medium or mid-cap blend
- SB Small-cap blend
- LV Large-cap value
- MV Medium or mid-cap value
- SV Small-cap value
- SP Specialty-precious metals
- SN Specialty-natural resources
- ST Specialty-technology
- SU Specialty-utilities

- SH Specialty-health
- SF Specialty-financial
- SR Specialty-real estate
- SC Specialty-communications
- SS Specialty-unaligned (one that invests in a sector other than those listed above)
- DH Domestic hybrid (invests in both stocks and bonds)
- CV Convertibles (invests in convertible bonds)
- FS Foreign stock
- WS World stock (invests in both

the U.S. and abroad)
- ES Europe stock
- DP Diversified Pacific stock·
- PJ Pacific stock excluding Japan
- JS Japan stock
- EM Diversified emerging markets
- LS Latin America stock
- IH International hybrid
- GL Long government bond
- GI Intermediate government bond
- GS Short government bond
- CL Long corporate bond

- CI Intermediate corporate bond
- CS Short corporate bond
- UB Ultrashort bond
- HY High yield bond
- MU Multisector bond
- IB International bond
- ML Muni national long bond
- MI Muni national intermediate bond
- SL Muni single-state long bond
- SI Muni single-state intermediate bond
- MS Muni short bond

READING A MUTUAL FUND'S ANNUAL REPORT

Annual reports contain a great deal of valuable information for every shareholder. It's a pity that so few people take the time or make the effort to read them, or in some cases even to look at them. *Every* shareholder receives an *annual report.* The Security and Exchange Commission (SEC) *requires it.* Some mutual funds even provide quarterly and semiannual reports as well.

MOST ANNUAL REPORTS WILL PROVIDE ALL OF THE FOLLOWING INFORMATION

The Fund's Investment Portfolio: (1) This section lists all of the securities held by the fund. (2) An alphabetical breakdown of *all the investments* held at the close of the fiscal year. (3) The face value of the bonds and/or the shares held by the fund. (4) The *cost* of the portfolio, i.e., the amount the fund actually paid for the listed securities. (5) The *market value* of the securities in the fund's portfolio, i.e., the current *worth* of each security.

The Financial Statements: These are records of the financial status of the organization. They are produced by a firm of Certified Public Accountants and must conform to Generally Accepted Accounting Principals (GAAP) established by the Securities and Exchange Commission (SEC). Included are statements of Assets and Liabilities as follows:

Assets show the market value of anything owned on the last day of the fiscal year and include cash reserves and receivables. Receivables include (1) investments sold, for which the fund will receive payment at a later date; (2) fund shares sold and payment for which is pending (usually institutional investments); (3) dividends and interest earned but not yet paid to the fund; and (4) expense reimbursements due from the fund manager.

Liabilities are claims against the assets, and include (1) investments purchased but not paid for as yet; (2) fund shares redeemed, but not yet paid to shareholders; (3) dividends declared but not yet paid to shareholders; (4) management fees; (5) shareholder servicing fees incurred but unpaid at fiscal year end; (5) administrative expenses; (6) other accrued expenses; and (7) accumulated undistributed net investment gain.

The *Statement of Assets and Liabilities* will sometimes show the net asset value (NAV) of the fund's shares as of the end of the fiscal year.

Other Sections include (1) Report of Independent Accountants, (2) List of Officers and Trustees, (3) Program services, and (4) Tax Information.

CHAPTER 14

Services Provided by Mutual Fund Companies

The services provided by various mutual fund investment companies should be reviewed to make certain that the fund under consideration offers all that you may require. All mutual funds do not provide the same roster of shareholder services. A complete program of investment services should include at the very least the following four types.

ACCUMULATION PLANS

1. Automatic Reinvestment Plan

The most common accumulation service, offered by virtually all mutual funds, is the automatic reinvestment of all income and capital gains. This investor option allows for the easy, systematic accumulation of additional shares of the fund.

Automatic reinvestment is always a voluntary option. Distributions may always be taken in cash, if so desired; but the benefits of compounding will be lost. However, in either case, all distributions, whether reinvested or taken in cash, are subject to certain tax liabilities. (See Chapter 16 for a discussion of tax responsibilities.) In most cases, reinvested dividends and capital gains are not subject to the load charge levied by load mutual funds. Be certain to check the prospectus to learn whether the load is added to reinvested distributions. Better still, buy no-load funds and you can be absolutely certain there will be no charge for reinvesting any distributions.

Each time any distribution is reinvested in your account, you will receive a confirmation statement showing the amount of the distribution, the current NAV, the number of additional shares your distribution purchased, and the total shares currently owned by you.

2. Contractual Accumulation Plan

A contractual accumulation plan requires the investor to commit to purchasing a predetermined, fixed dollar amount on a regular basis for a specific period of time. With such a plan, the investor decides on the dollar amount, the frequency, and the length of time the plan is to continue. I would caution you to avoid this type of plan, because you may find yourself obligated to complete it. Too often, investors lose the incentive that induced them to adopt a contractual accumulation plan in the first place, or some other problem arises that makes the payments burdensome, and they wish to discontinue the plan. However, if you can keep up with the plan, consistency in investing is assured, and you are guaranteed to reap the benefits of dollar-cost averaging described in Chapter 12. On the other hand, if you are a self-disciplined person and make regular purchases, a better accumulation plan is described below.

3. Voluntary Accumulation Plan

A more flexible plan is the voluntary accumulation plan. With this plan in place, you, the shareholder, decide the amount and the frequency of each periodic purchase. For the plan to be effective, you must commit yourself to send a check for the plan you've decided upon on a regular basis. The success of a voluntary plan depends entirely on your commitment and resolve to stay with it. With this plan, as with the previous one, the amount of each additional purchase must meet the fund's minimum investment requirement for the type of account you have. (IRA accounts have lower minimums.) For regular accounts, the minimum purchase is usually $100. Of course, a voluntary plan allows you to change the amount you invest each time, the frequency with which you make your investments, and the duration of your plan. In addition, you may discontinue at any time with no further obligation on your part.

Figure 14–1 shows how an accumulation plan plus automatic reinvestment of distributions substantially increases the value of your account vs. a fixed monthly investment without reinvestment of distributions. Figure 14–2 shows how the dollar-cost averaging benefit of an automatic accumulation plan reduces the average cost per share over a period of time. Figure 14–3 illustrates how easily an accumulation plan may be established.

There is yet another valuable benefit frequently overlooked by investors who fail to establish an automatic accumulation plan. If the fund in which you establish an account is a tax-free municipal bond fund, for example, you enjoy *triple compounding:* the principal amount of your investment compounds, your reinvested distributions and additional investments compound, and the money you don't have to give the IRS stays in your account to compound.

FIGURE 14–1

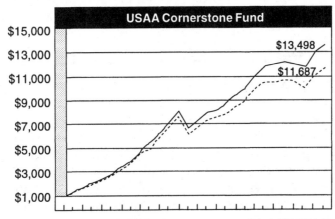

Value of $1,000 initial and $100 subsequent monthly investment with reinvestment dividends and capital gains

Value of $1,000 initial and $100 subsequent monthly investment

FIGURE 14-2

The chart illustrates monthly investments of $100 in a hypothetical fund. Over seven months, the fund's average price per share was $42.86. But an investor employing dollar-cost averaging paid only $40.39 per share.

Date	Amount Invested	Price Per Share	Shares Purchased
1/7/91	$100	$50	2
2/7/91	$100	$40	2½
3/7/91	$100	$30	3⅓
4/7/91	$100	$30	3⅓
5/7/91	$100	$40	2½
6/7/91	$100	$50	2
7/7/91	$100	$60	1⅔

Average price per share for period = $42.86
Average price paid by periodic investor = 40.39

Historically, investors who used dollar-cost averaging came out ahead of those who didn't.

$300 ÷ 7 = $42.86 average price per share
$700 ÷ 17.32 shares = $40.34
Savings of $2.44 per share
Saved $41.91 on just 17.32 shares

4. Retirement Plans

Most, if not all, mutual funds include among their services the administration of a variety of tax-deferred retirement plans. These include Individual Retirement Accounts (IRAs), Keogh plans (for the self-employed), and 401(k) and 403(b) plans. The 401(k) plan is set up by the employer and employee and is available to most companies. Frequently, the employer will also contribute to an employee's 401(k) plan. The 403(b) plan is open only to employees of tax-exempt organizations such as schools and hospitals.

IRA and Keogh plans are established by the investors themselves and are subject to certain government regulations. The rather complex topic of retirement planning is best left to other sources, since they do not come within the scope and purpose of this book. Suffice it to say that choosing a mutual fund that offers retirement plan services is wise and prudent. Such plans offer not only all the advantages of mutual funds in general, but provide a number of additional advantages for retirement plan investors.

FIGURE 14-3

What is EasiVest?

Setting aside money can appear next-to-impossible with today's high-priced lifestyles. But this needn't be the case if you use EasiVest — a simple, systematic way to build for your future.

By activating a Financial EasiVest program, you arrange to have a specific sum of money automatically transferred from your bank checking account to your Financial account, on the same day every month.

What are the benefits?

1. **Investment Discipline.** The best way to build for your future is to "pay yourself first," by investing money regularly. But how many of us have the discipline to do that? EasiVest is an effortless way to start a regular investment program.

2. **Dollar-Cost Averaging.** By investing a fixed amount regularly, your average purchase price will tend to offset market fluctuations. Sometimes you will buy more and sometimes fewer shares with that fixed amount of money; however, over a sufficient period of time, your average cost per share will be less than the actual average price per share.

EasiVest Instructions:

1. Complete both sections of the EasiVest authorization and sign it exactly as you sign your personal checks. Specify the amount ($50 or more) to be transferred. Pick the day of the month (either the 7th or 21st) you wish to have the money transferred.

2. Attach an unsigned, personal check marked "VOID." We'll imprint the identical checking account number in magnetic ink on the EasiVest checks to be submitted to your bank by us every month.

3. If you're a current Financial shareholder: Send us the entire EasiVest authorization form, voided check, and the stub portion of a recent Financial confirmation or statement of account.

If you're not already a Financial shareholder: Complete the fund application and return it to us with your initial investment of $250 or more; also enclose the entire EasiVest authorization form and personal check marked "VOID."

4. Mail to: **The Financial Funds**
P.O. Box 2040
Denver, CO 80201

Please allow at least four weeks for your EasiVest program to become effective.

Notice to Bank:
There is an indemnification on the reverse side.

EasiVest
Check Authorization

INVESCO Funds Group, Inc.
Post Office Box 2040
Denver, Colorado 80201

Bank Name

Bank Address	Street	City	State	Zip

As a convenience to me, I hereby request and authorize you to pay and charge to my account drafts on my account by and payable to the order of INVESCO Funds Group, Inc. provided there are sufficient collected funds in said account to pay the same upon presentation. I agree that your rights in respect to each draft shall be the same as if it were a check drawn on you and signed personally by me. This authority is to remain in effect until revoked by me in writing and, until you actually receive such notice, I agree that you shall be fully protected in honoring any such draft. I further agree that if any such draft be dishonored, whether with or without cause and whether intentionally or inadvertently, you shall be under no liability whatsoever.

Date	Bank Signature of Depositor(s)
Checking Account No.	(Both Signatures Required if Joint Checking Account)

EasiVest
Check Authorization

Home Office Record (Please Print)

Names as Shown on Checking Account	Financial Funds Account No.		
	$	7th	21st
Name of Bank	Amount of Drafts	Date of Draft (Circle One)	
Bank Address: Street	City	State	Zip

INVESCO Funds Group, Inc.
I have given authority to the above bank to honor the drafts drawn on my personal account by INVESCO Funds Group, Inc. Should any draft not be honored by said bank upon presentation, I understand that this method of payment may be terminated. I understand also that shares credited to my account when a draft is deposited will be removed from my account if said draft is returned unpaid by my bank.

Reprinted with permission of INVESCO.

The plan offered by the mutual fund must:

1. Meet all legal requirements for every type of retirement plan offered.
2. Notify shareholders of any legal changes relating to their retirement plan as they occur.
3. Provide assistance to shareholders in meeting all legal reporting requirements.

4. Offer investment vehicles that are suitable for the long-term growth so important to retirement plans.
5. Administer the plan so all distributions (dividends and capital gains) accrued on retirement plans are reinvested in the retirement plan and are tax-deferred until such time as withdrawals begin.

To sum up, the U.S. government has provided a measure of tax relief for the wage earner through IRAs and Keogh plans. Both of these tax-relief measures are available to individuals. The former (IRA) is a personal savings plan that offers tax advantages for setting aside money for one's retirement. In order to qualify, one must receive taxable compensation (earned income) from wages, tips, commissions, etc., and be under the age of 70-1/2. A Keogh plan is similar to an IRA except that it applies to individuals who derive their income from self-employment.

As noted earlier, it is not the purpose of this book to cover all the complexities of retirement plans. There are free federal income tax publications (Publication 590, "Individual Retirement Arrangements," and Publication 560, "Retirement Plans for the Self-employed") that are readily available from the Internal Revenue Service merely for the asking. These two publications provide a comprehensive analysis of the two plans discussed. They do not, of course, advise you where or what kind of retirement account to establish. That, hopefully, is what this book will help you to do.

Most mutual fund companies have provisions for establishing and managing tax deferred retirement accounts of all types. By utilizing their services, not only do you achieve IRS tax relief, and provide for a solid retirement nest egg, but also enhance the prospects of compounding the growth and capital of your retirement plan whereby it accumulates tax-free until you are eligible to draw upon it. Early withdrawals may be subject to penalties and taxes.

It would be wise to consider a *moderate-risk growth fund* for retirement planning purposes. You don't want to be in a position where you have to worry about whether your money will be there when you retire. Chapter 6 provided insights into risk levels and how to handle them for short- and long-term investing. A *New York Times* article appearing in 1987 estimated that one-third of all families participated in IRA plans and that assets in these plans had grown to more than $30 billion. It was further pointed out that fully 11% of these assets were invested in mutual funds. That amounts to $3.3 billion that have been entrusted to mutual funds for retirement. This is just another example of the trust and confidence the public has placed in the mutual fund industry—a well-deserved trust, I might add. By the year 2000, the $3.3 billion had reached $15.5 billion in IRAs alone.

CHECK WRITING

Many mutual funds and all money market mutual funds offer the convenience of free check writing. Should you wish to exercise this option, indicate so on the application form. (It is not available for tax-deferred retirement accounts.) The fund will in turn send you a free book of checks that may be used for any purpose you wish. Additional checks are provided free of cost as needed. If the fund on which you are to write checks is registered as a joint account, you may indicate on the application whether you wish to permit either owner to sign checks, or whether you require that both signatures be on the checks.

There is no restriction governing how many checks you may write each month (as there is with bank money market accounts), as long as you do not reduce your account balance below the minimum required to maintain the account, and you do not write checks for less than the minimum amount stipulated by the fund. Most funds require that checks be written for $500 or more. However, there are funds that have dropped the minimum to $250, such as the Vanguard Money Market Fund. Recently, the Franklin Tax-Exempt Money Fund has dropped its minimum to $100. Of course, in any case, you may always write checks for more than the minimum as long as there is sufficient money in your account to cover the checks, and your fund balance meets the minimum requirement. Your account continues to earn full interest until your checks clear.

SWITCHING WITHIN A FAMILY OF FUNDS

Most mutual fund investment companies permit shareholders to switch from one fund to another within their family of funds. Usually, all that is required is a telephone call from the investor to the fund's toll-free number. This feature is offered at no cost by most funds. (Under certain circumstances, the fund may impose a small fee for this service—check the prospectus.)

Simply put, telephone switching is a strategy whereby you attempt to capitalize on the cyclical swings in the stock market. It means keeping your entire investment in equity (stock) funds when the market trend is "bullish" (moving up), and switching everything into the fund family's money market fund when the stock market shows signs of becoming "bearish" (moving down).

The theory upon which the strategy is based is as follows. When a bear market threatens and stock prices are falling, your investment should be switched to a money market. Such a move will protect your principal from a loss, because money market funds' NAVs rarely, if ever, fluctuate. A thousand shares of a money market fund with an NAV of one dollar will be worth $1,000 whether the price of stocks is rising or falling. While your principal is "parked" in the money market fund, it will still be earning interest. When a "bull" market is signaled, a telephone call will enable you to switch from your money market back to your equity funds. This maneuver will enable you to be in a position to profit from the rising market. The trick, of course, is to know when to initiate the switches in order to profit or protect. Few investors, especially novices, are able to predict with absolute certainty the market trends. Not even the professionals are always right. However, switching funds to increase your profits and safeguard your gains is a technique you should definitely look into and employ as opportunities arise.

Fund switching is a fairly sophisticated technique and expert help should be sought. There are dozens of readily available sources of switching advice to assist you in utilizing telephone switching. A number of mutual fund telephone switch newsletters are published; most of them purport to have good track records. Below are some of those available:

Donoghue'$ Moneyletter
360 Woodland Street
Box 8008, Holliston, MA 01746
1-800-343-5413

Fabian Telephone Switch Newsletter
P.O. Box 2538
Huntington Beach, CA 92647-9880
1-800-950-8765

InvesTech Market Letter
522 Crestview Drive
Kalispill, MT 59901
(406) 755-8527

Professional Timing Service
P.O. Box 7483
Missoula, MT 59801
(406) 543-4131

Time Your Switch
P.O. Box 673
Andover, MA 01810
(617) 470-3511

Most of the above newsletter sources will be happy to provide a sample copy of their publications. (Make the request in writing.) The authors of these publications track the stock market and generate appropriate "buy" and "sell" signals, which are published in newsletters mailed to subscribers. When the market is poised for an upswing, you are advised to "buy"—that is, to have all of your funds' assets fully invested in equity funds. When the market shows signs of a downturn, you are advised to "sell"—that is, to switch all of your assets out of the equity funds and sweep them into the money market fund available in your fund family. In this way you are able to preserve your principal and profits.

The telephone switch newsletters listed above (and others) all claim to have excellent records of accuracy in predicting changes in the market. Unfortunately, I have found their claims to be greatly overstated. As has been repeatedly noted in these pages, "No one can accurately time the market short-term." Save your money. These newsletters cost quite a bit. Be selective in the funds you choose, invest for the long-term, reinvest your distributions, and you won't need the newsletters to advise you.

VOLUNTARY WITHDRAWAL PLANS

Voluntary withdrawal plans are also available through most mutual funds. These plans are just the opposite of the voluntary accumulation plans. A voluntary withdrawal plan requires the shareholder to initiate the request for regular, periodic redemptions which will be sent directly to the shareholder. Shareholders may, instead, establish a plan whereby the fund will redeem a prearranged fixed dollar amount to be wired to the shareholder's bank monthly, quarterly, semiannually, or annually. The necessary arrangements have to be made between the fund and the bank in accordance with the written instructions of the shareholder.

The usual minimum redemption for a voluntary withdrawal plan is $50 monthly. Of course, withdrawals may be for more as long as you maintain the required account minimum balance.

Retirees, especially, appreciate the voluntary redemption plan because it provides them with a fixed amount of income at regular intervals. Surprisingly, during a bull market when the fund's NAV is rising, the net value of the investor's fund from which redemptions are being made may not appreciably decrease, as one would expect. As a matter of fact, a rising NAV, plus the regular dividends and capital gains credited to the investor's account, may actually result in the value of the account *increasing*, despite the regular redemptions.

REDEEMING SHARES

You may redeem shares at any time through one of several easy methods provided by the fund:

1. *Written redemption requests by mail or fax.* You must include:
   a. account number and name of the fund from which you are redeeming
   b. number of shares to be redeemed, or dollar amount desired
   c. each owner's name as registered on the account
   d. your address and daytime telephone number
   e. signatures of all owners.
2. *Telephone redemption requests.* As long as prior authorization has been established, a simple phone call is all that is necessary. Checks will be mailed to you or credited to your bank account. (See "Voluntary withdrawal plans.")

3. *Systematic withdrawal plan.* It is possible to set up automatic withdrawals. (See "Voluntary Withdrawal Plans.") Generally, a $5,000 minimum account balance is required to set up such a plan. This may vary from fund to fund. Check the prospectus, or call the fund directly for particulars.

STUDY GUIDE FOR CHAPTER 14

1. Besides the fund's performance, what else is it important to know about the fund?
2. What are the advantages of an automatic investment plan?
3. Compare the contractual accumulation plan with the voluntary accumulation plan. Which would you choose?
4. How is it possible to achieve triple compounding?
5. What advantages are there in having your retirement plan in a mutual fund?
6. In what type of fund is it best to invest your retirement plan?
7. Being able to write checks against your fund is a convenience. What are some of the constraints imposed by most funds?
8. How do you effect switching within a family of funds?
9. What circumstances might cause you to want to change the composition of your portfolio?

POSTSCRIPT 14–1

UTILIZING SPECIAL MUTUAL FUNDS SERVICES

AUTOMATIC INVESTMENT PLANS

Check your fund's prospectus to determine whether such plans are available. Most funds offer them. Generally, they operate in conjunction with either your bank checking account or savings account. Such plans are an excellent means of dollar-cost averaging, i.e., buying low and selling high. You set up an automatic investment plan with your fund and your bank. Your bank must be a member of the Federal Reserve System in order for the plan to operate. Based on the specifics of the plan you select, your bank will wire on a regular basis sums from your designated bank account to be deposited into your mutual fund account.

In addition, a mutual fund will permit anyone who establishes such a plan to open an account with a much lower initial deposit than would be required when opening an account without an automatic investment plan. Again, check the fund's prospectus. The fund will provide the form necessary to open such a plan.

AUTOMATIC WITHDRAWAL PLANS

Such plans are also set up between your fund and your bank. A form will be provided upon request. Automatic withdrawal plans are used to ensure that an exact amount will be wire-transferred from your fund to your bank account on a regular basis. You determine the amount and the frequency to be withdrawn from your fund account. Generally, such plans are initiated by retirees who have need to supplement their Social Security and pension income checks.

In essence, this is dollar-cost averaging *in reverse*. Let's say you want your fund to wire $200 monthly to your bank account. In order to do this, two conditions must be met: (1) You must have a sufficient amount in your fund to cover the withdrawals, and (2) you should understand the effects of *reverse dollar-cost averaging*. In order to effectuate the plan, the fund will *redeem* from your fund account a sufficient number of shares to provide the $200 monthly transfer to your bank account. Thus, the fund will have to redeem more shares when the NAV is low in order to generate the $200 each month. When the NAV is high, the fund will redeem fewer shares. This is precisely the *opposite* of what you want to do moneywise. Add to that the horrendous job of figuring your taxes on the redemptions when the number and value of redeemed shares may fluctuate every month.

It is preferable to take charge of the withdrawals yourself by instructing your fund to redeem the specific shares that will benefit you most, i.e., by redeeming the shares with the highest NAV so that fewer shares will need to be redeemed in order to cover the $200 withdrawal.

EARLY START IRA: HOW $6,750 GROWS TO OVER $1 MILLION

This table shows four ways to accumulate approximately $1 million in an IRA by age 65 at 10% a year compounded. Investor A contributes $2,000 at the beginning of each year for forty years (ages 26–65); Investor B, $2,000 a year for only seven years (19–25); Investor C, $2,000 a year for only five years (age 14–18); and Investor D smaller sums still from age 8 through 13. Finally, Investor E shows the IRA growth achieved by making all of these contributions at every age from 8 to 65.

Early Start IRA: How $6,750 Grows To Over $1 Million

This table shows four ways to accumulate approximately $1,000,000 in an IRA by age 65 at 10% a year compounded. Investor A contributes $2,000 at the beginning of each year for forty years (ages 26-65); Investor B, $2,000 a year for only seven years (19-25); Investor C, $2,000 a year for only five years (age 14-18); and Investor D smaller sums still from age 8 through 13. Finally, Investor E shows the IRA growth achieved by making all of these contributions at every age from 8 to 65.

	INVESTOR A		INVESTOR B		INVESTOR C		INVESTOR D		INVESTOR E	
Age	Contri-bution	Year-End Value	Contri-bution	Year-End Value	Contri-bution	Year-End Value	Contri-bution	Year-End Value	Contri-bution	Year-End Value
8	-0-	-0-	-0-	-0-	-0-	-0-	500	550	500	550
9	-0-	-0-	-0-	-0-	-0-	-0-	750	1,430	750	1,430
10	-0-	-0-	-0-	-0-	-0-	-0-	1,000	2,673	1,000	2,673
11	-0-	-0-	-0-	-0-	-0-	-0-	1,250	4,315	1,250	4,315
12	-0-	-0-	-0-	-0-	-0-	-0-	1,500	6,397	1,500	6,397
13	-0-	-0-	-0-	-0-	-0-	-0-	1,750	8,962	1,750	8,962
14	-0-	-0-	-0-	-0-	2,000	2,200	-0-	9,858	2,000	12,058
15	-0-	-0-	-0-	-0-	2,000	4,620	-0-	10,843	2,000	15,463
16	-0-	-0-	-0-	-0-	2,000	7,282	-0-	11,928	2,000	19,210
17	-0-	-0-	-0-	-0-	2,000	10,210	-0-	13,121	2,000	23,331
18	-0-	-0-	-0-	-0-	2,000	13,431	-0-	14,433	2,000	27,864
19	-0-	-0-	2,000	2,000	-0-	14,774	-0-	15,876	2,000	32,850
20	-0-	-0-	2,000	4,620	-0-	16,252	-0-	17,463	2,000	38,335
21	-0-	-0-	2,000	7,282	-0-	17,877	-0-	19,210	2,000	44,369
22	-0-	-0-	2,000	10,210	-0-	19,665	-0-	21,131	2,000	51,006
23	-0-	-0-	2,000	13,431	-0-	21,631	-0-	23,244	2,000	58,306
24	-0-	-0-	2,000	16,974	-0-	23,794	-0-	25,568	2,000	66,337
25	-0-	-0-	2,000	20,872	-0-	26,174	-0-	28,125	2,000	75,170
26	2,000	2,200	-0-	22,959	-0-	28,791	-0-	30,938	2,000	84,888
27	2,000	4,620	-0-	25,255	-0-	31,670	-0-	34,031	2,000	95,576
28	2,000	7,282	-0-	27,780	-0-	34,837	-0-	37,434	2,000	107,334
29	2,000	10,210	-0-	30,558	-0-	38,321	-0-	41,178	2,000	120,267
30	2,000	13,431	-0-	33,614	-0-	42,153	-0-	45,296	2,000	134,494
31	2,000	16,974	-0-	36,976	-0-	46,368	-0-	49,825	2,000	150,143
32	2,000	20,872	-0-	40,673	-0-	51,005	-0-	54,808	2,000	167,358
33	2,000	25,159	-0-	44,741	-0-	56,106	-0-	60,289	2,000	186,294
34	2,000	29,875	-0-	49,215	-0-	61,716	-0-	66,317	2,000	207,123
35	2,000	35,062	-0-	54,136	-0-	67,888	-0-	72,949	2,000	230,035
36	2,000	40,769	-0-	59,550	-0-	74,676	-0-	80,244	2,000	255,239
37	2,000	47,045	-0-	65,505	-0-	82,144	-0-	88,269	2,000	282,963
38	2,000	53,950	-0-	72,055	-0-	90,359	-0-	97,095	2,000	313,459
39	2,000	61,545	-0-	79,261	-0-	99,394	-0-	106,805	2,000	347,005
40	2,000	69,899	-0-	87,187	-0-	109,334	-0-	117,485	2,000	383,905
41	2,000	79,089	-0-	95,905	-0-	120,267	-0-	129,234	2,000	424,496
42	2,000	89,198	-0-	105,496	-0-	132,294	-0-	142,157	2,000	469,145
43	2,000	100,318	-0-	116,045	-0-	145,523	-0-	156,373	2,000	518,269
44	2,000	112,550	-0-	127,650	-0-	160,076	-0-	172,010	2,000	572,286
45	2,000	126,005	-0-	140,415	-0-	176,083	-0-	189,211	2,000	631,714
46	2,000	140,805	-0-	154,456	-0-	193,692	-0-	208,133	2,000	697,086
47	2,000	157,086	-0-	169,902	-0-	213,061	-0-	228,946	2,000	768,995
48	2,000	174,995	-0-	186,892	-0-	234,367	-0-	251,840	2,000	848,094
49	2,000	194,694	-0-	205,581	-0-	257,803	-0-	277,024	2,000	935,103
50	2,000	216,364	-0-	226,140	-0-	283,358	-0-	304,727	2,000	1,030,814
51	2,000	240,200	-0-	248,754	-0-	311,942	-0-	335,209	2,000	1,136,095
52	2,000	265,420	-0-	273,629	-0-	343,136	-0-	368,719	2,000	1,251,905
53	2,000	295,262	-0-	300,992	-0-	377,450	-0-	405,591	2,000	1,379,095
54	2,000	326,988	-0-	331,091	-0-	415,195	-0-	446,150	2,000	1,519,425
55	2,000	361,887	-0-	364,200	-0-	456,715	-0-	490,766	2,000	1,673,567
56	2,000	400,276	-0-	400,620	-0-	502,386	-0-	539,842	2,000	1,843,124
57	2,000	442,503	-0-	440,682	-0-	552,625	-0-	593,826	2,000	2,029,636
58	2,000	488,953	-0-	484,750	-0-	607,887	-0-	653,209	2,000	2,234,800
59	2,000	540,049	-0-	533,225	-0-	668,676	-0-	718,530	2,000	2,460,480
60	2,000	596,254	-0-	586,548	-0-	735,543	-0-	790,383	2,000	2,708,728
61	2,000	658,079	-0-	645,203	-0-	809,098	-0-	869,421	2,000	2,981,800
62	2,000	726,087	-0-	709,723	-0-	890,007	-0-	956,363	2,000	3,282,180
63	2,000	800,896	-0-	780,695	-0-	979,008	-0-	1,052,000	2,000	3,612,598
64	2,000	883,185	-0-	858,765	-0-	1,076,909	-0-	1,157,200	2,000	3,976,058
65	2,000	973,704	-0-	944,641	-0-	1,184,600	-0-	1,272,920	2,000	4,375,864
Less Total Invested:		(80,000)		(14,000)		(10,000)		(6,750)		(110,750)
Equals Net Earnings:		893,704		930,641		1,174,600		1,266,170		4,265,114
Money Grew:		11-fold		66-fold		117-fold		188-fold		38-fold

IRA CHOICES

CHARACTERISTICS	TRADITIONAL IRA 1998 RULES	ROTH IRA
Who Is Eligible to Invest?	• Individuals under age 70½ who have earned income or whose spouses have earned income, regardless of amount.	• Individuals (and their spouses) of any age with earned income, whose adjusted gross income is below $110,000 (single) or $160,000 (joint). • Individuals age 70½ and over **may** contribute. • An individual's participation in an employer-sponsored plan is immaterial to Roth contribution eligibility.
Deductibility of Contribution	• Subject to limitation, contributions are deductible. Deductibility depends on income level for individuals who are active participants in an employer-sponsored retirement plan. • Full deductions are permitted if taxpayer is not an active participant of an employer-sponsored plan. • Partial deduction permitted for active participants of an employer-sponsored plan, who meet the Adjusted Gross Income (AGI) limits ($30,000 to $40,000 for single filers; $50,000 to $60,000 for joint filers).	• No deduction permitted for amounts contributed.
Annual Contribution Limits	• Individuals (and their spouses) may contribute up to $2,000 annually (or 100% of compensation, if less).	• Individuals (and their spouses) may generally contribute up to $2,000 (or 100% of compensation, if less). • Ability to contribute phases out at income levels of $95,000 to $110,000 (individual) and $150,000 to $160,000 (joint). • *Overall limit for contributions to all IRAs (Traditional and Roth combined) is $2,000 annually (or 100% of compensation, if less).*
Rollover/Conversion	• Individuals may rollover amounts held in employer-sponsored retirement plans (401k, SEP IRA, etc.) tax-free to Traditional IRAs.	• Rollovers from other Roth IRAs or Traditional IRAs only. • An individual whose adjusted gross income is higher than $100,000 is **not permitted** to rollover a Traditional IRA to a Roth IRA. • Amounts rolled over (or converted) from Traditional IRAs are subject to income tax in the year rolled over or converted, except if the conversion or rollover is done within 1998, then the tax liability is spread over a four-year period (1998 through 2001).
Tax Advantage	• Tax-deferred investment growth.	• Tax-free investment growth if account is open for 5 years or more.
Tax Treatment of Distributions	• Total deductible contributions and all earnings taxed as ordinary income in the year of withdrawal. • Distributions attributable to nondeductible contributions are considered a (nontaxable) return of capital. • Distributions made before age 59½ may be subject to a 10% penalty. • Early withdrawal can be made penalty-free prior to age 59½ upon death, disability, the purchase of first-time home (up to $10,000 lifetime maximum), higher education expenses, medical expenses in excess of 7.5% of AGI, or health insurance premiums (for unemployed more than 12 weeks).	• Distributions made after age 59½ are tax-free if the Roth IRA has been held for more than five years. • Distributions made before age 59½ may be subject to a 10% penalty. • Early withdrawal can be made penalty-free prior to age 59½ if the *Roth IRA is held* more than five years, upon death, disability, the purchase of first-time home (up to $10,000 lifetime maximum), higher education expenses, medical expenses in excess of 7.5% of AGI, or health insurance premiums (for unemployed more than 12 weeks). • Also, you can withdraw your **contributed principal** from a Roth IRA without tax or penalty at any time.
Minimum Distribution Requirements	• Distributions must start by age 70½.	• No requirements to begin withdrawal at age 70½.

POSTSCRIPT 14–4

QUESTIONS AND ANSWERS ABOUT ROTH IRAs Do you have to be working to get a Roth IRA? How do you purchase one? What are the fees?

The Roth IRA, which became available in 1998, does not allow you to claim a tax deduction on the money you put into it, as the traditional IRA does. However, you may withdraw everything tax-free at retirement if the account has been open at least five years, and you are at least 59-1/2 years of age. With a traditional IRA you may qualify for a tax deduction, but you must pay taxes when you take the money out.

To open any kind of IRA, you must have "compensation," meaning "earned income." Basically, that means money from *work*. It does not, however, have to be full-time work, and compensation can be from self-employment, anything from running your own business to baby-sitting for a fee. The rule is that each person can put a maximum of $2,000 a year into an IRA, but no more than the total amount of the compensation.

There is an important exception, though. If you are married and your spouse works, you qualify to make an IRA contribution even if you have no compensation. The maximum for a married couple in which only one spouse has compensation is $4,000 a year, or $2,000 per person but no more than the compensation of the working spouse.

You can open an IRA on your own, or through a bank, a broker, and many other financial institutions. However, opening one *on your own* will generally save you money in commissions, fees, and other transaction costs. And the process is quite simple. Any mutual fund company will provide you with the necessary details and an application with which to open the IRA account. Incidentally, you "open" an IRA as opposed to "buying" one, because an IRA is a legal arrangement, not a particular investment. You can find any number of ads in magazines, newspapers, and financial publications that will indicate that the company posting the ad offers IRAs to individuals wishing to open an account.

Fees are another matter. Each institution sets its own. Many have eliminated fees in order to entice consumers. *No-load mutual fund companies* are probably your best way to reduce and / or eliminate fees as well as eliminate transaction costs.

CHAPTER 15

Costs of Ownership

MANAGEMENT FEES

All mutual funds, including no-load funds, have certain fixed expenses that are built into their per share net asset value. These expenses are the actual costs of doing business. They are deducted from the assets of the fund. It is advisable to check the prospectus to determine the percentage of the fund's total net assets that is paid out for expenses. Additionally, shareholder services provided by the fund, investment adviser's fees, bank custodian fees, and fund underwriter costs also come out of the fund's assets. These charges vary from fund to fund; however, they are clearly spelled out in the prospectus.

To get some idea of the variations that exist in the operating expenses between two funds, see the examples provided in Figure 15–1. Example A is from the Dreyfus New Leaders Fund Prospectus of May 1, 1990. Example B is from the Value Line High Yield Fund Prospectus of July 1, 1991.

The two examples cited in Figure 15–1 by no means represent the highest nor the lowest annual fund operating expenses charged by mutual funds. Because these expenses are spelled out in the prospectus, you can understand how important prospectuses are and why they must be read carefully before investing or sending money.

Other things being equal, you should seek to invest in funds

FIGURE   15-1

Example A: DREYFUS NEW LEADERS FUND
Annual Fund Operating Expenses
(as a percentage of average daily net assets)

Management Fees 75%
12b-1 Fees 25%
Other Expenses 37%
Total Fund Operating Expenses 1.37%

In the above example, you would pay the following expenses on a $1,000 investment, assuming (1) 5% annual return, and (2) redemption at the end of each period:

1 Year	3 Years	5 Years	10 Years
$14	$43	$75	$165

Example B: VALUE LINE HIGH YIELD FUND
Shareholder Transaction Expenses
(as a percentage of average daily net assets)

Management Fees 50%
12b-1 Fees 00%
Other Expenses 10%
Total Fund Operating Expenses 60%

In the above example, you would pay the following expenses on a $1,000 investment, assuming (1) 5% annual return, and (2) redemption at the end of each period:

1 Year	3 Years	5 Years	10 Years
$6	$19	$33	$75

with low operating expenses. A fund's operating expenses can amount to millions of dollars annually. Thus, they adversely affect the fund's net asset value and its yield, because they are paid from the total assets of the fund. All funds subtract expenses—salaries, services, administrative costs, and so on—from their assets, thereby reducing the value of your shares as well as the amount of your return.

On a per-share basis, however, management expenses are usually quite small, because they are spread over the tens of thousands, or the millions, of shareholders in the fund. The formula for determining the cost of a fund's management expenses is simple: From the current value of the fund's total assets subtract liabilities and expenses, and divide the result by the number of outstanding shares. The fund's prospectus and/or annual reports often provide this data. Management fees and expenses are usually expressed as a ratio of expenses paid out to total assets. Generally, the prospectus will show these expense ratios. Invest in funds with low ratios, as long as they meet all of your other investment criteria.

REDEMPTION FEES

All load funds levy a sales charge when purchasing shares (see Chapter 4). Some load and some no-load funds also charge a redemption fee when you take money out (redeem shares). The redemption fee is a percentage of the amount redeemed, usually 0.05% (1/2 of 1%).

If your fund levies such a charge, and you were to redeem 100 of your shares with an NAV of $12.50, your total redemption cost would amount to $1,250. The redemption fee of .05% would come to $6.25. This amount would be subtracted from the $1,250, and you would receive a net of $1,243.75 instead of the $1,250 you would have received from a fund with no redemption fee. *Avoid funds with redemption fees.* There are excellent funds available that will meet your objectives and do not levy redemption fees. In my opinion, redemption fees are levied only with the intent to cut down on the number of redemptions the fund experiences. The bottom line is that you are entitled to the *full value* of the shares you redeem.

Redemptions may be made in the following ways:

1. By writing a check, if you have chosen the check-writing option when you opened your account; however, you may not close an account by writing a check, nor may you write checks for less than the minimum amount indicated in the prospectus.
2. By telephone; however, the proceeds will be sent only to the shareholder's address of record.
3. By wire, if you have selected this method on your application when you opened your account; the proceeds will be wired to your bank account.

If the redemption amount is for $10,000 or more, or if the proceeds are to be sent to anyone other than the shareholder, the signature(s) on the request must be guaranteed by a commercial bank or a member of a stock exchange. The fund's prospectus will carefully spell out redemption procedures for you.

12b-1 FEES

Many funds to charge a fee known as the 12b-1 fee, which was created in 1980 and authorized mutual funds to charge an additional fee to cover marketing and distribution costs. These fees range from .1% to 1.25%. The 12b-1 fee is in addition to the adviser's management fee. In order for a fund to adopt a 12b-1 plan, shareholders must vote approval, unless it was included in the fund's charter at the inception of the fund. Again, this information must be provided in the prospectus. No-load funds rarely, if ever, charge 12b-1 fees— another argument in favor of buying them! Stick with no-load funds, and you will always be ahead of the game.

SWITCHING FEES

Most, if not all, open-end mutual funds permit you to transfer all or any part of your investment from one fund to another fund within its family. This kind of transfer is commonly called "switching" (see Chapter 14).

For many years there was no charge required to switch funds. In recent years, however, some funds have started to charge for switching. It is usually a flat fee. The few funds that are charging the investor for this service say it is to discourage too frequent moving in and out of funds. Constant switching of funds increases the administrative costs involved in keeping track of customer accounts and in providing confirmation statements each time a switch is made. The investor pays directly for this service, because the fund charges it against the account from which the switch was made.

I do not expect to see switching fees proliferate, however. Market timers and newsletter publishers like Dick Fabian, who publishes the *Fabian Telephone Switch Newsletter,* are telling their thousands of subscribers to move completely out of funds that charge switching fees and move into funds that do not. Astute investors who use telephone switching as a technique for improving their positions and profits are strongly against the imposition of switching fees.

MAINTENANCE FEES

Be on the lookout for a fee that is being assessed against the shareholder's account(s) directly. It is called an "account maintenance" fee. According to prospectuses of the funds that levy this fee, it is to "offset the costs of maintaining shareholder accounts." The $10 fee is deducted from the dividends earned by each account the investor owns at the rate of $2.50 per quarter, or $10 per year. If the account does not generate enough dividends to cover the maintenance fee, enough shares or fractions of shares will be automatically redeemed from the account to make up the difference.

Strangely, the addition of the maintenance fee has done nothing to eliminate or even lessen the accounting cost fee, which continues to be listed among the fund's annual operating costs. It seems to me the funds that charge this fee are asking investors to pay twice for the same service. Avoid funds that charge the investor a separate maintenance fee.

Figure 15–2 shows a list of usual and justifiable fees charged by virtually all mutual funds. Expect to pay these fees; they are minimal and necessary. On the other hand, the other fees about which I have cautioned you are not, in most cases, justifiable.

Finally, I do not suggest that you use the costs of ownership described in this chapter as the only criteria for selecting a fund in which to invest. There are other criteria upon which to base decisions. For example, a fund with low expense charges may have a poor performance record, or a low rate of return, both of which are more significant than expense charges alone. Your selection must always be based upon a variety of criteria; among them are the fund's:

- Objective
- Yield
- Load
- Portfolio diversification
- Long-term track record
- Management expertise
- Risk level
- Services provided
- Annual total return

F I G U R E　15-2

Customary Fees Charged by Most Mutual Fund Companies

Investment Advisory Fees: The fund pays a set fee, stated in the prospectus, for investment management. This allows the fund the use of the advisor's investment research staff, equipment, and other resources. Administrative and accounting services, such as data processing, pricing of fund shares, and preparing financial statements, are included in this fee.

Transfer Agent Fees: The fund pays a set fee for each account for maintaining shareholder records and generating shareholder statements, plus answering your phone inquiries and correspondence.

Audit Fees and Expenses: Each fund is audited annually by an internationally recognized, independent accounting firm which is not affiliated with the fund.

Custodian Fees and Expenses: The fund's assets, represented by stock certificates and other documents, are held by an outside source for safe-keeping.

Directors' Fees and Expenses: The fund's directors are compensated for their time and travel. The Board meets at least quarterly, as a whole and in subcommittees, to review the fund's business. (Directors or officers who are employed by the fund receive no compensation from the fund for serving as directors.)

Registration: The SEC and various state securities agencies charge fees permitting a fund's shares to be sold.

Reports to Shareholders: Annual, semiannual, and interim reports are printed and mailed to shareholders on a periodic basis. The postage for mailing shareholder statements and confirmations is also included here.

Other Expenses: Miscellaneous small items, such as pricing services.

The nine criteria listed above are among the many to be considered before investing in any mutual fund.

STUDY GUIDE FOR CHAPTER 15

1. How do all mutual fund companies secure the money necessary to cover the costs of doing business?
2. Where can you obtain information regarding the management fees charged by mutual funds?
3. In the two funds shown in Figure 15–1, other things being equal, in which fund would you invest? Why?

4. What is a redemption fee?
5. How may shares be redeemed?
6. For what reason is the 12b-1 fee charged?
7. How may you avoid being charged a 12b-1 fee?
8. What are "switching" fees, and why do some funds levy them?
9. Why do some funds impose a maintenance fee?

Fees make a big difference

If an investor put $10,000 in a fund with a return of 10%, before expenses, and the fund had annual operating exopenses of 1.5%, after 20 years the investor would end up with roughly $$49,725. However, if the $10,000 were deposited in a fund with a similar return, but with an expense ratio of only .05% then the investor would end up wirth $60,858 -- an **18%** difference.

$49,725 $60,858

1.5% fee   .05% fee

HOW FUND EXPENSES AFFECT RETURNS

Fund expenses include fees that pay salaries, research expenses, telecommunications charges, 12b-1 marketing and distribution costs, shareholder statements, research expenses, check processing, tax reporting, overhead expenses, transfer agent fees, and all other operating costs involved in keeping the fund running.

To determine the fund's expense ratio, divide the amount of total expenses by the amount of total dollars under management. Therefore, a fund with $10 million in assets and $120,000 in operating expenses will have a 1.2% expense ratio ($120,000 divided by $10,000,000).

Is a 1.2% expense ratio good? It all depends on how well the fund does. To deliver a 10% return to you, the fund manager would have to earn 11.2% before expenses in order for you to have an ROI (return on investment) of 10%. A lower cost fund with expenses of 0.5% would only have to earn 10.5% to generate the same 10% return.

For example, let's say you expect the market to return 10% a year (its actual long-term norm) for the next 25 years, and you are considering making a long-term investment in three funds with similar objectives. Fund A has a modest 0.5% expense ratio; Fund B has about an average 1.5% expense ratio; and Fund C, a high 2.5% expense ratio (not a far-fetched example—more than 150 funds have expense ratios of 2.5% a year or higher).

After deducting expenses from portfolio earnings, Fund C will return just 7.5% a year. At that rate, your $10,000 will produce a cumulative 25-year profit of $50,983. Fund B will leave you with a 1% higher return, or 8.5%. But thanks to the magic of compounding, your 25-year earnings at that rate are nearly a third greater, $66,868. Finally, Fund A nets you 9.5% a year, which produces $20,000 of extra compound earnings, or $86,684. The difference between Fund A and Fund C? A staggering *$325,701.* All told, Fund A earns you *70% more than Fund C.*

Or look at it this way. A 2.5% expense ratio for a fund that earns 10% a year on its portfolio means that *one-fourth* of your annual earnings are eaten up by expenses.

You may be wondering at this point which fund family has the industry's lowest expense ratios for its equity funds. The clear champ is the Vanguard Family of Funds. Its expense ratio for all its equity funds averages only .37%. Its nearest rival is the American Family of Funds, with an average expense ratio of .73% for its equity funds. Which fund has the highest expense ratio for its equity funds? GT Global, with an expense ratio of 2.06%.

POSTSCRIPT 15–2

TIPS FOR SELECTING A MUTUAL FUND

When faced with over 10,000 different mutual funds that are available, far too often the vast majority of investors narrow their options by looking at *past performances.* In many cases there is nothing terribly wrong with such a strategy. However, it is only one criterion in selecting a winning fund for your portfolio—one that will continue to provide profitable returns into the future.

Many financial experts are predicting that slower times lie ahead in the financial market. The 20% to 30% returns of the past few years may soon vanish, and the 10% to 11% *historical average returns* in the market are due to return.

Therefore, in addition to past performance, other statistical criteria should be considered when selecting a mutual fund (assuming, of course, you have previously factored in your risk tolerance, time horizon, and objectives). Criteria such as *fund fees,* e.g., expense ratios, management fees, 12-b 1 fees, and sales loads, are worth considering. When the market was sailing along to 20% to 30% gains, a 1% difference in expense ratios may not have seemed a big deal. However, should the market return to its historical averages, even a 1% difference may become a serious factor.

In addition to searching for low expense ratios, it pays to heed my oft-repeated advice to eschew load funds in favor of pure no-load funds. A front-end load can put you in a deficit situation from the very start. For instance, if you pay a 5% sales charge, and add to that a 1.5% expense ratio, your money has to gain *6 1/2%* just to break even.

Another way to cut costs is to consider *index funds.* The average domestic equity fund charges 1.5% in management fees. Index funds can offer excellent returns with half the expenses. The Vanguard S & P 500 Index Fund, for example, has a minuscule 0.19% expense ratio. That is less than two tenths of 1%.

Let me do a little math for you. If you were to invest $10,000 in a no-load mutual fund with an expense ratio of 1.5% in 1999 and the fund returned an average of 11% a year, your nest egg will amount to $61,415 in the year 2010 (11 years). Put the same $10,000 into a low-cost, no-load index fund with an expense ratio of 0.2%, such as the Vanguard S & P 500 Index Fund, and assuming the same 11% annual return, your nest egg will amount to $69,109 in the same 11 years. That's a difference of $7,693. Expense ratios do make a difference in fund returns!

Many investors tend to look down on unmanaged index funds because they hardly ever beat the market. Statistically, however, fewer than *one in five* actively managed equity funds do that anyway. According to Lipper Analytical Services, the one in five actively managed funds that did beat the market over the past 20 years averaged a return of 1.5% a year better than index funds—barely enough to justify their higher expenses. The vast majority of managed funds (the four out of five) that trailed the market came in at an average 3% a year *worse* than their index counterparts.

Like most investors, you probably do not have the expertise to properly research thousands of stock funds, even though you realize investing in stock funds is the best way to secure a rewarding financial future. What do you do?

The simplest and cheapest way to invest in the *entire* stock market is through an index fund that tracks the entire stock market such as the Wilshire 5,000 Index. Between the S & P 500 Index Fund and the Wilshire Index Fund, you have a stake in approximately 7,300 regularly traded domestic stocks.

If you were to invest in a total market fund such as the Fidelity Spartan Total Market Fund, or the Vanguard Total Stock Market Index Fund, or the T. Rowe Price Total Equity Market Index Fund, you would essentially buy the *entire stock market.* Talk about diversification!! These funds are the epitome of diversification, and broad diversification provides a safety net against falling market prices.

CHAPTER 16

Tax Issues

Mutual funds do not pay taxes on their earnings. Instead, the fund periodically distributes to its shareholders substantially all (98%) of the investment income and net realized capital gains it generates. Thus, the fund itself is not subject to federal income or excise taxes.

Shareholders do pay taxes on the income the fund distributes to them. As owners of fund shares, investors pay taxes on the income they receive as though they themselves owned the securities in the fund's portfolio. Depending on the fund, shareholders may receive two kinds of income from their mutual fund investments: dividends and capital gains, both of which may be taxable. Dividend income from tax-free municipal bond funds, however, is not subject to *federal taxes*, although it may be taxable by *some states*. (There are municipal bond funds that are free of state taxes also.) Capital gains income, on the other hand, is taxable by federal and state governments even when earned on tax-free funds.

IRS 1099 FORMS

Form 1099-B—Capital Gains or (Losses)

A 1099-B form will be sent to you by the end of January each year, if your fund distributed capital gains income during the preceding year. In the case of fund-distributed capital gains income, your

1099-B form will show the exact amount you received. In the event that you have a capital gain (or loss) as a result of redeeming shares or switching shares, you will be required to determine the taxable amount by yourself. It is then reported on Schedule D of your IRS Tax form even though you may have suffered a loss. As noted before, you must also report capital gains (or losses) on your tax-free funds. Your 1099-B form will remind you that the IRS has received a copy of this form also. Therefore, be sure to keep the confirmation slips you received from the fund. They serve as proof of transactions you made that may have resulted in capital gains (or losses) during the year.

There are several methods of determining your tax liability should you redeem shares that have appreciated (or depreciated) in value since their purchase or if you have transferred shares to another fund:

1. First in—first out (FIFO) (most costly)
2. Last in—first out (LIFO) (least costly)
3. Identifying specific shares (identifying the exact shares involved by sending a letter to the fund designating exactly which shares to redeem or switch)
4. Average cost basis (calculate average cost of all shares owned)

For the novice investor, the easiest method of calculating capital gains (or losses) and the least apt to be questioned by the IRS is by the average cost basis. The way to determine the average cost of your shares in the fund is to first calculate your total cost of purchasing all the shares you owned on the date of your redemption or switch. If you sold 100 shares of XYZ Fund on April 10, 1991, you would use the following simple formula to determine your average cost: AC = CP + DR divided by TS (AC = average cost, CP = cost of purchases, DR = distributions received, TS = total shares).

For example, assume that you spent $3,150 in purchasing your shares of XYZ Fund. During the period that you owned the shares, you received $275 in dividends and capital gains. Then on April 10, 1992, the date on which you redeemed 100 shares of XYZ Fund, you owned 250.25 shares, and you received $1,520 (NAV: $15.20 per share) for the shares you redeemed. Our formula looks like this:

Average cost: ($3,150 + $275) ÷ 250.25 = $13.69 avg. cost/share

The average cost of the shares sold was 100 × $13.69 = $1,369. Therefore, the capital gain would be $1,520 (amount received) minus $1,369 (average cost) equals $151: your capital gain on the transaction. If the shares were held for more than one year, the $151 is treated as a long-term capital gain for income tax purposes. A capital loss would be figured in exactly the same way. Both would have to be reported on Schedule D of your IRS return.

Capital Gains Tip

Avoid buying mutual funds just *prior* to the ex-dividend date (usually near the end of the year). This is the date on which a fund sells "ex" or without the dividend. On or after this date, the buyer receives the shares "ex" or without the dividend. You will be taxed on the gain as though you had use of it for the entire year. Secondly, since the NAV will be automatically decreased by the amount of the capital gains distribution, you gain nothing and have taxes to pay to boot.

It is better to buy just *after* the ex-dividend date. The NAV is reduced by the amount of the distribution. Therefore, your investment dollars will buy *more* shares, and you will avoid paying capital gains taxes on the distribution. Even if the fund performs well between the time you planned to buy and the distribution date, the extra tax is likely to exceed the gain.

Say, for example, you bought shares in a fund at $10 each just before a capital gains distribution of $1 per share. You will receive the $1 per share pay-out, but you will be no richer because the NAV will be reduced by an equal amount. So your $10 a share is still only worth $10 (the $9 NAV plus the $1 distribution you received). But you wind up *poorer,* because the $1 per share distribution represents *taxable* income to you.

A simple call to the fund's toll-free number will give you the ex-dividend date and the size of the distribution. If the distribution is very small, don't hesitate to buy. The effect on your taxes will be negligible. Base your decision on the amount of the distribution, the number of shares you own, and your tax bracket.

As this is not a book on tax reporting, I shall not go into the intricacies involved in filing your tax return. Your accountant, tax adviser, and/or the IRS Tax Information Booklet will provide that information. There are any number of fine books that will assist you in filing your tax return, as well as an excellent *free* publication from the IRS called "Your Federal Income Tax—Publication 17." An updated version is available each year. You may write for it, or call the IRS toll-free number 1-800-829-3676 to request it and other helpful, free tax preparation materials.

Form 1099–DIV

This form, which you will also receive by the end of January each year, reports to you *and* the IRS the amount of income you received from your fund's dividend distributions. You must report this amount on your tax return. If your dividends were paid to you from a tax-free fund, you are not required to pay federal taxes on the amount received; however, it must be reported. There is a line on the 1040 Income Tax form where you record the total amount of tax-free dividends received. It is not taxed or figured in with your earnings; therefore, it does not add to the amount of your income subject to federal taxes.*

You will receive a confirmation statement each time you receive dividends or capital gains distributions (or have them reinvested in your account, if this is your option). Save each statement you receive during the year until you receive the year-end statement; then dispose of the others. Be sure to save your year-end statements, however—they are very important for tax purposes and for evaluating your fund's overall performance. (The latter should be done at least once a year.)

TAX RELIEF WITH TAX-FREE MUTUAL FUNDS

Most investment companies offer tax-free mutual funds. Basically, the portfolios of these funds consist of municipal bonds. The volatility (riskiness) of "munis," as they are called, varies with the maturity dates of the bonds in the portfolio. Short-term municipal bond funds—up to four-year maturities—are the least volatile. Interme-

---

* It is figured on your SS at 85%.

diate-term bond funds—up to ten-year maturities—have greater price volatility and somewhat higher yields. Long-term bond funds—maturities up to thirty years—have the greatest price volatility and risk, but do have the highest yields. Your risk tolerance level will determine which you should choose. There are also *insured* tax-free municipal bond funds. The insurance protects you against default by the bond issuers. It does not insure the NAV of the fund, which will generally fluctuate with prevailing interest rates.

Municipal bond funds offer several advantages over taxable mutual funds. The tax advantages are obvious. Normally, you pay absolutely no federal taxes on dividends received or reinvested. There are other subtle tax savings that accrue. Consult with your accountant or tax adviser on these tax advantages.

The second major advantage obtained through tax-free mutual funds is their increased earning potential. For example, a tax-free fund yielding 6% would be equivalent to a taxable yield of 8.3% for someone in the 28% tax bracket (for someone in the 31% tax bracket, even higher: 8.7%). A low-risk, tax-free mutual fund yield of 7% (and there are many available) equals a taxable yield of 10.4% for the 28% taxpayer. If you are able to tolerate a fair degree of risk, there are some tax-free, high-yield, long-term mutual funds yielding 10%—the equivalent of a 13.9% taxable yield for the average taxpayer.

If you would like to work the figures out for yourself, here's the formula. To determine the equivalent *taxable yield* on a tax-free municipal bond mutual fund, divide the stated yield by 1.00 minus your tax bracket. Thus, for someone in the 31% tax bracket, a yield of only 6.5% from a tax-free mutual bond fund would be equivalent to 9.4% on a taxable fund. Here is the computation:

$$0.065 \text{ (fund yield): } 0.065 \div (1.00 - .31) = 9.4\%$$

You would have to earn 9.4% on a taxable investment to match the 6.5% on the tax-free fund (assuming the 31% tax bracket). See also Table 3–1.

What does this mean in actual dollars? Look at Figure 16–1. Assume you had invested $1,000 in this fund on January 2, 1985. By the end of 1990 your account would have grown to $1,849 as a result of reinvested dividends and capital appreciation. The fund

F I G U R E 16–1

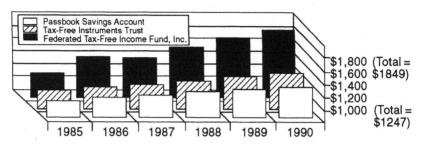

Compares the return on tax-exempt investments with the after-tax return on a passbook savings account at 5 percent. Assumes the initial investment of $1,000 on January 2, 1985, with dividends reinvested. Returns for passbook savings assume the same initial investment for an investor in the 28% tax bracket.

showed a total return of 6.5% for the five-year period. On the other hand, if you had put the same $1,000 in a taxable passbook account earning 5% interest compounded daily, the account would be worth only $1,247 after taxes, versus an account value of $1,849 for the Federated Tax-free Fund. Thus, at the end of the same five-year period, you would have earned a total of *$602 more* in the tax-free fund, or over $120 more *tax-free each year* on the same investment: two and a half times as much!

Many investors are turning to municipal bonds because of the tax advantages. However, individual municipal bonds usually are available in $5,000 denominations only. This makes it difficult for the novice investor to achieve much in the way of diversification. Further, municipal bond issuers have occasionally defaulted, and bond holders have lost their entire investment. While it is almost impossible to find an *individual* municipal bond that is insured against default, it is very easy to find *municipal bond funds* that are so insured.

Furthermore, no-load municipal bond funds will provide excellent diversification. Their portfolios will consist of *many* bonds; therefore, a greater degree of safety is assured—much more than you will ever get in an individual municipal bond. In addition, you will have the benefit of professional management. As I advise throughout this book, stick with mutual funds: they are practically the only financial investments that merit your complete trust.

FIGURE 16–2

Effect of Federal Income Taxes on Yields of Tax-exempt and Taxable Instruments

	7$\frac{1}{2}$% Tax-exempt Bond	9$\frac{1}{4}$% Taxable Investment	Stock Paying 4% Dividend
Cash Investment	$30,000	$30,000	$30,000
Interest	2,250	2,775	1,200
Federal income tax in the 33% marginal tax bracket	0	915.75	396
Net return	$2,250	$1,859.25	$804
Yield on investment after taxes	7.5%	6.2%	2.7%

*the top marginal tax rate effective 1994. Currently it is 39.6%.

Figure 16–2 provides additional verification, if you still require it, of the valuable benefits of tax-free mutual fund investing.

There are some who maintain that federally tax-free mutual funds are only for taxpayers in the top tax brackets. This is not true. A taxpayer in any bracket at today's rates will find some after-tax benefit in owning tax-free municipal bond mutual funds. Until tax rates take a substantial drop, or the IRS adopts a flat-tax system, tax-free municipal bond funds will offer the average taxpayer a definite tax break.

In comparing return on investment, always look at the *after-tax* return. That is the only way you can get a true sense of how much will finally end up in your pocket as a *net profit.*

STUDY GUIDE FOR CHAPTER 16

1. Mutual funds do not pay taxes on their earnings. Why?
2. What two kinds of earnings do holders of mutual funds generally receive?
3. Is all income received by shareholders of tax-free mutual funds nontaxable?

4. What is the purpose of the 1099-B form?
5. List the four ways that may be used to calculate tax liability for capital gains or (losses).
6. What does the form 1099-DIV show?
7. What determines the risk level of municipal bond funds?
8. What are the advantages to be realized by owning tax-free municipal bond funds?
9. Why is it important to know the "after tax" return on your funds?

P O S T S C R I P T   16–1

YEAR-END TAX FORMS SCHEDULE

Mutual fund shareholders should receive a tax form for any taxable income distributed by their funds, for any redemptions, and for switches (which are the same as redemptions) that took place during the year and may have resulted in capital gains or (losses). Tax forms for the previous year should reach you *by the end of January.* If you fail to receive the necessary forms by February 15, call your mutual fund's toll-free number and report the problem. Duplicate forms will be provided.

1999 TAX UPDATES

The chart below describes the types of tax forms you may receive from your mutual fund companies. In addition to sending the forms to shareholders, they are also sent to the Internal Revenue Service (IRS). The taxpayer prepares and sends Schedule D to the IRS.

FORM	WHO WILL RECEIVE
1099-DIV	Shareholders who earned $10 or more in taxable dividends or capital gains distributions (whether taken in cash or reinvested)
1099-B	Shareholders who redeemed or exchanged shares from a taxable account in 1999. May also include average cost basis information
1099-R	Shareholders who received distributions from retirement accounts (IRAs)
1099-INT	Investors who received interest from bank accounts, CDs, annuities, etc.
Schedule D (this form is secured from	Must be filed if you realized capital gains or capital (losses) from any sources.

P O S T S C R I P T   16–2

FEDERAL INCOME TAX CHANGES APPROVED

The oft-proposed and long-awaited tax changes are finally to become a reality. President George W. Bush has signed into law sweeping changes in the Federal Income Tax laws. The most *immediate* effect is the creation of a 10% income tax rate retroactive to January 1, 2001.

Rebates

The Treasury Department will mail taxpayers' rebate checks beginning in the year 2001. An individual will receive $300, a single parent $500, and a married couple $600. Rebates are not linked to income.

Tax Rates

Rate cuts begin July 1, 2001. The new 10% tax rate applies to the first $6,000 of taxable income for single persons, and $12,000 for married couples filing jointly. The present 39.6% top tax rate drops to 35% by 2006. Other rates drop gradually, and by 2006 the 36% rate will drop to 35%, the 31% rate to 28%, and the 28% rate will drop to 25%. The 15% rate will not change. Income limits on itemized deductions will be adjusted upward beginning in 2006. Personal exemption phase-out repealed gradually beginning in 2006.

Child Credit

Child credit rises from $500 to $600, effective in 2001, meaning it could be claimed on 2001's tax returns. The credit rises to $700 in 2005, $800 in 2009, and $1,000 in 2010. Taxpayers earning more than $10,000 could claim a credit of 10% of earnings, rising to 15% over time, above that income level. They cannot claim the credit now.

Marriage Penalty

The standard deduction for married couples will be gradually raised so that it is equal to twice that of single taxpayers. If it were to be in effect this year, the deduction would be $9,100 instead of $7,600 for married coulples. The 15% tax rate will be gradually enlarged so it applies to more of a married couple's income, equal to twice that of singles. If it were fully in effect in 2001, the deduction would be $9,100 instead of $7,600 for married coulples. The 15% tax rate will be gradually enlarged so it applies to more of a married couple's income, equal to twice that of singles. If it were to be in effect in 2001, the lowest tax rate would apply to $54,100 of a couple's income instead of $45,200. The income limit for earned income tax credit will be expanded by $3,000 and fully phased in by 2008.

Estate Tax
The tax will be repealed in 2010. The top 55% rate will be immediately dropped to 45%. The current $675,000 individual exemption will be raised to $1 million in 2002, $1.5 million in 2004, $2.6 million in 2009. The tax on certain gifts will be retained, but the rate will be reduced to 40%.

Retirement
Tax-favored contribution limits for individual retirement accounts and Roth IRAs will be gradually raised from $2,000 to $5,000. No change in income limits. Tax-deferred contribution limits for 401(k)-type plans gradually increased from $10,500 to $15,000.

Education
Maximum $5,000 deduction for higher education tuition will be lowered to $2,000 for incomes between $130,000 and $160,000. Phases out above that level. Limitation on deductibility of student loan interest removed. Contribution limit for tax-favored education savings accounts raised from $500 to $2,000.

Source: The Associated Press

CUTTING YOUR CAPITAL GAINS TAX

If you are going to sell a winner, you most likely want to pay the least amount of taxes possible. As a general rule, try to sell long-term winners (those held over 12 months) first to benefit from the new, lower 20% maximum capital gains rate.

If you are not in a loss position, think twice about selling shares held for 12 months or less because of the higher short-term rate which could be as high as 39.6%, depending on your regular income tax bracket.

Another way to reduce capital gains taxes is to sell the underperformers in your portfolio as early as feasible, rather than wait until January. Under federal tax law, if you have some clear loss leaders in your portfolio, you can sell enough shares of these losers to wipe out all of your realized capital gains for the year plus up to $3,000 in regular income ($1,500 if married and filing separately). A note of caution: If you are selling a loser to offset capital gains, you cannot buy the same security within 30 days before or after the sale. In that situation "wash sale" tax rules will disallow the loss. So far so good, but which losers should get the boot? Remember, you can always buy the fund back after 30 days in order to avoid the wash sale restrictions, but you have to be comfortable with being out of the market for that period of time.

To get the most out of your losses, you may want to sell short-term losses. Your short-term losses will offset any of the more expensive short-term gains, which, again, are taxed at your regular income tax rate. Any short-term losses left over will then offset long-term gains (maximum 20% tax rate), and lastly up to $3,000 of regular income.

On the flip side, long-term losers first offset long-term gains (20%), then short-term gains, and lastly, up to $3,000 of regular income. If you are still confused, you may want to consult your accountant, tax preparer, or financial planner.

Calculating Capital Gains

Assets held for period of	Maximum Capital Gains Tax Rates
12 months or less	39.6%
More than 12 months but less than 60 months	20%
More than 60 months (and acquired after 2000)	18%

CAPITAL GAINS TAX ADDENDUM

At the end of every year your mutual fund company will send you a statement showing the amount of capital gains and dividends that were distributed during the year. In addition, it sends you IRS tax forms, either a 1099-DIV, a 1099, or both, even if you reinvested all the distributions. *Do not forget, the IRS receives copies of these forms also.*

In addition to the capital gains that the fund may have distributed, you may have redeemed shares worth more when you redeemed them than they cost when you purchased them, resulting in *additional* capital gains you earned. If, on the other hand, the shares were worth *less* when you redeemed them than when you purchased them, you have a capital loss. Remember also, if you *switch* shares out of one fund into another, the switch is considered a redemption of shares from the fund which you switched out of, and therefore may also result in a capital gain or capital loss.

Capital gains are taxed generally at 20% if the investment was held for one year or more (long-term gain). If the investment was held for less than one full year, the gain is treated as a short-term gain and is taxed at your regular tax rate (15%, 28%, 31%, 36%, or 39.6%). Capital gains and capital losses are reported on Schedule D of your tax return. Capital losses can be used to offset capital gains up to $3,000 per year. If your capital losses exceeded $3,000, you may carry the excess over to succeeding years until it is completely written off. (NOTE: Capital gains tax legislation is pending, therefore, check for any changes in the law which may occur during or after 1995.)

However, it is possible that you may owe no capital gains tax if either of the following situations apply to you:

1. Your capital losses exceed your capital gains.
2. Your overall tax deductions are high enough so you are not required to pay *any* taxes. Remember, however, you must file a tax return even though you may owe no taxes.

Be sure to complete a Schedule D showing all capital gains and losses, even though it turns out that you owe *no taxes* for either of the above two reasons. Failure to report will get you into a lot of trouble. Maintain careful records, in the event that you are audited.

Dividends and interest you may have received are reported on Schedules A and B, not on Schedule D. I hope all the above will be helpful, because if you apply what you learn from this book, I am sure that you *will have* capital gains to report.

THREE METHODS OF CALCULATING CAPITAL GAINS TAXES (Assuming shares were held more than one year)

Note: Capital gains taxes on shares held *more* than one year are currently taxed at 20%. This is the new IRS long-term rate adopted in 1998 for shares held more than one year.

Capital gains taxes on shares held *less* than one year are taxed at the taxpayer's *regular tax* bracket—15% to 39.6%—since they are considered short-term gains. There are three IRS-accepted-methods of calculating capital gains taxes. Each is illustrated below.

Example of a Shareholder's Mutual Fund Account

Date	Action	Cost
12/10/96	Bought 1,000 shares at $10 per share	$10,000
6/1/97	Reinvested $1.50 dividend per share at $13.50 per share on 1,000 shares this purchased 111.111 additional shares	$1,500
12/1/97	Bought 1,000 shares at $18 per share	$18,000
4/15/98	Sold 1,000 shares at 20 per share received $20,000	
	Total cost of the 2111.111 shares	$29,500

Tax Consequences of Each Method When Used to Calculate Capital Gains Taxes (using the example account shown above)

FIFO (First in–first out) (The IRS loves this method! It's the most costly!)

First 1,000 shares at $10 per share	$10,000
Sold 1,000 shares at $20 per share	$20,000 proceeds
Net gain	$10,000
Tax on long-term capital gain at 20%	$2,000

Average Cost Method

First 1,000 shares at 10 per share	$10,000
Dividend of $1.50 per share × 1,000 shares	$1,500
at $13.50 per share: the $1,500 purchased 111.111 shares	
Next 1,000 shares at $18 per share	$18,000
TOTAL COST	$29,500

Average cost per share = $29,500 divided by 2111.111 = $13.97
Average cost of $13.97 per share × 1,000 shares = $13,970

Sold 1,000 shares at $20 per share = $20,000 − $13,970	$6,030
Tax on long-term capital gain at 20%	$1,206

Specific Shares Method

Sold 1,000 shares costing $18,000 on 12/1/97 at $20 per share	$20,000
Net capital gain = $2,000 ($20,000 − $18,000 = $2,000)	
Tax on $2,000 capital gain at 20%	$400

P O S T S C R I P T   16–6

DON'T "BUY" A DIVIDEND

It is important to know the exact date on which a mutual fund is scheduled to make any substantial distributions such as may be the case when year-end capital gains distributions are to be paid to shareholders of record. Armed with this information, it is possible to avoid "buying a dividend." (*Note:* the following does not apply to tax-deferred investments such as IRAs, 401(k) plans, etc.) However, for investors who must pay taxes on distributions whether they are reinvested or received in cash, keeping an eye on end-of-the-year distribution dates can mean a substantial tax saving in the spring.

Let's examine the following scenario in order to see exactly why it is to one's advantage to avoid "buying a dividend." On December 20, 1993, the Vanguard Explorer Fund paid a $5.24 per share capital gain distribution (true fact). This meant if you were a shareholder on that date you would receive the distribution. To make the math easier, let's assume that the fund also paid a $.01 per share income dividend for a total distribution of $5.25.

Jim, investor # 1, liked the Vanguard Explorer Fund, but didn't know when the fund was to declare its year-end distributions. He therefore, made his investment of $3,000* in the Explorer Fund on December 19, 1993, the day before the distribution. That means that Jim will receive the distribution. On December 12, 1993, Explorer shares had an NAV of $45.00. Jim received 66.667 shares for his $3,000. The very next day, the Explorer Fund paid out the $5.25 per share distribution, and Jim received his $350 distribution (66.667 shares × $5.25) which he wisely had reinvested. However, because of the distribution, Explorer's share price (NAV) dropped by $5.25 to $39.75. (We will assume that Explorer Fund's portfolio experienced no other changes that day.) Jim's reinvestment bought him an additional 8.805 shares ($350 divided by $39.75). He now owns a total of 75.472 shares of the Explorer Fund.

Jane, Investor # 2, on the other hand, knew about the distribution date and invests her $3,000 in the Explorer Fund *the day after* the distributions were made, i.e., December 21, 1993. Therefore, she did not receive the $5.25 distribution, however, her $3,000 buys shares at the new NAV of $39.75 for a total of 75.472 shares. Jane and Jim have both

---

* Minimum initial investment for the Explorer Fund

invested the exact same amounts, and each has the exact same number of shares in the Explorer Fund.

However, Jane is in much better shape. Jim, who invested before the ex-dividend date will have to pay over $100 in taxes ($108.50 to be exact) on the $350 distribution he received (31% tax bracket). Jane who invested after the ex-dividend date has no tax liability, and yet has the same number of shares as Jim. It really pays to wait!!

A SCENARIO BASED ON THE NEW 20% CAPITAL GAINS TAX FOLLOWS*:

Consider the example of the imaginary XYZ fund, a no-load fund with an NAV of $10 a share when you invest $10,000 on December 14.

A day later, the fund goes "ex-distribution" for a payout of $2 a share, reducing the NAV to $8 (no other changes occurred in the fund that day).

You have arranged, like most investors, to have your fund distributions automatically reinvested. So the $2,000 you get on your new investment is plowed back into additional shares at the $8 price, and your investment is still worth $10,000

Come income tax time, you will have a $2,000 gain to report. Assuming you are in the 20% bracket for long-term capital gains, you will owe Uncle Sam $400, not to mention any state or local taxes that may apply.

You can avoid these taxes by ducking the distribution, and instead making your $10,000 investment afterward at the $8 NAV.

---

*Scenario # 2 is from the Associated Press

TURNING MUTUAL FUND LOSSES INTO TAX BREAKS

Stock market slumps prompt a great number of investors to dump their losing investments. When large numbers of people decide to bail out in fear of sustaining even greater losses during bear markets, it impacts the market unfavorably. Wall Street analysts attribute a great part of the market's pullback to *year-end, tax-loss selling.*

What should you do when faced with the badly slumping mutual funds in your portfolio? Since you cannot control the market, begin to weed out those funds that are dragging down the *returns* on your portfolio. Toward the end of the year is generally a good time to sell or switch your losers. This strategy enables you to realize tax losses, which will serve to minimize the taxes you would ordinarily have to pay on the distributions that most mutual funds normally make in December.

Capital gains and losses are reported on Schedule D of your tax return. When preparing your Schedule D keep in mind that up to *$3,000 in capital losses* may be used to *offset capital gains,* dividends, salary, and any other income you may have received. Losses in excess of $3,000 (hopefully you will not be faced with that problem) can be carried forward to future years. Therefore, if you have a fund that is selling for less than you paid for it (within the guidelines described in the book) selling in late November or early December can yield some extra tax deductions. In essence, this strategy makes it possible to recoup some of your investment losses.

Another strategy might be to sell shares of a fund that shows *steady losses* over a *three-month period.* You can write off the loss at tax time. The proceeds from the sale of the shares that you sold should be deposited in a mutual fund *money market.* This will maintain your investment position and protect your principal against further erosion.

Later, you can repurchase the same fund if it has gone up again. However, you must wait *30 days* in order to repurchase the *same fund* or another fund having *similar characteristics* to the fund that you sold, otherwise the IRS will consider it a "wash sale" and deny your tax deduction.

The only risk in using the above strategy is that the fund you sold may *rebound* during the 30 day waiting period. However, don't fret over the potential gain you may have missed. Remember, your money market shares will have earned very generous interest during the month, thus moderating any serious risk to your earnings.

CHAPTER 17

Developing a
Model Portfolio

FOUR-STEP PROGRAM

Figure 17–1 depicts a model portfolio that the novice investor would be wise to work toward developing. It represents a long-term, balanced, step-by-step plan for growth and income. The representative funds listed in the upper left side of the chart have been selected from just two highly regarded investment companies' funds (Vanguard and Fidelity) and are to be used for the final phase in the development of your model portfolio. Vanguard is strictly a no-load company. Fidelity offers both load and no-load funds. Remember, these are only suggestions; there are hundreds of other investment companies that offer equally worthwhile funds from which to choose.

The four-step program consists of:

Step One: Goal Setting
Step Two: Asset Distribution
Step Three: Sector Distribution
Step Four: Mutual Fund Selections

Setting objectives is fundamental to all successful investment programs. Before buying a single fund, you, as an investor, must decide on both your short- and long-term objectives. Being without objectives is like being a ship without a rudder. You will not be able to steer a course that will enable you to reach your destination. As noted in the very first chapter of this book, mutual fund investing is not a "get-rich-quick scheme." It is therefore important to keep your sights on long-term objectives. Even during the *early* stages in the development of your portfolio, your decisions should be based on your long-term goals.

Goal setting should not be based on the belief that you will achieve *dramatic* results overnight, or even in a year or two. Plan on reaching your *ultimate* objectives in no less than five to ten years. With this in mind, you can expect to achieve annualized returns of 15% to 20% compounded over any five-year period, especially if the suggestions presented in Chapter 12 are followed consistently.

MAKING ADJUSTMENTS

The percentages projected in Figure 17–1 are flexible and should be adjusted to meet your particular needs and objectives. The examples shown in Figure 17–2 are meant to show long-term goals, and should be developed gradually as finances permit.

As the examples illustrate, retirees would be wise to increase the percentage of income-producing funds shown in Figure 17–2 in order to ensure enough steady, sufficient income to maintain their accustomed lifestyles. On the other hand, a young couple looking at the long-term picture (15 to 20 years to retirement) would be justified in assuming a higher risk level and, therefore, increasing the percentages allocated to growth funds.

Allocating specific percentages does not mean that changes cannot be made as financial and personal conditions change. Continuous monitoring of your portfolio (as described in Chapter 13) is a must, even with the best of portfolio allocations.

IMPLEMENTATION

When selecting the actual mutual funds to be used in assembling your model portfolio, proceed slowly, according to the guidelines outlined in the preceding chapters. As a novice, avoid buying more funds than you are able to monitor. Give yourself time to do the job properly. Rome wasn't build in a day—nor will be your model portfolio.

Developing a Model Portfolio

Money Market Funds: 10%
Fund 1: Vanguard Money Market - Federal Portfolio
Fund 2: Fidelity Cash Reserves

Fixed Income Funds: 25%
Fund 3: Vanguard U.S. Treasury Bond Portfolio
Fund 4: Fidelity Capital & Income Fund
Fund 5: Vanguard GNMA Portfolio

Equity Income Funds: 20%
Fund 6: Vanguard Wellington Fund
Fund 7: Fidelity Ginnie Mae Portfolio

Conservative Growth Funds: 35%
Fund 8: Vanguard Index Trust Portfolio
Fund 9: Vanguard U.S. Growth Portfolio
Fund 10: Fidelity Megellan Fund

Aggressive Growth Funds: 10%
Fund 11: Vanguard Explorer Fund
Fund 12: Fidelity Medical Delivery Fund

Step One
Goal Setting

Balanced/Diversified
Portfolio

Step Two
Asset
Distribution

10% Liquid
45% Income
45% Growth

Step Three
Sector
Distribution

10% Money Market
25% Fixed Income
20% Equity Income
35% Conservative Growth
10% Aggressive Growth

Step Four
Mutual Fund
Selections

10% M.M.   25% F.I.   20% E.I.   35% C.G.
Fund 1   Fund 3   Fund 6   Fund 8
Fund 2   Fund 4   Fund 7   Fund 9
            Fund 5   Fund 10

10% A.G.
Fund 11
Fund 12

FIGURE 17–2

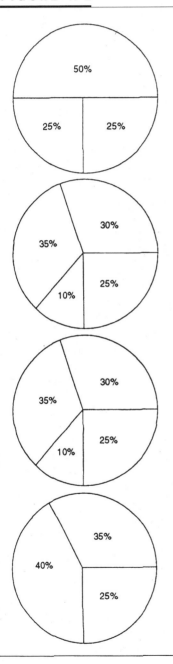

1. A young single professional might set up a portfolio with 50% in several aggressive equity funds, 25% split between high-yield bond funds and growth and income funds; and the remaining 25% in conservative money market funds.

2. A young couple with two incomes and one or two children might consider a slightly different portfolio, consisting of a 10% investment in a tax-free money market, 30% in aggressive equity funds, 25% in moderately aggressive funds such as high-yield bond funds and long-term growth funds, and the remaining 35% allocated to long-term municipal bond funds.

3. An older couple with a single income should be moving toward a more conservative, income oriented position in order to preserve their capital and reduce their tax liabilities. In this case, 30% might be invested in short-term, tax-free municipal funds, 35% in a moderately conservative fund concentrating on longer-term municipal obligations, 25% in a moderately aggressive equity fund which emphasizes growth, and 10% in an equity fund focused on emerging growth companies.

4. A recently retired couple should be thinking of capital preservation and current income as their objectives. With these goals in mind, 35% of their investment should be in strictly conservative equity funds for capital preservation and income, no more than 25% in moderately aggressive funds for estate planning and modest capital growth, and the remaining 40% invested in money market funds.

There are a half-dozen broad guidelines to make certain that you are providing for high levels of safety, diversification, and performance in the funds you select for your portfolio:

1. Preferably, select no-load funds.
2. Invest only in funds that have been in operation for at least five years.
3. Choose funds that regularly show an expense ratio of 1% or less.
4. Check the fund's track record. Has it consistently outperformed similar funds for at least a year or more?
5. Pick funds whose managers have better-than-average track records over a period of years.
6. Buy funds that are large enough in size (assets of at least $100 million) to offset sudden sell-offs.

STUDY GUIDE FOR CHAPTER 17

1. What are the four steps in creating a model portfolio?
2. Based on your personal goals and needs, describe a suitable asset distribution for your own mutual fund portfolio.
3. What steps should be taken before buying any funds for your portfolio?
4. How might it be possible to achieve annualized yields of from 15% to 20%?
5. What circumstances might cause you to wish to change the allocation of your portfolio's funds?
6. How can you ensure safety and high performance for your own portfolio?

HOW TO BUILD A WINNING PORTFOLIO

1. *Establish Your Goals* What do you want to get out of your portfolio? By explicitly defining your goals, even to the point of writing them down, you establish two critical elements: When you'll need the money, and how much you will need. The important thing is to estimate the amount of money you will need in the time frame you have established. Then you can either develop a plan to give you the necessary capital or, as may be necessary, adjust your goals to a more realistic level.

2. *Assess Your Finances* You now know where you want to go and when you want to get there. Now it's time to determine what you have to work with.

   First, make a list of all your liquid assets: cash, stocks, bonds, funds, etc. Then list your short-term debts. Subtract the liabilities from the assets to determine your net liquid worth. Next, examine your income and expenses, and track your spending for at least a month. You may be surprised to see that a significant portion of your earnings are wasted on frivolous pursuits that could be converted to savings instead.

3. *Determine Your Risk Tolerance* Assessing your risk tolerance may be the single most important decision you can make regarding your investments. If retirement is your goal, you need to take as much risk as necessary to avoid outliving your capital. Younger investors can usually be more aggressive, because they have more time to ride out the rough spots in the market. But older investors shouldn't get timid and put 100% of their assets in money market funds the minute they turn 65. (Of course, if more risk today means an ulcer tomorrow, forget it; it's not worth it!)

4. *Make Taxes Work for You* Know your marginal tax rate. This will help you decide whether taxable or tax-free investments are best suited for your portfolio. (Bond funds and money market funds are available as either taxable funds or tax-free funds.)

5. *Define Your Strategy* In the mutual fund arena, most investors commonly use four strategies: fund timing, market timing, dollar-cost averaging, or buy and hold. One of mutual fund investors' more common mistakes is failing to stick with

a plan. Long-term winners are invariably those investors that define an approach and adhere to it consistently over the long term.

6. *Diversify* Mutual funds are the embodiment of diversification. In addition, you have got to think of asset allocation—another form of diversification. The premise: Funds perform well at different times, providing balance to an investment portfolio. The driving force in building a winning portfolio is getting the asset allocation right.

7. *Education* If financial experts agree on anything, it is this: Do your homework. Fortunately, we live in an information age. Go to the library, dig up some information on the different types of funds, and really look at what they are all about. Look at more than just the return. Look at the risk they are assuming. Look at the manager's tenure and the rating he or she has earned over the years. Also look at the expense ratios, and the load, and evaluate all those things. Naturally, you should also examine the prospectus carefully of any fund in which you might consider investing.

8. *Put Your Plan into Action* Having acquainted yourself with the necessary background of information, you can now do business with no-load fund families directly and avoid fees and commissions.

9. *Maintenance* The pros say you should sit down every six to 12 months to review your master plan and your progress toward your goals. At this time, it would be wise to reconfigure your investments in order to maintain your allocation. The individual investments in your portfolio grow at varying rates, causing your portfolio to change shape over time; hence the need for rebalancing it at regular intervals. Maintaining your fund portfolio is as important as keeping up with the repairs and maintenance of your home or car. In both cases you preserve the value of your investment.

TRYING TO TIME THE MARKET

At one time or another, investors may be tempted to try to outguess the stock market by aggressively shifting assets from equity funds to cash (money market funds) in anticipation of a market downturn, and then back again to stock funds just before the upturn. Fortunately, most mutual fund investors realize that such a strategy is not likely to succeed over the long run. Studies have shown how risky it can be. That's because it is absolutely impossible to *accurately* predict the *short-term* swings in the market.

Figure 17–3 shows how much lower the return on $1.00 would have been if an investor missed some of the best days to be in the market between 1963 and 1993. For example, if the investor missed just 90 of the best days, or only 1.2% of the total trading days, the $1.00 invested would have grown to only $2.10. That is well below the $24.30 of a buy-and-hold strategy, and certainly less than would have been earned on one month Treasury bills. Further, in this case the in-

F I G U R E   17–3

THE RISK OF MARKET TIMING: 1963–1993
Value of $1.00 invested at the start of the period

Entire 31-Year Period (7,802 Trading Days)

$24.30

Miss 10 Best Days

$15.40

Miss 40 Best Days

$6.50

Miss 60 Best Days

$4.10

Miss 90 Best Days

$2.10

vestor would have incurred 93.5% *more risk* than the risk posed by U.S. Treasury bills.

The data show that the returns from trying to be an outstanding market timer are most likely to be even less than simply owning Treasury bills. This does not mean that investors should necessarily keep all or most of their assets in stock mutual funds; a portfolio should always be diversified. But a disciplined, *long-term approach* for that portion of the portfolio committed to *equity funds* clearly pays off.

CHAPTER 18

Is Mutual Fund Investing for Me?

Before you attempt to answer that question with a yes, ask yourself:

1. Is my income sufficient to meet basic needs (food, clothing, and shelter)?
2. Is my insurance coverage (life, health, and casualty) adequate?
3. Am I in a position to assume some level of financial risk?
4. Would my savings enable me to take care of emergencies?
5. Am I able to put aside a portion of my income on a regular basis?

Assuming that you are able to answer yes to these questions, you are definitely ready to assume a strong position in the world of mutual fund investing. Every day you delay is a day of lost opportunity.

SUMMING UP

A note of caution is perhaps in order at this point. Never plunge; start your investment program on a gradual basis. By following the guidelines offered in this book, you will be ready to take advantage of the investment opportunities that present themselves. Remember: *You must invest, if your fortune is to grow.*

As a further incentive to starting an investment program, consider the statistics shown in Figure 18–1. The chart shows how mutual funds fared during the *recessionary period* of the early nineties. The figures shown on the chart are as of May 1991.

If mutual funds can produce the kinds of gains shown in Figure 18–1 during a deep recession, just imagine the growth potential during periods of prosperity. Over the years, mutual funds have proved to be the safest and most reliable investment medium during good times *and* bad.

In Chapter 12, "Strategies to Maximize Return on Investment," it was pointed out that too many investors, especially novices, tend to "fall in love" with their portfolios. They hold on to them without

F I G U R E 18–1

How Mutual Funds Fared—Mutual Fund Performance
for Periods Ended May 30, 1993

Type of fund (no. of funds)	Total return[1]		
General stock funds	Week	1991	12 mos.
Capital appreciation (146)	+2.82%	+22.40%	+8.79%
Equity-income (73)	+2.44%	+15.25%	+8.65%
Growth (275)	+2.77%	+21.47%	+10.04%
Growth and income (217)	+2.78%	+18.10%	+9.97%
Small-company growth (91)	+3.07%	+29.79%	+11.03%
Gen. stock fund avg. (802)	+2.79%	+21.13%	+9.78%
Specialized funds			
Balanced funds (61)	+2.01%	+12.91%	+10.87%
European region funds (22)	+0.45%	+2.68%	−8.52%
Fixed income (561)	+0.42%	+6.29%	+10.23%
Gold funds (37)	+4.55%	−4.95%	−16.36%
Health/biotechnology (9)	+2.66%	+35.19%	+46.31%
International funds (68)	+0.55%	+9.28%	−3.72%
Pacific region funds (18)	−0.12%	+14.17%	−1.66%
Science & technology (21)	+3.43%	+26.48%	+9.09%
Utility funds (23)	+0.64%	+6.04%	+10.07%

[1]Total return is the change in price plus all dividends and capital gains reinvested.
Source: Lipper Analytical Services Inc.

determining whether their investments are productive, and if they are not, what to do about it.

You must not become lazy or complacent. Buying mutual funds puts you in the investment business. Therefore, just as in any business, *you must take charge.* You must determine if your business is profitable, is stagnating, or losing money. Then, based on your findings, you must take *some* kind of action—whether to buy, sell, or hold. As the chief executive officer of your business, the decisions are yours and yours alone to make.

Throughout this book, suggestions have been presented to help you make the decisions necessary to maintain a position of *profitability.* Isn't that the reason you are planning to invest in mutual funds in the first place?

Let me offer an analogy which, hopefully, will make my point.

I trust that in the interest of your physical health you visit your physician at least annually for a medical examination and that you visit your dentist semiannually. It's equally important to conduct a periodic checkup of your investment program to help keep it in tip-top condition.

You should by now have your own measures for determining the "health" of your investment plan, but here are some critical signs you may wish to evaluate.

Objective

Make sure your fund's objectives as stated in the prospectus still suit your specific financial goals. (See Chapter 3.)

Performance

Compare your fund's total returns (distributions plus change in NAV) with other funds having the same objectives over time periods that cover bull as well as bear markets. (See Chapter 13.)

Risk

How much does the fund's NAV fluctuate? Do you lose sleep over it? (See Chapter 6.)

Cost

Check the "Summary of Fund Expenses" found in the fund's latest prospectus. Understand that escalating fees, charges, and expenses will reduce the return on your investment. (See Chapter 15.)

Service

Make sure the fund continues to offer all the services you need. (See Chapter 14.)

Tracking Your Investments

Lastly, novice investors have a tendency to watch over their investments on a daily basis. Checking once a week is sufficient. Remember, however, whatever your investment goals may be—income, growth, or a combination of both—periodic checking *is necessary.* Do not skip fund-tracking altogether, but don't overdo it either. Think long-term!

When you have mastered the fundamentals presented in this book, you will be ready for the more complex aspects of mutual fund investing. Books for the advanced investor are plentiful, but they only tend to confuse if used during the beginning stages of your investing adventure.

If some aspects of mutual fund investing remain unclear, do not hesitate to reread chapters of this book that relate to your still unanswered questions. Now that you have completed a first reading, rereading will reinforce the many important concepts presented throughout this book.

May you become a prosperous investor and a happy one! Good hunting and good luck.

STUDY GUIDE FOR CHAPTER 18

1. Before you initiate a mutual fund investment program, what questions should you answer?
2. Why should you start your investment program on a gradual basis?

3. Are mutual funds able to perform satisfactorily during periods of recession?

4. How often should you monitor your portfolio?

5. What are some of the critical signs to be aware of in measuring a fund's suitability for your portfolio?

6. How do you go about ensuring a position of profitability for your portfolio?

7. If you haven't already done so, would you now begin a mutual fund investment program? Why?

INVESTING RULE

Too frequently investors tend to think in terms of fixed-rate investments when they plan to rely on investment earnings as a major source of income. Obviously the logic behind this is understandable. Fixed-rate investments make sense because they generate a predictable amount of income. This is reassuring and convenient for budgeting.

But important factors are overlooked in this type of thinking, namely the effects of inflation and fluctuating interest rates. If the dollar amount you need for living expenses would always stay the same over the years—as does the dollar amount of your fixed income—there would be no problem. But, in reality, the number of dollars you need goes up as inflation increases your expenses. If interest rates go down, you may have to reinvest the principal of your maturing fixed-rate investment (such as a CD or a bond) at a lower current interest rate.

Reinvesting dividends, which compounds the growth of the investment, is the only way to produce growth in a fixed income investment. If the dividend is spent instead of being reinvested, then the growth potential is *gone.* Further, if you were investing in fixed-rate items in order to produce needed or spendable income, you would not be able to reinvest the dividends, since you need the income. Thus, *your principal would continue to erode until you lost your entire source of needed income.*

However, adding mutual funds invested in securities adds the potential for growth plus dividend income, which may be spent without eroding the principal of your portfolio. There are countless mutual funds whose objective is to create *growth and income.* Mutual funds with a portfolio of stocks have consistently outpaced inflation and reaped higher long-term returns. Of course, how much of your total retirement portfolio is allocated to this type of investment depends on your *personal risk tolerance.* Stock mutual funds do fluctuate. But they do invariably overcome the disadvantages of fixed-income investments when held for the long term (three to five years). Lastly, in my opinion, you should continue to invest in stock-based mutual funds *even after you retire.*

MY PERSONAL PHILOSOPHY REGARDING INVESTING

1. We *all* need a sound, long-term retirement plan. Social Security and company pension plans alone are not sufficient to maintain one's preretirement lifestyle and to offset the effects of inflation.

2. As a rule of thumb, for every two years you put off investing, you may need to almost double your monthly investing amount to achieve the same retirement income. This is especially true the closer you are to retirement.

3. Choose investments with a level of risk that makes you feel comfortable and that are appropriate for your long-term goals.

4. I believe in the wealth-generating power of mutual funds whose portfolios consist of the stocks of growth-oriented companies. Over time, stocks have outperformed all other investments and compensated for inflation. Keep in mind, however, that stocks present greater risks.

5. Cash, bonds, and CDs don't grow, they only pay interest. I include fixed-income investments and money market mutual funds in my portfolio only for diversification and liquidity.

6. Investing requires patience and the discipline to hold on to or add to investments through down markets as well as up markets.

7. For more consistent and reliable outcomes, use asset allocation and mutual funds to create a broadly diversified portfolio—spreading risk over a variety of investments.

8. Investing doesn't stop when you retire. To make your money continue to work for you, don't shift all of your money automatically into fixed-income and money market investments too early.

Note: Chapter 6 covered the risk-reducing potential of diversification. Think about the following when investing in mutual funds.

Can you name all the different stocks in which you are invested? Before you start, don't forget to count all those you own through your mutual funds. For example, if you owned the Fidelity Value Fund, there would be 284 names you'd need to tick off. If you own the Vanguard S&P Index 500 Fund, it might take you at least 15 minutes to name all 500 stocks you own in this one fund. There are mutual funds that have portfolios invested in *all the stocks* in the United States. Don't even *try* to name the approximately 10,000 stocks in such a portfolio. *Now that's Diversification with a capital D!*

SERIOUS INVESTMENT ERRORS YOU CAN'T AFFORD TO MAKE

It is a known fact that most investors fail to make any money over any given five-year period, simply because they make all or most of the errors noted below:

1. *Investors have no financial goals. Without a goal you don't know where to start, which course to take, or where to go next.* No plan can be adopted, no results can be measured, any investment, therefore, can be good or bad. Without a goal you can't know! The effect is like sailing a ship without a compass. Sooner or later such a ship will founder.

2. *Investors do not understand the laws of compounded growth. If they did, more investors would be wealthy.* Over time, compounding converts small sums of money into a fortune. The fastest way to wealth is to make consistent gains, adding profit on top of principal, all steadily compounding over the long term.

3. *Investors follow complex and inappropriate strategies. It is important to consider just how much time you can devote to your investment strategy.* If you can follow a difficult strategy, if the risks are tolerable, if you have enough money to make it work, if you have the patience and emotional strength to see it through—you may succeed. On the other hand, if it causes too much anxiety, or family disharmony, you may have to abandon it. Abandoning difficult and stressful strategies is often the cause of investor failure.

4. *Investors are greedy, impatient, unwilling to work for long-term results.* In attempting to make a fast buck, you are likely to get a fat loss. Remember the Aesop fable of the tortoise and the hare. The moral of this story is extremely valuable to investors.

5. *Investors are influenced by, and act upon, what they read in the financial press.* The objectives of the financial press are not the same as yours. You want to make money. They want to sell newspapers, magazines, and television shows. Consider these oft seen headlines: "The 20 Best Mutual Funds to Buy Now," "15 Hot Stocks to Buy Now," "Seven Smart Ways to Invest for Income Now," etc. Next month they'll give you another 57 things to buy NOW. What are you supposed to do, sell the previous month's recommendations and start over? Or just keep buying?

6. *Investors rely on brokers, financial planners, money managers, or friends and relatives for investment advice.* Even the best guru predictions are accurate only half the time. Brokers and financial planners give advice based on sales commissions. And finally, even though friends and relatives are well-meaning, blaming them after you've lost money won't be much consolation. Use a *mutual funds consultant.* They have nothing to gain from the investments you make; since the honest ones do not work for any particular mutual fund or brokerage firm, they will allow you to make your own decisions free from bias and profit.

POSTSCRIPT 18–4

WHAT IS THE MOST IMPORTANT FACTOR FOR FINANCIAL SUCCESS?

This question was put to 1,000 people by Opinion Research Corporation of Princeton, New Jersey. Surprisingly (or not so surprising) *more than two-thirds of Americans* could not identify this crucial factor for financial success.

- It is not the ability to pick good investments—chosen by 18%.
- It is not having a high paying job—favored by 29%.
- It is not "marrying well," chosen by (believe it or not) 5%.
- The correct answer, picked by only 32% of Americans, is *"having clearly defined goals."*
- Author Harold Evensky in his new book, *Wealth Management,* reiterates the thrust of Opinion Research's findings. Evensky points out, "Most people if they think about financial goals at all, tend to think of them in very generalized ways. Goals must be time and dollar-specific and prioritized."
- In discussing the time factor, Evensky points out that, "No investment that puts your principal at risk should be made for a goal less than five years away; and that's a 'rolling' five years, because if you invest today, you only have four years and 364 days left tomorrow."
- In commenting on risk, the author says, "Risk is critical to investing. If an investor needs only 9% return to meet his goals, for example, a portfolio designed to return 10% but taking on more risk would not be appropriate." The worry and anxiety are not worth it!
- Trying to evaluate the specific dollar goal is impossible until specific long- and short-term objectives are determined. Investing to buy a new car presents a far different goal from investing to finance a child's college education. Each goal in the examples given will have significantly different dollar amounts.
- Prioritizing goals is a very personal matter and should be done by the investor himself. Financial guidance may be sought if the individual's investment profile points to a conflict between investment profile and investment goals.

ROTH'S RULES REGARDING RISK

Rule 1: *Every Investor Has to Determine His Own Threshold of Pain.*
"Understand which risks your investments have before you buy them. Imagine which ones will keep you awake at night. If you can't sleep; then don't keep! Take a long-term attitude toward investing aimed at keeping and enhancing the real value of your money."

Rule 2: *Any Nondiversified Portfolio Is Risky.*
"Like interest rates, financial markets move up and down. You can expect *daily* changes in the market value of investments. My advice is not to overreact when markets are moving *up or down*. Make diversified investments with a long time horizon in mind."

Rule 3: *Don't Let Your Emotions Control Your Investing.*
"Remove emotions from your investment decisions. Diversify your portfolio. Invest some money in equity funds as well as fixed-income vehicles."

Rule 4: *Doing Nothing Is an Investment Decision.*
"The return on stocks, bonds, and money markets can vary widely in any period. Stocks were basically flat in 1994, but had risen about 18% in only six months of 1995. Bonds were down sharply in 1994, but had recouped all of their losses by the end of April 1995. Most significantly, I do not know of anyone who predicted these trends. I believe that stocks and long-term bonds will provide higher returns than very low-risk investments. I build my personal portfolios accordingly."

Rule 5: *Investing Is Not Gambling.*
"We have at least 70 years of data with which we can mathematically describe both the expected returns of stocks and bonds and the standard deviation* of those returns. Add to this the fact that the past 70 years encompasses both the best and the worst of economic times in this country, and you have a powerful case for potentially successful investing."

---

* Standard deviation measures how much an asset's actual return can vary from its expected return.

POSTSCRIPT 18–6

THE HEART OF THE BOOK
(If You Remember Nothing Else, Remember This!)

N.L.	L.T.
NO-LOAD	LONG TERM
D	R
DIVERSIFY	REINVEST

CHAPTER 19

Mutual Fund Investing via the Internet

Buying stocks and mutual funds by means of the Internet is a powerful investing tool. Of the 48 million U.S. households that own mutual fund shares, 68% use the Internet, and 47% of those—15.3 million households—visit the Internet websites of companies that offer mutual fund shares. These statistics, as startling as they may appear, were reported in a recent release by the prestigious Investment Company Institute. The report was compiled from data gathered in April 1998.

Just two years later, fund-owning, Internet-using households increased by 6 million, or 65%.

Why such a large increase? Part of the reason, of course, is due to the *4 million* increase in the number of mutual-fund-owning households. A bigger reason is due, in part, to the rapid growth of the Internet. However, the biggest reason for the huge increase in Internet use is the availability of vast amounts of mutual fund information and help provided on numerous Internet websites. Today a mutual fund investor can use a website to:

- Check the market
- Read about investing for retirement
- Order a prospectus
- Use a calculator to determine portfolio asset allocations
- Review recent press releases from mutual fund companies

- Purchase fund shares in one portfolio and redeem shares in another—all with the click of the mouse

What types of mutual fund information do website users look at most often?

1. *Fund Performance* (72%) Recognizing the importance of *historic fund performance data,* it is little wonder that this feature would be the most sought after information by mutual fund investors.

2. *Share Prices* (66%) When daily newspapers provide fund prices, it should be unnecessary to look them up on a website, unless, of course, you want to know the latest share prices before the morning paper is delivered.

3. *Personal Account Information* (63%) No feature of a website is more important than this one. When you click your mouse, you can instantly evaluate your fund portfolio in just an hour or two after the market closes. Just be sure that you have previously correctly entered and updated the number of shares you own.

4. *Fund Educational Information* There is an abundance of valuable material that leading mutual companies offer on the Internet. For example, one can find out about fund objectives and policies; types of risks to which a fund exposes its shareholders; expense costs and fees; manager tenure; and much more. Websites also enable investors to open accounts and buy and redeem shares.

The Vanguard Group gives the types of investors for which a particular fund is and is not suitable; portfolio composition by sectors; names the ten top holdings in a fund's portfolio; lists income and capital gains distributions; alphas and betas; and last but not least, vital tax information.

Fidelity Investments noted that about 40% of its mutual fund trades made during June 2000 were conducted online. This figure represents *millions of shares* traded with Fidelity in just *one month.* Yet, this mutual fund company is just one of hundreds of fund companies that permit online trading. Figures such as these give you some idea regarding the tremendous amount of mutual fund activity conducted on the Internet.

Perhaps you haven't been using the Internet for your mutual fund investing, because you are not familiar with the websites that provide such features. If that is the case, here are a few excellent websites to help you get started.

> *www.wordalarm.com* keeps you up-to-date on funds you might consider selling. Remember, it is just as important to know when to sell as it is to know when to buy.
>
> *www.fundspot.com* lists mutual funds' phone numbers and has links to fund websites. It also features informative articles on investing on the Internet.
>
> *www.kiplinger.com* offers investors access to fund performance and expense data. Portfolio links to Kiplinger fund manager interviews are also frequently provided as well.
>
> *www.morningstar.com* contains many helpful articles about investing in mutual funds. It has a fund selector and portfolio tracker and also enables you to download and print hard copies of a large number of different mutual fund reports, called "Morningstar Quick Take Reports." In addition, Morningstar has an excellent glossary of typical mutual fund expenses and fees. This glossary is more informative than the data on this subject found in most mutual fund prospectuses.

By using the valuable information to be found on these and other websites, a would-be investor should not find it difficult to build a rewarding, personal, mutual fund portfolio.

THE DOT.COM REVOLUTION

Among the many marvels of the new technology age are the number and variety of websites available to investors. The Internet has spawned a formidable array of websites that lure the novice as well as the experienced investor to their dot.com portals.

Virtually all major mutual fund companies offer websites via the Internet, as with the Vanguard Group's *www.vanguard.com*, Fidelity Investment's *www.fidelity.com*, etc.

Once you have established a mutual fund account with a company that has a website, you can log on to your own account(s) and see the full history of your account(s): a record of all transactions made, and almost any other information you wish to have. This data serves as a valuable tool in the management of our account(s).

In addition to providing a complete and accurate record of all the activity that has occurred in your account(s), many mutual fund websites serve as valuable Learning Centers. Scudder Mutual Funds manages a number of AARP mutual funds and has a Learning Center that addresses the following topics:

Retirement Living: Information to help you plan, invest, and become financially organized after you retire.

Legacy Planning: Learn how to put your financial affairs in good order so your family is protected in the event of your death.

Long-Term Care Planning: Information on how to meet the financial demands of long-term care—such as nursing homes, assisted-living facilities, and in-home services.

Investing Fundamentals: Information on investing basics, mutual funds, IRAs, and taxes. Worksheets are provided to help you allocate your investments toward various goals, such as college expenses, retirement planning, or building a legacy for your heirs, as well as other useful tools.

Note: The Scudder AARP website is focused on older investors who are nearing retirement or are already retired. AARP is an acronym for the American Association of Retired People. There are many other mutual fund websites that focus on investors of all ages. For more about no-load mutual fund basics, you should check out the following websites:

Findafund.com
www.findafund.com/topperformers.htm
Lists top no-load fund performers by fund type and time period

Mutual Fund Education Alliance
www.mfea.com/learn/noload.htm
Details no-load mutual fund features and benefits

Investorama
www.investorama.com/story/funds/loadnoload
Article on the advantages of no-load mutual funds

MutualFundsCentral.com
Mutualfundscentral.com/news/top10bnl.html
Provides monthly round-up of the top 10 best-performing no-load mutual funds

Wall Street City
www.wallstreetcity.com/funds/Funds_Tech_Load_No_Load.asp
Examines the load vs. no-load mutual fund question

Epilogue

This section will serve as a brief refresher—sort of a booster shot—to get you started on a profitable mutual fund investment program. The preceding chapters explained all the "how-to" methods of mutual fund investing. However, knowing what to do and actually doing it are two entirely different things. You now possess the keys to an investment vehicle, but like the keys to any vehicle, they do absolutely no good unless you use them to start the ignition.

Let us review the highlights of the preceding chapters.

A REVIEW

1. *A wide variety of open-end, no-load mutual funds are available.* For the investor, this means no commissions, no early withdrawal penalties, no record keeping, and no salesmen to pressure you to buy. A no-load fund puts *all* of your investment dollars to work for *you*. In addition, the variety of fund types available is almost unlimited. There are stock funds, bond funds, money market funds, international funds, sector funds, tax-free funds; income, growth, and balanced funds; conservative funds and aggressive funds. There is something for everyone who wishes to invest in mutual funds.

2. Every January, *mutual fund companies provide detailed, tax*

reporting information for each account that shareholders have. This service saves time, record keeping, and frustration at tax filing time.

3. Another often overlooked service provided by mutual funds is the manner in which they handle their *management fees for tax purposes.* On all investments *other* than mutual funds, management fees are deductible on your tax return only to the extent that they exceed 2% of your adjusted gross income. Mutual funds report *net yield* (after fees). This automatic deduction relieves the investor of the worry and work of reporting it at tax time.

4. A fairly subtle type of *tax deferment* also accrues to mutual fund owners. The *unrealized capital gains* on a fund's portfolio grow tax-free until you redeem your shares or switch them into another fund in the same fund family.

5. *Low initial investment.* Some funds require an initial investment of only $100, and subsequent investments as low as $25. Thus, for an investment as low as $100, you can participate in a billion-dollar mutual fund portfolio.

6. *Extensive research and analysis are performed by professional management teams.* In order to perform these services, experience, knowledge, and technical skill are required. Few, if any, of us have the time, expertise, or patience needed to successfully manage a large, diversified portfolio such as is found in a mutual fund. Thus, mutual fund investors are provided with the finest kind of professional management at virtually no cost to themselves.

7. *Budget-priced diversification* is achieved through mutual fund investing. Diversification, as has been pointed out, is the key to reducing risk. In order to diversify a portfolio by purchasing even *one share* of the stocks that make up a mutual fund's portfolio, an individual investor would pay many thousands of dollars. However, broad diversification can be achieved with a mutual fund investment of $250, or less. In fact, mutual funds—by definition and by *law*—must diversify their portfolios.

8. *Liquidity* is another feature inherent in mutual funds. All open-end funds will redeem their shares at *any time* without penalty. It is as easy as making a telephone call, sending a letter, or writing a fund check. You *cannot* redeem a bank CD before it matures, unless you are willing to incur a substantial penalty. Neither can you sell stocks, unless you pay a hefty broker's commission. The mutual funds advantage is clear.

9. *Investment flexibility.* Most mutual funds are part of a "fund family," consisting of a variety of different types of funds, usually with different goals. Fund families generally permit their investors to switch from one fund to another within the same family just by making a phone call, without sales charges or transfer fees. This feature allows you to change your investment strategy as the need arises, without the high commission costs which would be incurred in stock switches. With mutual funds, you can move your money when you feel that the return will be greater in a different fund, or your goals change, or for any other reason; it makes no difference to the company.

10. *All kinds of retirement programs are available.* With mutual funds you can set up IRA, Keogh, and other tax-sheltered plans very easily: Administrative fees for these types of accounts are substantially less than the fees charged by other institutions.

11. The benefits of *dollar-cost averaging* may be achieved through mutual fund investing. Most funds will, with proper authorization, regularly debit your bank checking account for you, and invest the money in the funds of your choice, thus making disciplined investing *automatic.* (Or you may do it on your own.) Remember, dollar-cost averaging pays off in long-term gains, thanks to the power of compounding and the rise and fall of the fund's NAV.

12. *Reinvestment of dividends and capital gains.* Every mutual fund with which I am familiar allows, if not encourages, reinvesting the dividends and capital gains it distributes,

as a way to harness the many benefits of compounding. Very few corporations will do this for you as a stockholder, even if you wanted it.

13. *The fund provides adequate, accurate, and explicit information* to its investors through its prospectuses, reports, and advertising. In addition to detailing the benefits of investing in the fund, these releases also will advise prospective investors of the risks and costs of buying shares in the fund. What could be more fair?

14. *Mutual funds are subjected to strict, independent scrutiny* through regular audits by reputable accounting firms and by government regulatory agencies. Mutual funds are independent of "outside" corporate control or external investment advisers. Control of the fund company rests entirely with its executive officers, fund managers, and the board of directors for whom you, as a shareholder, vote.

15. *Mutual funds are managed solely in the interest of their shareholders.* You, their customers, are the fund's owners, and you vote on any proposed changes in fund policies (usually by proxy).

16. *Safeguarding your investments.* While in possession of the fund, your account is insured up to $2 million against theft, fraud, or embezzlement.

17. *Fractional share purchases permitted.* Mutual fund companies will sell fractional shares, thereby allowing you to invest any amount desired (as long as it meets the investment requirements stipulated in the prospectus). For example, if you decide to invest $250, and the current NAV of the fund in which you are investing is $11.50, you will receive 21.739 shares. You *cannot* buy fractional shares of stocks or bonds. The fractional share purchases allowed by mutual funds permits you to implement a dollar-cost averaging plan, or any other investment plan you might wish to use based on *your* budget. This is a great help when trying to expand your portfolio, or to further diversify it by increasing the number of funds you include.

18. *Prompt response to any inquiry or complaint* that you may have regarding your account is assured: All it takes is a toll-free phone call (or a letter), and appropriate action will be taken.

FIVE MAJOR MISTAKES

I'm confident that by applying the information provided in the preceding chapters, you *will* become a successful investor. However, it is possible to defeat the entire purpose of this book if you begin by committing any of the five common mistakes made by many experienced investors—to say nothing of novice investors.

Mistake Number One: Failure to Think Long-Term

Don't be in a hurry to make money. You will not make a fortune in mutual fund investing if you think only in the short term. To avoid mistake number one, seek carefully for funds that satisfy the following criteria of a good investment:

1. Fund objectives that match your own goals
2. A stable management team
3. Low management fees
4. A risk level with which you are comfortable
5. A dividend reinvestment policy that provides the benefits of compounding
6. Funds that have ranked among the most consistent money makers
7. Funds that have averaged at least 16% annualized growth over the last five to ten years

Mistake Number Two: Relying Too Heavily on Recent Performance

All too often, last year's big winners end up as next year's big losers. This is especially true of sector and international funds, as well as such flash-in-the-pan funds as gold, pharmaceuticals, and computers, to name but a few. It is almost a truism that funds with short-term, meteoric rises frequently fall just as rapidly. That is why relying on short-term performance (say, one year), even if the fund achieves a 50% gain in one year, is not the only criterion that must be considered when selecting a fund. It is important to consider as well the fund's midterm (five years) and, where possible, long-term performance (10 years or more). You must evaluate carefully all of these factors when selecting the funds in which you decide to invest. Invest only in high-quality funds with *proven long-term results.*

Mistake Number Three: Being Underdiversified and/or Overdiversified

If you own only *one* fund, you risk suffering a major capital loss should that fund suffer a serious slump. With no other funds in your portfolio with which to offset the loss, you've risked everything. To cite another cliché: Don't put all your eggs in one basket. On the other hand, you can own *too many funds.* If you read popular publications such as *Money, Forbes, Financial World,* and *Kiplinger's Personal Finance* magazine, you will usually find tables that list the top-performing mutual funds each month (Table EP-1). The temptation to invest in these "top picks" is great. However, the listings change from month to month, and by trying to profit by investing in such "headliners," you will wind up with so many funds that you may be unable to carefully monitor each one. Such a mistake can be costly, because rarely do these popular magazines tell you when to *sell* these once-top performers. Eventually you wind up with a number of *former* great picks and no real, long-term winners. Remember, owning a mutual fund is not like owning shares of a stock, which is an investment in a *single* corporation; thus, you have no diversification. On the other hand, every mutual fund is required by *law* to be *highly diversified.* Therefore, you can limit the number of funds you own and still be well-diversified. Five or so good funds are all that are really necessary, and they should generally be from two or three *different* fund families.

Mistake Number Four: Paying High Fees

Many investors foolishly believe that funds charging a load (commission) must, *ipso facto,* be superior to no-load funds. This is not so! As was pointed out in Chapter 4, a load of 8.5% can eat up as much as 9.3% of your investment before it buys a single share. Why buy load funds when there is no statistical evidence to show that they perform one iota better than no-load funds? If you must buy a load fund, never pay more than a 2% to 3% load fee.

Because of the commission, which is deducted from the total amount invested, a load fund will always be playing catch up, and more times than not will never make it. For example, if you had made a single investment of $1,000 in 1991 in the no-load Oakmark Fund versus the same amount invested in the 6.5% load Merrill Lynch Phoenix A Fund, you would automatically start out with $65 less in the load fund. By 1992 the no-load Oakmark Fund was worth $1,563 and the Merrill Lynch load fund was worth only $1,291. In just one year the no-load fund was worth $272 *more* than the load fund. At this rate, the load fund would have had to earn almost 30% more just to equal the no-load fund's return. That's a tough challenge! And in just *five years*, with compounding, the no-load fund would be ahead by as much as *$1,800*. Avoid load funds!

Mistake Number Five: Starting Out Without a Plan

A ship without a rudder may never reach port, and an investment program without a plan will rarely reach the goal you have set. Your plan must take into account (1) your risk tolerance level, (2) the purpose for which you are investing, and (3) the way your money is to be allocated. (See Chapters 6 and 17.) If your portfolio is a blend of these critical factors, *you will be a successful investor.*

STUDY GUIDE FOR THE EPILOGUE

1. How do mutual funds relieve you of the necessity of reporting their fees for income tax purposes?
2. Who is responsible for doing the research that goes into establishing a mutual fund?
3. Why are you assured of some diversification even when purchasing one mutual fund?
4. What is meant by liquidity in connection with open-end mutual funds? Why is this not always true for closed-end funds?

5. Is it an easy matter to switch your funds within a fund family? What is required?

6. What are two important benefits of reinvesting distributions?

7. How are mutual funds supervised, and by whom?

8. How much insurance do mutual funds provide while your money is in their custody?

9. What is the most common mistake made by mutual fund owners?

10. What are the best criteria to use in checking a fund's performance?

11. Is it necessary to have a great number of funds in order to achieve diversification in your portfolio? Why?

12. Where do you find information on the fees charged by funds?

TABLE EP-1

This Month's Top All-Star Funds

Top Five-Star Common Stock Funds

All-Star Rating	Mutual Fund (Share class in quotes)	Inv. Obj.	Type of Investments	Safety Rating	Market Rankings Up	Down	Worst-Ever Loss (1981–2000)	Corr. vs S&P	Corr. vs Bonds	Yield	1 mo.	3 mo.	6 mo.	12 mo.	3 yrs.	5 yrs.	10 yrs.	Telephone	Minimum Initial Invest.	Telephone Switching (freq; cost)
*****	Adams Express	GI	Diversified sound-co stocks	7.3	C↑	B	-29% 10/87-1/87	57%	1%	1.2%	+8%	+25%	+23%	+36%	+112%	+213%	+387%	Closed-end NYSE 17% discount		
*****	Berger Growth & Income	GI	Highly predictable firms	7.0	C↑	B	-27% 8/87-1/87	81%	3%	0.0%	+19%	+41%	+36%	+61%	+142%	+247%	+502%	800-333-1001	2,000	4@yr; free
*****	Bergstrom Capital	G	Long term growth stocks	7.4	D	A	-36% 1/93-4/94	19%	-1%	0.1%	+6%	+22%	+26%	+47%	+140%	+293%	+513%	Closed-end AMEX 15% discount		
*****	Central Securities	GI	Stocks; leveraged	6.4	D	A	-39% 1/97-1/98	22%	-1%	1.0%	+5%	+15%	+7%	+22%	+34%	+140%	+499%	Closed-end AMEX 22% discount		
*****	Ellsworth Conv Grth & Icm	GI	Convertible securities	7.0	E	A	-32% 8/86-1/87	18%	2%	7.1%	-4%	+2%	0%	+2%	+36%	+112%	+216%	Closed-end AMEX 24% discount		
*****	Fidel Adv 'T' Eqty Growth	G	Inst:stks;EPS-gr abv S&P 500	6.7	A	D	-30% 7/90-1/90	91%	3%	0.0%	+10%	+23%	+20%	+37%	+138%	+290%	+768%	800-843-3001	2,500	4@yr; free
*****	Fidelity Fund	G	Stocks & cmvts; pfds & bonds	7.1	A	D	-34% 8/87-1/87	95%	4%	0.7%	+11%	+20%	+12%	+24%	+114%	+241%	+429%	800-544-8888	2,500	4@yr; free
*****	Fidelity Growth Company	G	Hi earnings or sales growth	6.5	A	E	-41% 8/87-1/87	82%	2%	0.0%	+22%	+45%	+50%	+79%	+172%	+343%	+734%	800-544-8888	2,500	4@yr; free
*****	Fidelity Mid-Cap Stock	G	Stks w-mkt cap $109mil-$5bil	6.9	A	D	-30% 7/98-1/98	71%	2%	0.0%	+16%	+28%	+23%	+40%	+105%	+224%		800-544-8888	2,500	4@yr; free
*****	Fidelity OTC	G	Over-the-counter securities	6.0	A	A	-39% 1/87-1/87	73%	0%	0.0%	+21%	+46%	+46%	+73%	+166%	+355%	+684%	800-544-8888	2,500	4@yr; free
*****	Fidelity Retirement Grth	G	For retirement accts only	6.8	E↓	D	-37% 8/87-1/87	82%	3%	0.2%	+23%	+36%	+29%	+47%	+150%	+219%	+464%	800-544-8888	500	4@yr; free
*****	Franklin 'A' Calif Growth	G	Non-dvsf;sm-med cap CA stks	6.6	A	C	-29% 4/98-1/98	66%	1%	0.2%	+22%	+56%	+67%	+95%	+171%	+329%	+534%	800-342-5236	1,000	Unlim/free
*****	Gabelli Growth	G	Grth stks w-good earnings	6.4	A	C	-27% 7/98-1/98	90%	3%	0.0%	+11%	+26%	+25%	+46%	+155%	+261%	+513%	800-422-3554	1,000	Unlim/free
*****	General American Invstrs	G	Long term capital apprec	7.3	C	B	-39% 8/87-12/87	82%	0%	1.2%	+9%	+24%	+23%	+38%	+169%	+284%	+474%	Closed-end NYSE 11% discount		
*****	Heritage Captl Apprec 'A'	G	Undervl growth stocks;cmvts	6.9	B	D	-29% 8/87-1/87	82%	6%	0.0%	+13%	+27%	+23%	+40%	+163%	+318%	+474%	800-421-4184	1,000	1@mo; free
*****	Invesco Dynamics	G	Dvsf equities; up to 25% fgn	6.4	A	E	-44% 10/87-1/87	74%	2%	0.0%	+15%	+39%	+37%	+72%	+163%	+318%	+764%	800-525-8085	1,000	4@yr; free
*****	Janus Enterprise	G	Mid-cap eqtys; S&P 400 cap	5.8	A	C	-33% 7/98-1/98	55%	1%	0.0%	+24%	+58%	+71%	+122%	+229%	+367%		800-525-3713	2,500	4@yr; free
*****	Janus Fund	G	Diversified growth stocks	6.6	A	B	-28% 7/98-1/98	84%	4%	0.0%	+11%	+23%	+47%	+114%	+151%	+288%	+545%	800-525-3713	2,500	4@yr; free
*****	Janus Growth & Income	GI	Dvsf grth stks 25% icm-prod	6.4	A	C	-26% 7/98-1/98	86%	6%	0.2%	+12%	+29%	+29%	+51%	+175%	+372%		800-525-3713	2,500	4@yr; free
*****	Janus Mercury	G	Non-dvsf; good fundamentals	5.9	A	A	-26% 7/98-1/98	73%	3%	0.0%	+20%	+43%	+48%	+96%	+248%	+444%		800-525-3713	2,500	4@yr; free
*****	Janus Olympus	Gr	Growth stocks;bonds;hedging	6.0	A	D	-29% 7/98-1/98	72%	1%	0.0%	+20%	+52%	+57%	+100%	+298%			800-525-3713	2,500	4@yr; free
*****	One Group 'T' Lrg Cap Gr		Tnst: frg-cap grm stk;opin	6.?	A	U	-18% 7/98-1/98	92%	4%	0.0%	+8%	+20%	+15%	+28%	+146%	+265%		800-480-4111	1 mil.	Unlim/free
*****	Price Blue Chip Growth	GI	Med-lrg estb cos;grwth potl	7.1	A	D	-24% 7/98-1/98	96%	4%	0.1%	+7%	+17%	+9%	+20%	+97%	+247%		800-638-5660	2,500	1@4mo;free
*****	Rainier Core Equity	GI	Diversified stocks	7.0	A	D	-23% 4/98-1/98	93%	2%	0.0%	+11%	+22%	+15%	+27%	+105%	+271%		800-248-6314	25,000	4@yr; free
*****	Reynolds Blue Chip Growth	GI	Well establishd growth cos	6.2	A	D	-22% 7/98-1/98	87%	4%	0.0%	+13%	+34%	+29%	+51%	+206%	+421%	+569%	800-773-9665	1,000	Unlim/free
*****	Strong Growth & Income	GI	Div-pay grwth stks;bds;deriv	6.9	A	C	-22% 7/98-1/98	96%	2%	0.0%	+9%	+21%	+17%	+32%	+129%		+472%	800-368-1030	2,500	See prosp.
*****	Strong Total Return	GI	Stks;corps;govts;mny mkts	6.7	D	B	-21% 8/87-1/87	81%	6%	0.0%	+24%	+42%	+38%	+60%	+162%	+279%	+264%	800-368-1030	2,500	See prosp.
*****	TCW Convertible Secs	GI	Value stocks;estab-cos	7.1	A	C	-40% 3/87-1/87	6%	3%	8.8%	+5%	+12%	+7%	+15%	+41%	+109%	+264%	Closed-end NYSE 16% discount		
*****	Thornburg Value 'A'	GI	Sectr-dvsf stks; 10% ADRs	7.2	A	A	-24% 3/87-1/87	79%	0%	0.8%	+10%	+22%	+15%	+37%	+125%			800-847-0200	5,000	Unlim/free
*****	Turner Growth Equity	GI	Emerging growth eqtys;deriv	6.4	A	E	-26% 7/98-1/98	84%	4%	0.0%	+18%	+40%	+38%	+54%	+179%	+332%	+823%	800-224-6312	2,500	Unlim/free
*****	United New Concepts 'A'	G	Top Value Line ranks	6.5	A	B	-36% 10/87-12/87	52%	0%	0.0%	+18%	+46%	+46%	+64%	+166%	+273%	+452%	800-366-5465	500	Mail only
*****	Value Line Special Situat	G	Convertible securities	6.7	A↑	E	-42% 10/87-1/87	64%	0%	0.0%	+19%	+38%	+39%	+62%	+177%	+284%	+210%	800-223-0818	1,000	8@yr; free
*****	Van Kampen Convert Secs	GI	Convertible securities	7.6	E	A	-27% 2/87-12/87	10%	1%	3.3%	+10%	+26%	+25%	+38%	+67%	+137%		Closed-end NYSE 23% discount		
*****	Vanguard Growth Index	G	Match S&P-BARRA Grth Idx	6.7	A	D	-18% 7/98-8/98	93%	5%	0.6%	+8%	+20%	+16%	+29%	+149%	+327%	+503%	800-523-1154	3,000	Mail only
*****	Warb Pinc Cap App 'Com'	G	Dvsf hi-eqs growth eqtys	6.7	A	B	-30% 8/87-12/87	84%	3%	0.0%	+19%	+33%	+32%	+48%	+145%	+317%	+271%	800-927-2874	2,500	3@mo; free
*****	Weitz Partners Value	G	Low PE stks;conv;optns;fgn	7.4	B	B	-25% 7/98-1/98	61%	7%	1.0%	+1%	+6%	+3%	+22%	+125%	+271%	+430%	800-232-4161	100,000	Unlim/free
*****	Weitz Value	G	Dvsf stocks; cnvrts; optns	7.5	C	A	-22% 7/98-1/98	61%	8%	1.1%	+1%	+7%	+4%	+21%	+117%	+256%	+493%	800-232-4161	25,000	Unlim/free
*****	Wilmington Large Cap Grth	G	3 independent portf mgrs	6.5	D	E	-26% 7/98-1/98	80%	1%	0.0%	+22%	+41%	+36%	+48%	+133%	+272%		800-336-9970	1,000	Unlim/free

Performance Scoreboard – Through 12/31/99 (Top 10% of funds in bold type)

Note: Lists such as the above change almost monthly.

Non-Technical Magazines and Newspapers

Barron's
200 Burnett Road
Chicopee, MA 01021

Financial World magazine
1450 Broadway
New York, NY 10018

Forbes magazine
60 Fifth Avenue
New York, NY 10114-0034

Kiplinger's Personal Finance magazine
Editor's Park, MD 20782-9960

Money magazine
1271 Avenue of the Americas
New York, NY 10020

Mutual Funds magazine
2200 SW 10th Street
Deerfield Beach, FL 33442

Note: The public library carries copies of the periodicals listed above, as well as many others. It might be a good idea to check them out in order to determine which ones best fit your needs before subscribing to any of them.

Mutual Fund Listings in Newspapers

Explanation of Daily Newspaper Mutual Fund Listings

1. The first column (in Table B–1) shows the names of the investment companies (bold type), followed by the names of the funds offered by that company. The fund name, in many cases, is followed by a letter symbol. (See below for an explanation of the symbols.)

2. The second column shows the "sell" price. This is the amount you would receive if you were to redeem any of your shares. (Sell price is the same as the bid price.)

3. The third column shows the "buy" price. This is the amount you would pay in order to purchase shares. (The asked price.) The difference between the buy and sell price represents the load charged by the fund or the broker selling shares of the fund (broker's commission).

4. The last column shows the amount of change in the fund's price from the previous day's NAV. Plus signs show gains; minus signs show losses.

Note: Where a fund's buy price and sell price are the same, it indicates a no-load fund.

Mutual Fund Listings Found in Weekly Newspapers

1. The first column (in Table B–2) is the same as number one above.

TABLE B-1

Daily Mutual Fund Listings

IDS GROUP	SELL	BUY	CHANGE
*Blue Chip	$ 6.75	$ 7.10	+ .87
Growth	$19.00	$18.28	-. 42
Income	$ 1.64	$ 1.75	+. 05
International	$ 6.25	$ 6.75	+ .85
Realty	$ 4.81	$ 6.35	- .35
Oil Refinery	$ 7.63	$ 7.98	+ ,.93
etc.			

LORD ABBETT			
*Affiliated	$ 10.55	$ 11.19	+ 1.05
Growth & Income	$ 10.51	$ 11.15	- .61
Health Sci.	$10.70	$ 11.32	- 1.33
etc.			

PUTNAM			
*Genesis	$ 5.94	$ 6.30	+ .12
Global Equity	$ 1.16	$ 1.96	- .15
Growth and Income	$ 2.25	$ 2.98	+ .06
New Opportunity	$ 3.09	$ 3.19	- .08
Research	$ 1.12	$ 1.47	+ .05
Vista	$ 6.10	$ 6.40	- .14
Voyager	$ 7.30	$ 7.55	+ .11
etc.			

CALCULATING A FUND'S LOAD

✻IDS GROUP – Blue Chip Fund
$ 6.75(sell) $ 7.10 (buy) =difference of $ .35
$.35 divided by $ 7.10 = **5% load** .

* LORD ABBETT – Affiliated Fund
$ 10.55 (sell) $ 11.19 (buy) =
a difference of $ .64
$ .64 divided by $ 11.19 = **5.7% load**

*PUTNAM – Genesis Fund
$.5.94 (sell) $ 6.30 (buy) =
a difference of $ ..36
$ .36 divided by $ 6.30 = **6% load**

NOTE: Buy, Sell & Change figures are for illustrative purposes only.

2. The second column shows the highest NAV for the week.

3. The third column shows the lowest NAV for the week.

4. The fourth column shows the closing NAV for the week.

5. The last column shows the amount of gain or loss in the NAV for the week.

Key to Letter Symbols

a: fee covering marketing costs paid from the fund's assets

d: deferred sales charge or redemption fee

f: front-end load (sales charge)

TABLE B-2

Weekly Mutual Fund Listings

	High	Low	Close	Chg
AggGrowC	m33.28	32.19	33.22	+1.01
AmerValA	m22.98	22.59	22.98	+.37
AmerValB	m22.41	22.03	22.41	+.37
AmerValC	m22.42	22.04	22.42	+.36
ComstockA	m15.63	15.43	15.43	-.20
ComstockB	m15.62	15.41	15.41	-.20
EmgGrA	m105.27	103.44	104.96	+1.69
EmgGrB	m95.77	94.12	95.49	+1.53
EmgGrC	m97.68	95.99	97.38	+1.55
EnterprsA	m24.68	24.37	24.62	+.36
EnterprsB	m23.58	23.28	23.52	+.35
EqIncomeA	m8.46	8.39	8.46	+.10
EqIncomeB	m8.36	8.29	8.36	+.10
FocusEqA	m28.56	28.28	28.56	+.37
FocusEqB	m27.52	27.25	27.52	+.35
GlobEqAlA	m17.86	17.72	17.86	+.14
GlobEqAlB	m17.05	16.93	17.05	+.13
GlobEqB	m11.10	11.05	11.10	-.01
GovtSecsA	m9.79	9.75	9.78	+.02
GrowIncA	m19.97	19.79	19.92	+.22
GrowIncB	m19.81	19.63	19.76	+.22
HarborA	m21.71	21.22	21.71	+.40
HiYldMuA	m10.72	10.71	10.72	+.01
HiYldMuB	m10.71	10.70	10.71	+.01
HighIncA	m5.24	5.22	5.24	+.02
HighIncB	m5.25	5.23	5.25	+.02
HighYldA	m8.13	8.10	8.13	+.02
InsTaxFA	m18.51	18.45	18.51	+.07
MuniIncA	m14.25	14.21	14.25	+.04
PATaxFA	m16.85	16.81	16.85	+.05
PaceA m	14.18	14.08	14.14	+.14
SelGrB m	10.65	10.50	10.55	+.05
StratIncB	m10.23	10.21	10.22	-.02
TaxFHiInA	m13.41	13.39	13.41	+.02
TaxFHiInB	m13.41	13.39	13.40	+.01
TechA m	25.67	24.86	25.56	+.64
TechB m	25.47	24.66	25.36	+.64
TechC m	25.47	24.66	25.36	+.64
USGovA	m13.67	13.62	13.67	+.03
Van Wagoner				
EmgGrow	b59.35	58.08	59.10	+1.13
MicroCpGr	b47.52	46.55	47.32	+1.11
MidCapGr	b34.47	33.75	34.35	+.70
PostVent	b46.70	45.56	46.55	+1.12
Tech b	74.59	72.76	74.31	+1.83
Vanguard				
500Idx	139.42	138.48	139.26	+1.36
AdmIntTm	10.19	10.15	10.19	+.04
AdmLgTm	10.78	10.73	10.78	+.04
AdmShTm	9.93	9.91	9.93	+.02
AstAlc	25.55	25.40	25.54	+.19
BalIdx	20.81	20.65	20.80	+.20
CAInsLgTm	11.39	11.34	11.39	+.05
CATxFIns	10.87	10.83	10.87	+.04
CapOpp d	33.24	32.49	33.24	+.92
ConvSec	15.13	14.82	15.13	+.35
EmMktIdx	d10.93	10.85	10.92	-.01
Energy d	28.50	27.83	28.08	+.31
EqIncome	23.83	23.78	23.79	+.06
EurStkIdx	27.59	27.32	27.59	-.12
ExMkIdx	37.96	37.11	37.96	+.90
ExMkIsIdx	38.01	37.16	38.01	+.90
Explorer	80.92	78.78	80.92	+2.27
FLInsTxF	11.09	11.06	11.09	+.04
FixILTTrs	10.48	10.42	10.48	+.04
FixISTCls	10.51	10.48	10.51	+.03
FixISTCor	10.51	10.48	10.51	+.03
FixISTFd	9.95	9.94	9.95	+.01
GNMA	10.03	10.00	10.03	+.02
GldPrM d	7.31	7.20	7.31	+.09
GroInc	37.37	37.13	37.31	+.35
GrowIdx	40.70	40.03	40.59	+.68
GrowIsIdx	40.71	40.04	40.60	+.68

	High	Low	Close	Chg
MuShTm	15.50	15.50	15.50	...
NJInsLT	11.53	11.48	11.53	+.05
NYInsLTrm	10.82	10.79	10.82	+.03
OHInsLT	11.53	11.48	11.53	+.05
PAInsLT	10.97	10.93	10.97	+.04
PacStkIdx	11.10	10.65	11.10	+.37
PrefStk	8.89	8.86	8.89	+.03
Primecap	75.49	74.04	75.37	+1.13
REITIdx d	11.64	11.41	11.41	-.26
STTrs	10.07	10.05	10.06	+.01
SelValue	11.15	11.02	11.02	-.09
ShTmBdIdx	9.78	9.76	9.78	+.02
SmCpGrIdx	12.62	12.25	12.62	+.39
SmCpIdx	24.58	24.18	24.58	+.44
SmCpIsIdx	24.61	24.20	24.61	+.45
SmValIdx	9.18	9.09	9.18	+.09
Star	18.55	18.44	18.55	+.13
StratgcEq	d18.05	17.95	18.05	+.10
TaxMgdApl	d36.79	36.34	36.78	+.59
TaxMgdBal	d19.93	19.78	19.93	+.21
TaxMgdCap	d36.76	36.32	36.75	+.58
TaxMgdGro	d32.76	32.54	32.72	+.32
TaxMgdInt	d11.21	11.07	11.21	+.08
ToBdIdx	9.73	9.70	9.73	+.03
ToBdIsIdx	9.73	9.70	9.73	+.03
ToStIsIdx	34.04	33.73	34.02	+.44
ToStkIdx	34.03	33.72	34.02	+.45
TotIntIdx	13.33	13.17	13.33	+.09
TxMgdSmCp	d14.11	13.83	14.11	+.30
USGrowth	48.38	47.34	48.22	+1.06
UtlInc	15.08	14.92	14.92	-.23
ValIsIdx	23.15	23.04	23.06	+.04
ValueIdx	23.15	23.04	23.05	+.03
Wellesin	19.71	19.67	19.71	+.03
WelIngtn	28.56	28.49	28.56	+.04
Windsor	16.06	16.00	16.06	+.02
WindsorII	26.85	26.65	26.65	+.10
Vantagepoint				
AggrOpp	17.42	17.03	17.42	+.46
AstAlloc	11.07	11.02	11.07	+.08
BrMktIxl	12.64	12.52	12.64	+.17
BrMktIxII	12.10	11.99	12.10	+.16
CorBdIxl	9.64	9.60	9.64	+.04
EqInc	7.67	7.62	7.62	-.03
Growth	14.75	14.55	14.73	+.26
Intl	13.13	12.97	13.13	+.11
Victory				
Bal A f	14.51	14.48	14.50	+.07
DivrStkA	f17.77	17.63	17.77	+.16
EstValue	b32.79	32.62	32.62	+.04
GrowStk	f26.27	25.95	26.27	+.48
IntInc f	9.28	9.25	9.26	-.02
SpecValA	f15.28	15.22	15.28	+.01
StockIdx	f25.07	24.90	25.04	+.24
Value f	17.83	17.72	17.78	+.13
Vintage				
EquityS b	24.80	24.57	24.80	+.36
W&R Funds				
IntlGrowC	m23.91	23.72	23.91	-.11
SciTechC	m35.14	34.34	35.13	+.82
CapAprC	m18.78	18.48	18.78	+.40
TotalRetC	m14.20	14.14	14.15	+.07
WM Str Asset Mgmt				
BalA m	13.89	13.78	13.89	+.14
BalB m	13.88	13.77	13.88	+.14
ConsGrowA	m16.04	15.89	16.04	+.20
ConsGrowB	m15.70	15.55	15.70	+.19
StrGrowB	m17.48	17.29	17.48	+.25
WM Trust I				
EqIncA	m14.86	14.86	14.86	...
GrFdNwstA	m40.15	39.55	40.15	+.56
GrowIncA	m26.99	26.77	26.88	+.37
GrowIncB	m26.40	26.19	26.29	+.36

	High	Low	Close	Chg
HiInclIA m	3.60	3.58	3.59	...
Income A	m9.38	9.34	9.34	+.05
Income Y	9.38	9.34	9.35	+.05
IntlGrowA	m11.99	11.93	11.98	-.08
MuniBondA	m6.81	6.79	6.81	+.02
MuniHiInA	m4.95	4.94	4.95	+.01
NewCncptA	m13.86	13.50	13.86	+.31
RetireA m	12.55	12.42	12.55	+.16
SciTechA	m18.82	18.51	18.80	+.35
SmCapA	m14.21	14.03	14.21	+.28
VanguardA	m14.56	14.48	14.56	+.10
Wanger				
IntlSmAdv	38.35	37.69	38.35	+.54
USSmCpAdv	19.23	19.08	19.23	+.12
Warburg Pincus				
AdvEmgGr	b52.10	50.86	52.10	+1.27
AdvIntlEq	b23.56	23.16	23.56	+.26
CapAprCmn	33.37	32.94	33.37	+.61
EmgGrCmn	54.45	53.16	54.45	+1.32
FixInCmn	9.82	9.78	9.82	+.03
GlPstVCmn	b31.09	30.28	31.09	+.88
GlobTlCmn	b67.92	66.71	67.92	+.35
IntlEq	14.89	14.70	14.89	+.12
IntlEqCmn	23.91	23.50	23.91	+.26
JapGroCmn	m15.63	14.22	15.63	+1.27
JapSmCmn	m6.88	6.36	6.88	+.45
PostVenCp	21.48	20.92	21.48	+.60
SmCoGr	26.33	25.36	26.33	+1.11
ValComm	15.22	15.10	15.12	+.11
Wasatch				
CoreGr	27.27	26.83	27.27	+.17
MicroCap	6.38	6.25	6.38	+.11
SmCapGr	34.06	33.21	34.06	+.60
Wayne Hummer				
Growth f	44.67	44.24	44.47	-.31
Weitz				
Hickory	27.50	27.35	27.50	-.23
PartVal	19.73	19.56	19.67	-.07
Value	32.66	32.35	32.51	-.19
Wells Fargo				
AstAlcA f	25.39	25.23	25.37	+.19
AstAlcB	m15.38	15.28	15.37	+.12
CATxFA f	11.09	11.05	11.09	+.05
DivEqI	54.57	54.40	54.56	+.37
DivrBondI	26.43	26.31	26.43	+.10
EqIdxA f	88.72	88.12	88.61	+.85
EqIncA xf	43.79	41.85	41.85	-1.62
EqIncI x	43.80	41.86	41.86	-1.62
GrBalI	33.45	33.33	33.45	+.16
GrEqI	41.51	41.36	41.51	+.23
GrowthA	f24.01	23.79	23.98	+.32
IncomeI	9.13	9.10	9.13	+.03
IndexI	62.65	62.22	62.57	+.60
IntGovInA	xf10.86	10.81	10.81	-.02
IntGovtI x	10.87	10.81	10.81	-.02
IntlI	26.56	26.30	26.56	-.01
LgCoGrA	f79.24	78.69	78.69	+.11
LgCoGrB	m73.73	73.22	73.22	+.10
LgCoGrI	74.66	74.15	74.15	+.11
Life2020A	m15.61	15.50	15.61	+.13
Life2040A	m20.16	19.98	20.16	+.22
MNIntTxFI	9.61	9.59	9.61	+.02
ModBalI	25.04	24.95	25.04	+.11
NaTxFIncI	9.99	9.95	9.99	+.04
SmCapGrA	f43.01	42.16	43.01	+.94

m: multiple fees charged (marketing, sales, or redemption fees)

NL: no-load (no sales charges)

Note: Different newspapers may use different symbols; be sure to consult the key employed by the newspaper you are using.

Addresses and Toll-Free Numbers of Selected Funds

Bull and Bear Mutual Funds
P.O. Box 928
Jersey City, NJ 07303
(800) 847-4200

The Dreyfus Family of Funds, Inc.
P.O. Box 9387
Providence, RI 02940-9821
(800) 373-9387

Fidelity Investments
82 Devonshire Street
Boston, MA 02109
(800) 544-8888

Invesco Funds, Inc.
P.O. Box 2040
Denver, CO 80201
(800) 525-8085

T. Rowe Price Investment Services, Inc.
100 E. Pratt Street
Baltimore, MD 21202
(800) 638-5660

Stein Roe Mutual Funds
P.O. Box 804058

Chicago, IL 60680
(800) 338-2550

Scudder Fund Distributors, Inc.
P.O. Box 2540
Boston, MA 02208-9911
(800) 225-2470

Strong Funds
P.O. Box 2936
Milwaukee, WI 53201-9986
(800) 368-1030

Janus Mutual Funds, Inc.
100 Filmore Street Suite 300
Denver, CO 80206-4923
(800) 525-8993

USAA Mutual Funds, Inc.
USAA Building
San Antonio, TX 78284-9863
(800) 382-8722

Tweedy Browne Funds, Inc.
52 Vanderbilt Avenue
New York, NY 10017
(800) 432-4789

Value Line Mutual Funds
711 Third Avenue
New York, NY 10017
(800) 223-0818

Vanguard Group of Investment Companies, Inc.
P.O. Box 2600
Valley Forge, PA 19482-2600
(800) 662-7447

Wasatch Mutual Funds, Inc.
68 South Main Street
Salt Lake City, UT 84101
(800) 551-1700

Warburg Pincus Mutual Funds
466 Lexington Avenue
New York, NY 10017-3147
(800) 927-2874

United Mutual Funds, Inc.
6300 Lamar Avenue P.O. Box 29217
Shawnee Mission, KS 66201-9217

Note: All of the funds listed are *no-load*, except Fidelity, which offers both load and no-load.

The Miracle of Compounding*
The Original Manhattan Project

The classic example of the virtues of compound growth is the Dutch purchase of Manhattan Island. When Peter Minuet, first Director General of the Dutch Province of New Netherland, bought the island from the Man-a-hat-a Indians in 1626 for 60 guilders, or about $22.50 at today's exchange rates, he probably had no idea what he was contributing to the economy of the investment world. Who got the better deal, the Indians or the white men? The settlers, of course, got land which is today part of a large metropolis.

But the Indians received 60 guilders! Had the Indians invested their 60 guilder fortune at, say, just 7% per year, by 1976 they would have had over $427 billion, which is well in excess of what Manhattan Island is worth today (land, buildings, and all).

Alternatively, had they invested the guilders in common stock on the "New Manhattan Stock Exchange" and earned a 9% yield year in and year out (as has been the American investing experience during the last 75 years), their original $22.50 would have grown to over $300 trillion(!), a sum many times greater than the value of all the world's assets. The fact that the Indians didn't make such investments in no way impugns the wisdom of their original sale of the land; it merely casts doubt upon the ability of their portfolio manager.

* From Fosback, Norman G., *Stock Market Logic,* The Institute for Econometric Research, 1993. Reprinted by permission.

TABLE D-1

Effect of Compounding
The amount to which $1 will accumulate at the end of the specified number of years

Year	4%	5%	6%	7%	8%	9%	10%	11%	12%	13%	14%	15%
1	1.04	1.05	1.06	1.07	1.08	1.09	1.10	1.11	1.12	1.13	1.14	1.15
2	1.08	1.10	1.12	1.14	1.17	1.19	1.21	1.23	1.25	1.28	1.30	1.32
3	1.12	1.16	1.19	1.23	1.26	1.30	1.33	1.37	1.40	1.44	1.48	1.52
4	1.17	1.21	1.26	1.31	1.36	1.41	1.46	1.52	1.57	1.63	1.69	1.75
5	1.22	1.27	1.33	1.40	1.47	1.54	1.61	1.68	1.76	1.84	1.93	2.01
6	1.26	1.34	1.42	1.50	1.59	1.68	1.77	1.87	1.97	2.08	2.20	2.31
7	1.32	1.40	1.50	1.61	1.71	1.83	1.95	2.08	2.21	2.35	2.50	2.66
8	1.37	1.48	1.59	1.72	1.85	1.99	2.14	2.30	2.48	2.66	2.85	3.06
9	1.42	1.55	1.69	1.84	2.00	2.17	2.36	2.56	2.77	3.00	3.25	3.52
10	1.48	1.63	1.79	1.97	2.16	2.37	2.59	2.84	3.11	3.39	3.71	4.05
11	1.54	1.71	1.90	2.10	2.33	2.58	2.85	3.15	3.48	3.84	4.23	4.65
12	1.60	1.80	2.01	2.25	2.52	2.81	3.14	3.50	3.90	4.33	4.82	5.35
13	1.66	1.89	2.13	2.41	2.72	3.07	3.45	3.88	4.36	4.90	5.49	6.15
14	1.73	1.98	2.26	2.58	2.94	3.34	3.80	4.31	4.89	5.53	6.26	7.08
15	1.80	2.08	2.40	2.76	3.17	3.64	4.18	4.78	5.47	6.25	7.14	8.14
16	1.87	2.18	2.54	2.95	3.43	3.97	4.60	5.31	6.13	7.07	8.14	9.36
17	1.95	2.29	2.69	3.16	3.70	4.33	5.05	5.89	6.87	7.99	9.28	10.76
18	2.03	2.41	2.85	3.38	4.00	4.72	5.56	6.54	7.69	9.02	10.58	12.38
19	2.11	2.53	3.03	3.62	4.32	5.14	6.12	7.26	8.61	10.20	12.06	14.23
20	2.19	2.65	3.21	3.87	4.66	5.60	6.73	8.06	9.65	11.52	13.74	16.37

FIGURE D-1

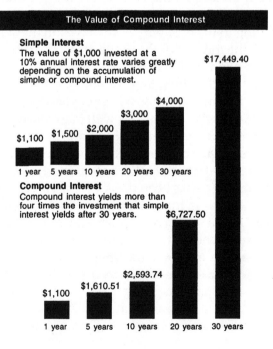

The Value of Compound Interest

Simple Interest
The value of $1,000 invested at a 10% annual interest rate varies greatly depending on the accumulation of simple or compound interest.

$17,449.40

$4,000

$3,000

$1,100 $1,500 $2,000

1 year 5 years 10 years 20 years 30 years

Compound Interest
Compound interest yields more than four times the investment that simple interest yields after 30 years.

$6,727.50

$2,593.74

$1,100 $1,610.51

1 year 5 years 10 years 20 years 30 years

Calculating Return on Investment

In order to completely evaluate a fund's performance, it is essential that you become knowledgeable about more than just its *yield*. You must also be able to determine its return on investment (ROI). This is the *critical* figure! It will tell you how well the fund is meeting its stated objectives, and how well it is meeting your expectations.

Calculating the ROI is simple. All that is needed is your latest investment account statement (IAS). You may use the quarterly, semiannual, or, best of all, the year-end IAS. The year-end statement will enable you to determine the fund's total return on your investment. (The quarterly IAS, for example, will give you a three-month ROI.)

In examining your account statements, you will find that IAS entries are always cumulative. Each new deposit, distribution, or redemption is displayed on a new line, and the total number of shares is adjusted to reflect the changes. Except for the year-end IAS, mutual funds will only list those transactions that can be reported on one page. Thus, you will need to retain one or more statements in order to have a record of transactions made earlier in the year which may have been dropped to make room for transactions made later in the year. To be on the safe side, retain all confirmations until the end of the year, before discarding those with repeated entries.

Before you can accurately compute your ROI or figure the taxes that may be due on your mutual fund investment, the cost basis for your shares must be determined. This is especially true if you have redeemed any shares during the year. Figure E–1 shows a sample year-end IAS for the XYZ Mutual Fund. You can see how the ROI, the cost basis, and the taxable amount due on your investment were derived. Note how imperative it is to determine the *cost basis* of any shares that were sold (redeemed) during the year. Only in this way are you able to accurately report the capital gain or loss for the year and avoid overpaying the amount of tax due.

Figure E–1 shows that $5,000 was invested on January 2, 1992.

FIGURE E–1

Sample Account Statement

XYZ MUTUAL FUND—P.O. Box 8910, Dallas TX 75266

Jane and John Doe JT TEN   Acct. No. 654321
1234 N.W. 105 Ave.
Miami, FL 33412
December 31, 1992 Investment Account Statement

Trade Date	Transaction	Dollar Amt.	Share Price	Shares Purch.	Shares Owned
Beginning balance					-0-
01/2	Shares pur. by ck.	$5000	$9.50	526.316	526.316
03/3	Income reinvest.	62.50	9.79	6.384	532.700
06/30	Income reinvest.	75.00	10.43	7.190	539.890
09/30	Income reinvest.	87.50	11.07	7.904	547.794
12/31	Income reinvest.	100.00	12.19	8.203	555.997
12/31	Cap. gain reinv.	100.00	12.19	8.203	564.200
12/31	ACCT. VALUE	$6877.60 (564.200 × $12.19)			
		(Tot. Sh. × NAV)			

ROI (Return on Investment) or (Total Annualized Yield)

(Taxable Income)		(Taxable Income if shares are sold at end of year)	
Income reinvest.	$325.00	1992 Acct. Value	$6877.60
Capital gain	$100.00	Cost Basis	$5425.00
Total taxable	$425.00	Total taxable	$1452.60
Original invest.	$5000.00	Yr. end Acct Value	$6877.60
Income reinvest.	325.00	Original invest.	$5000.00
Cap. gain reinv.	100.00	Total Return	$1877.60
Cost basis	$5425.00		

$$\text{ROI} = \frac{\$1877.60 \text{ (Tot. ret.)}}{\$5000.00 \text{ (Orig. inv.)}} = 37.55\%$$

The per share price at day's end for the XYZ Fund was $9.50. Therefore, the $5,000 purchased 526.316 shares. At the end of each quarter, the dividend was reinvested and credited to your account. These quarterly dividends purchased additional shares at the NAV on the day the dividends were credited to your account.

The sample account statement in Figure E–1 shows that the fund made a capital gains distribution of $100, which was credited to your account also.

Therefore, the accrued distributions increased the number of shares in your account to a total of 564.200. Dividends of $325 and a capital gain of $100 served to increase the cost basis to $5,425 for the 564.200 shares which you now own. However, only the $325 earned in dividends and the $100 capital gain are taxable for 1992, assuming that no shares were redeemed from this account.

If you were to sell all of your 564.200 shares at the end of 1992, you would *not* pay capital gain taxes on the $6,877.60 you would receive on the sale of your shares (your account value), but only on $1,452.60 (your account value less your cost basis). The $1,452.60 would become taxable as a long-term capital gain and reported on Schedule D of your tax return along with the $100 capital gain distribution.

The sample statement also shows that the XYZ Mutual Fund earned a "healthy" ROI of 37.55% for 1992. I think you will have to agree that this represents a hard-to-beat return on a $5,000 investment in just one year.

Bibliography

Brower, Kurt and Janachowski, Stephen. *Mutual Fund Mastery*. New York: Random House, 1997.

Cohn, Alan CFP and Cohn, Stephen CFP. *The Sage Guide to Mutual Funds*. New York: Harper Business Publications, 1999.

Hall, Alvin D. *Getting Started in Mutual Funds*. New York: John Wiley and Sage, Inc., 2000.

Levine, Alan and Liberman, Gail. *Making Money with Mutual Funds*. Alpha Books, Simon and Schuster: New York, 2000.

Mintzer, Rich. *The Everything Mutual Funds Book*. Adams Media Corp. Holbrook, Massachusetts, 2000.

Pettit, Dave and Jaroslovsky, Rich. *Guide to online Investing*. Crown Business, New York, 2000.

Rowland, Mary. *The Fidelity Guide to Mutual Funds*. Simon and Schuster, New York, 1990.

Glossary of Mutual Fund Terms

Account A mutual fund investor's record of investment transactions with the fund. A cumulative record of initial investment, distributions, reinvestments, redemptions, and changes in NAV (net asset value).

Accumulation Plan A relatively easy method of buying mutual fund shares through small, regular, voluntary purchases.

Aggressive Growth Fund A mutual fund that seeks a high level of capital growth through investment techniques involving greater than ordinary risk.

Adviser The investment organization engaged by a mutual fund to provide professional advice regarding the fund's investments and asset management practices.

AMEX American Stock Exchange.

Annual Report The formal financial statement issued yearly by a fund to its shareholders.

Appreciation Growth of capital or principal investment.

Asked or Offering Price The price at which a mutual fund's shares may be purchased. The asked price means the current net asset value per share plus sales charge, if any.

Asset Any item of value; an item that can be assigned a dollar value.

Automated Phone Messages A service provided by many mutual fund companies that allows anyone to use a touch-tone telephone to get current information about net asset values, yields, and other recorded information regarding their funds. In addition, investors with the company can get their account balance and switch money from one fund to another within its family of funds.

Automatic Reinvestment An option available to mutual fund shareholders in which fund dividends and capital gains distributions are automatically reinvested back into the fund to purchase new shares (at the current NAV) and thereby increase the value of their account.

Automatic Withdrawal   An arrangement offered by many mutual funds that enables shareholders to receive fixed payments, generally monthly or quarterly. The actual payment is determined by the investor.

Back-End Load   The fee paid when withdrawing money from a fund.

Balanced Fund   A mutual fund that diversifies its portfolio holdings over common stocks, bonds, preferred stocks, and possibly other forms of investment. Holdings of defensive securities are proportionately increased when the market outlook appears unfavorable, and aggressive positions are stressed when the market seems to be headed upward.

Basis Point   The term used to describe the amount of change in yield. One hundred basis points equal 1%. An increase from 6% to 8% would be a change of 200 basis points.

Bear   Someone who believes that the stock market is headed downward. A bear market is one that is moving lower on a fairly consistent basis for an extended period of time (see *Bull*).

Beta   A measure of the relative volatility of a stock or mutual fund. The higher the beta, the more volatile the stock or fund is considered to be relative to the market as a whole. The Standard and Poor's 500 Stock Index is assigned a beta of 1.

Bid Price   The price at which a mutual fund's shares are redeemed (bought back) by the fund. The redemption price is generally the current NAV per share exclusive of any load or commission.

Blue-Chip Stock   The common stock of a major corporation with a long, fairly stable record of earnings and dividend payments.

Bond   A security representing a debt; a loan from the bondholder to a corporation or a municipality. The bondholder generally receives semiannual interest payments, with the principal being repaid at maturity.

Bond Fund   A mutual fund whose portfolio consists primarily of fixed income securities such as bonds. The fund's objective is normally steady income rather than capital appreciation.

Broker   A member of a firm that buys and sells mutual funds as well as other securities.

Bull   Someone who believes that the stock market is headed upward. A bull market is one that is moving higher on a fairly consistent basis for an extended period of time (see *Bear*).

Buy Price   See *Bid Price*.

Capital Gains Distributions   Payments to mutual fund shareholders of profits realized by the fund on the sale of securities in the fund's portfolio. Such payments are usually distributed to the shareholders annually when such profits exist. These distributions are taxable to the shareholders (even in a tax-free fund).

Capital Growth   Represents an increase in the value of the fund's portfolio as reflected in the NAV of the fund shares. Such growth is the objective of many mutual funds and their investors.

Capital Loss   A loss from the sale of a capital asset.

Certificate of Deposit (CD)   A time deposit you make at a bank or savings and loan institution for a specific period of time, which may range from a week to several years. The bank, in turn, guarantees you a set rate of interest, usually somewhat higher than the passbook rate. If you withdraw your money, you pay a penalty. Bank CDs are insured by the Federal Deposit Insurance Company (FDIC).

Closed-End Investment Company   Unlike ordinary mutual fund companies, which are open-end investment companies, closed-end companies issue a limited number of shares and do not redeem them. Instead, closed-end shares are traded (bought and sold) in the securities markets, with supply and demand governing the price.

Commission   Portion of the purchase price that is paid to a salesperson (generally a stockbroker) on load funds.

Commodities   Bulk goods, such as metals, oil, grains, and cattle, traded on a commodities exchange. Funds that invest in commodities futures are very volatile.

Common Stock   A security that represents ownership in a company.

Compound Interest   Interest earned on the principal as well as on the previously accumulated interest.

Custodian   An organization (usually a bank) that keeps custody of securities and other assets of a mutual fund.

Deferred Sales Charge   Sometimes called a back-end load. This fee is used to discourage investors from switching in and out of their mutual funds too frequently (see *Exchange Privilege*).

Diversification   The policy followed by mutual funds to reduce the risk inherent in investing by spreading investments among a number of different securities in a variety of industries.

Dividend Distributions   Payments from net investment income designated by the fund's board of directors, to be distributed on a *pro rata* basis to shareholders of record.

Dollar-Cost Averaging   The investing of equal amounts of money at regular intervals regardless of whether share prices are up or down. This strategy reduces *average* share costs to the investor, who acquires more shares when the price is down and fewer shares when the price is up. Dollar-cost averaging is voluntary on the part of the investor.

Dow Jones Industrial Average   The average of 30 blue-chip stocks, originally published in 1897. With some revisions, it is still used today to show market trends.

Equity Fund   A mutual fund whose portfolio consists primarily of the stock (equity) of corporations. The term *equity* is often used interchangeably with the term *stock*.

Exchange Privilege   The right to exchange shares of one mutual fund for shares of another fund under the same sponsorship at net asset value. This privilege is valuable when using market timing as a technique to improve your position relative to the market, or when your objectives change. This privilege may be exercised several times yearly, usually with no fee or a very low fee.

Ex-Dividend   Effective date of a dividend distribution. When the dividend is paid, the NAV of the fund drops by the amount of the dividend; however, the total value of your investment remains unchanged if the dividend distribution is reinvested in the same account.

Expense Ratio   The percentage of a fund's assets that is paid out in expenses, including management fees, cost of distributing literature, and administration of the fund, divided by the average shares outstanding for the period. For most funds the expense ratios are usually low. The average is around 1.5%.

Family of Funds   A group of mutual funds managed by the same investment company. One company may manage several different funds, each with different investment objectives.

Federal Deposit Insurance Corporation (FDIC)   The federal agency that insures deposits up to $100,000 per account at member banks.

401(k)   A qualified employee benefit plan where employee contributions are made on a pretax basis. Both employer and employee contributions compound tax-free until withdrawn.

403(b)   A tax-sheltered plan open to members of certain professions, e.g., teachers and professors. It is similar to 401(k) plans; however, employers usually do not contribute to the 403(b) plan.

Fund Assets   The total market value of the assets invested by a fund.

Global Funds   Mutual funds that invest in stocks of companies from all over the world.

GNMA Funds   Mutual funds whose portfolios consist of Government National Mortgage Association securities, known as Ginnie Maes.

Growth Fund   A mutual fund that has as its principal objective long-term appreciation of principal. Growth funds are usually invested in common stocks.

Growth and Income Fund   A mutual fund that seeks both capital appreciation and current income. The portfolio of such a fund is balanced between stocks and fixed income securities.

Income Fund   A mutual fund which has as its primary objective the production of income in the form of interest or dividends. Mutual funds that invest in preferred stock, bonds, Treasuries, and money markets are characterized as income mutual funds.

Index Funds   Mutual funds whose portfolios duplicate the structure of either the Dow Jones Industrial Average or the Standard and Poor's 500 Composite Stock Price Index. The theory being that it is difficult to beat the average consistently, such a portfolio should at least match the performance of the indexes.

Individual Retirement Account (IRA)   A retirement account established by employees who have no company pension plan. Mutual funds have proved to be popular IRA investment vehicles. IRA accounts have several tax benefits as well.

Interest   Distributions made to shareholders that result from the fund's income on fixed income investments, such as municipal bonds, corporate bonds, and utility companies.

International Fund   A mutual fund that invests principally in the stocks and bonds of companies and countries outside of the United States.

Investment Company   An organization that invests the pooled funds of its shareholders in securities appropriate to the fund's objectives.

Investment Objective   The goal pursued by a mutual fund, e.g., long-term capital growth, current income, growth and income, etc. Each fund's objective is stated in its prospectus.

Junk Bonds   High-yielding, noninvestment-quality, lower-rated bonds of questionable worth.

Keogh Accounts   Retirement accounts for self-employed individuals, which are similar to IRA accounts.

Liquid   Assets that may easily be converted into cash or exchanged for other assets.

Load   The commission paid by the investor when purchasing mutual funds that are marketed through the use of salespeople.

Management Company   A company that is charged with the day-to-day management of a mutual fund investment company.

Management Fee   The amount paid by mutual funds to their investment advisers. The annual fee is generally about 0.5 percent of the fund's assets.

Market Timing   The use of economic and technical information or investment newsletters to guide your decision as to when to buy, sell, or switch mutual funds.

Money Market Deposit Account   Insured bank account that pays a market rate of interest. Depositors may write a limited number of checks on their accounts each month (usually three checks per month).

Money Market Mutual Fund   A mutual fund that invests in short-term debt obligations of governments and corporations. These accounts pay a market rate of interest that fluctuates from day to day. They always maintain a share price of one dollar. Although not insured, they are very safe. They are also completely liquid, which means you have ready access to your money by writing a check, transferring money into your bank account, or requesting by phone or letter to have a check mailed to you. There is no limit on the number of checks you may write, but each check amount must be for no less than the amount stipulated by the fund. (See Chapter 4.)

Municipal Bonds   Notes or other loans issued by state, city, or other local governments to pay for civic or other projects. All are exempt from federal taxes. Investors in municipal bond funds are also exempt from paying federal taxes on dividends.

Mutual Fund   A collection of stocks, bonds, or other securities purchased by a pool of investors and managed by a professional investment company.

Net Asset Value (NAV)   Market value of one share of a mutual fund. It is calculated at the close of each business day by taking the value of all the fund's assets, less expenses, and dividing by the total number of outstanding shares.

No-Load Mutual Fund   A fund that charges no fee or commission to sell or buy back its shares.

Open-End Investment Company   An investment company that continuously sells and redeems shares, i.e., a mutual fund.

Portfolio   The total securities held by a mutual fund or a private individual.

Preferred Stock Fund   A fund whose portfolio consists of shares of preferred stocks. Preferred stock is a class of stock that has prior claim on dividends before common stock.

Principal   Total amount of your initial investment plus subsequent investments. (The total value of one's account.)

Profit   The amount earned when the selling price is higher than the cost.

Prospectus   A formal printed document offering to sell a security. The Security and Exchange Commission (SEC) requires a prospectus to disclose *all* the pertinent information about a security.

Proxy   The written transfer of voting rights to someone who will then vote according to the wishes of the shareholder. Usually done when the shareholder cannot attend a shareholders' meeting.

Record Date   The date by which mutual fund, or other security, holders must be registered as share owners to receive a forthcoming distribution, e.g., dividends or capital gains.

Redemption Price   The amount per share mutual fund holders receive when they sell their shares (sometimes called the *bid price*).

Return on Investment (ROI)   Percent gain, including reinvestment of capital gains and dividends, if any.

Risk   The probability of loss associated with any investment.

Rule 12b-1 Fee   Fee charged by some funds and named after the 1980 Securities and Exchange Commission (SEC) rule that permits such fees to be charged to the shareholders. Such fees pay for the fund's advertising and marketing costs. The fund's prospectus discloses the existence of such fees if applicable. (Not all mutual funds charge such fees.)

Sales Charge   An amount charged to purchase shares in a load fund sold by brokers or other members of a sales force. (Also called a *commission*.) The sales charge is applied to load mutual funds even when purchased directly from the investment company.

Securities and Exchange Commission (SEC)   An independent agency of the U.S. government that administers the various security laws, the companies that manage mutual funds, and the salespeople who sell them. The SEC functions in the interest of shareholders.

Sector Fund   A mutual fund that invests in only one segment of the market, such as energy, transportation, precious metals, health sciences, or international stocks.

Securities   Publicly traded financial instruments such as stocks, bonds, and mutual funds.

Securities Act of 1933   The law that states what information is required to be included in the prospectuses of all mutual funds.

Sell Price   See *Asked Price.*

Short-Term Paper   Short-term loans to corporations or governments. Interest rates paid to mutual funds on such loans will vary with market conditions. Short-term paper is one of the primary sources of income for money market mutual funds.

Securities Investor Protection Corporation (SIPC)   A corporation backed by federal guarantees that provides protection for customers' cash and investments on deposit with an SIPC member firm, should the firm fail. Protection is generally provided up to $2.5 million.

Speculative   Considered to have a high degree of risk.

Systematic Withdrawal   Plan that permits you to withdraw a specified amount from your mutual fund account at regular intervals, generally on a monthly basis. This is a way of converting your investments into regular income.

Tax Avoidance   Legal action that may be taken to reduce, defer, or eliminate tax liabilities.

Tax-Deferred   Income on which tax is levied only when distributed.

Tax-Exempt (Tax-Free) Fund   A mutual fund whose portfolio consists of securities (usually municipal bonds or money market obligations) exempt from federal income taxes.

Tax Shelter   An investment used for deferring, eliminating, or reducing income taxes.

Tenancy in Common   Property or other capital assets jointly held by two people, usually unmarried, wherein each person retains control over his or her share of the property.

Tenancy by the Entirety   A joint form of ownership that exists when the names of both husband and wife appear on the title of the property, each having rights of survivorship.

Total Return   Profit realized on a mutual fund investment, which includes both the income it generates plus the change in the value of the principal (NAV).

Transfer Agent   The organization engaged by a mutual fund to assume responsibility for preparing and maintaining records relating to the accounts of all its shareholders, keeping a record of each registered owner, his or her address, the number of shares owned, purchases, and redemptions.

Volatility   Tendency of a fund to rise or fall sharply in value.

Wire Transfer   Use of a bank to send money to a fund or vice versa.

Withdrawal Plan   A mutual fund plan that provides for the automatic withdrawal of a specified amount of money at specified intervals as determined by the shareholder.

Yield   The dividends or interest paid by a mutual fund expressed as a percentage of the current per share price.

INDEX

INDEX

A B O U T   T H E   A U T H O R

Bruce Jacobs holds both bachelor's and master's degrees in Education and Economics from Temple University in Philadelphia, Pennsylvania. He currently resides in Delray Beach, Florida, where he is a member of the Free Lance Writers' Association. He has written numerous articles on mutual fund investing for local Miami and Fort Lauderdale newspapers.

Formerly, he was the administrator of several schools in his native Philadelphia. In this capacity, he was responsible for the management and implementation of million-dollar educational budgets.

The author has taught Mutual Investing courses at Broward Community College in Florida and currently conducts Investment Seminars at Piper Community School in Sunrise, Florida.

Mr. Jacobs also operates a financial consultation service devoted exclusively to preparing mutual fund investment portfolios for clients in Florida, Pennsylvania, and New Jersey.